Bhajan Supplement
2021

Mata Amritanandamayi Center
San Ramon, California, USA

Bhajan Supplement 2021

Published By:
Mata Amritanandamayi Center
P.O. Box 613
San Ramon, CA 94583-0613, USA

In India:
www.amritapuri.org
inform@amritapuri.org

In Europe:
www.amma-europe.org

In US:
www.amma.org

About Pronunciation

The following key is for the guidance of those who are unfamiliar with the transliteration codes used in this book:

A	-as	a	in America
AI	-as	ai	in aisle
AU	-as	ow	in how
E	-as	e	in they
I	-as	ea	in heat
O	-as	o	in or
U	-as	u	in suit
KH	-as	kh	in Eckhart
G	-as	g	in give
GH	-as	gh	in loghouse
PH	-as	ph	in shepherd
BH	-as	bh	in clubhouse
TH	-as	th	in lighthouse
DH	-as	dh	in redhead
CH	-as	ch-h	in staunch-heart
JH	-as	dge	in hedgehog
Ñ	-as	ny	in canyon
Ṣ	-as	sh	in shine
Ś	-as	c	in efficient
Ṅ	-as	ng	in sing (nasal sound)
V	-as	v	in valley
ZH	-as	rh	in rhythm
R	-as	r	in ride

Vowels with a line on top are pronounced like the vowels listed above but held twice as long.
The letters with dots under them (ṭ, ṭh, ḍ, ḍh, ṇ) are palatal sounds. They are pronounced with the tip of the tongue against the hard palate.

Table of Contents

abhangācyā rasāt (Marathi)

abhangācyā rasāt raṅgīlē man
tan man tsālē dēvā tutsyā caraṇī līn

O God, my mind is so immersed in singing Your praises that my body and mind are completely focused on Your lotus feet.

māyā ca tāvaḍīt sāpaḍla jīv
kṛpā asō dēvā tujhī man hō nisaṅg

O God bless me with grace that I may escape from the clutches of *maya.*

āḷa sācyā sākhaḷīla tōḍun dē gōvind
prakāśīt nirantar bōdha antaraṅg

O Lord, please break the shackles of my ignorance that awareness may dawn within me.

dēvācī mahima sāṅgumī kiti
he janm avagē nā karāyā tyāci kīrti

My entire life will not be enough for me to sing all your glory

bōlā viṭhal viṭhal viṭhal
jay viṭhal viṭhal viṭhal
māūlī viṭhal viṭhal viṭhal
jay viṭhal viṭhal viṭhal

Victory to Lord Vithala!

abhayārtthinī aham (Sanskrit)

abhayārtthinī aham āgatā-asmi
santaptāham nanmāya
nirguṇa-kāmkṣiṇī tava putrī
dhyāna-nimagnā nāsti gurō

I come before You seeking refuge. I have suffered many hardships trying to follow the good. O Guru, I am attracted to the attributeless, but the mind of your daughter is not immersed in meditation.

kim karaṇīyam mōkṣāya
duḥkha-nāśāya bravītu dēvī
vyartham gatāni janmāni
dīyatām sadgati kṛpayā

O Devi, what must I do to reach liberation and be freed from all suffering! So many births have gone in vain. Shower your grace and show me the right path.

arppaṇāya-aśru nāsti ambē
ajñānāndhyam mā grasa mām
ananta-ānandē layanāya
alam viḷambēna dēvi ambē

O Mother, I have no tears to offer you. Do not let the darkness of ignorance catch me. O Mother Goddess, may I merge in your infinite bliss without delay.

abhayattināyi (Malayalam)

abhayattināyi kēzhum ī ēzhayil
nin kṛpā-varṣam ēki kākkaṇamē
dīnar tan nōv-akaṫṫiṭunna janani
akhilarkkum āśvāsa tīramallō nī

Please shower your divine grace and save your children who cry for your protection. O Mother, you remove the suffering of the destitute, and you are the shore of consolation for all.

jani-mṛtikkayangaḷil muṅgiyum poṅgiyum
ēzhakaḷ ñaṅgaḷ kuzhaññiṭumbōḷ
tāngāy taṇalāy sāntvanam ēki nī
śōka tāpangaḷ keṭuttiṭunnu

As we toss about and flounder in the whirlpool of births and deaths, you support and save us. You console us and dispel our sorrows.

amma tan vātsalya tēn nukarnnīṭum ī
makkaḷ tan jīvitam śānti-pūrṇam
ammayām gaṅgayil muṅgi ī makkaḷ tan
pāpaṅgaḷ okke ozhiññuvallō

The honey of your motherly affection fills the lives of your children with peace. When your children swim in the Ganges of your love, all their sins are washed away.

advaita cintakku (Malayalam)

advaita cintakk-orākāram
vidyakaḷkk-ellāmē kēdāram
kanivatu pūṇḍatra sākāram
avaniyil amma tan avatāram

You are the embodiment of *advaita* and the home of all forms of knowledge. O Mother, you have incarnated on this earth in the form of compassion.

jīvanil ānanda varṣamāyi
hṛdayattil ōrunna vastuvāyi
nityatā-bōdhattin-attāṇiyāyi
ettunnu martyande hṛttil amma

You reside in the hearts of all and shower bliss in each life. You are the supreme consciousness in our hearts. O Mother, you are our support.

martya-hṛdaṅgaḷām vāpikūpādikaḷ
utsavam-ākkunnā tōṣavṛṣṭi
ēkātma bōdhattin nīrumōnti
pāritu pūvāṭiyāy lasippān

The lake of our hearts becomes festive in a shower of joy. Drinking the nectar of the one Self, our world becomes a joyful garden!

āgamakkātalāyi (Malayalam)

āgamakkātalāyi minni teḷiyum
kāruṇyattāl uḷḷil aṙiyum
mōhanāśini cinmayi ānandinī
hṛdayēśvarī vandanam

Through your compassion, You shine within as the essence of the Vedas. I bow to the Goddess of my heart, who is pure consciousness and bliss.

āgama-tikavuṫṫōr-amṛtin sattē
hṛttil teḷiyum azhakin niṙavē
uḷḷil teḷiyān sanmayī en
manaḥ karppūram uzhiyunnu
manaḥ karppūram uzhiyunnu

You are the immortal nectar of the Vedas. You are the immaculate beauty that fills my heart. I burn the camphor of my heart that you may shine within, O pure Existence!

āgamiccīṭukil janmam dhanyam
kāttu kātt-en manam iṭaṙunnu
inn-ende janmam saphalam ākku, janma-
sāphalya kaivalyamē
janma-sāphalya kaivalyamē

My life will be fulfilled if you enter my heart. My mind is losing courage as it waits for you. O Mother, please grant liberation and fulfill my life today!

innen teṫṫukaḷ poṙukkillē tāyē
abhayam nin padatāril allō
āśrayam ēkiṭū ennennum, nin
kṛpāvarṣa-prabha ēkiṭū
kṛpāvarṣa-prabha ēkiṭū

Won't you forgive my faults, O Mother? My shelter is your divine lotus feet. Shower your effulgent grace upon me and grant me refuge forever!

āgama-sāramē (Malayalam)

āgama-sāramē ānanda-dāyini
āgamiccīṭaṇe ende hṛttil
uḷḷam malarkkē tuṟannu vaccu
uḷlam uruki ñān kāttirippū

O essence of the Vedas, bestower of bliss, please come to my grief-seared heart. Keeping open the doors of my heart, I wait for you.

vēdavum śāstravum ētum aṟivīlā
dhyāna-japādikaḷ ētum illā
nityamām satyamē ninnil aliyuvān
nirmala-prēmam onnu mātram

I do not know Vedas or scriptures, nor do I practice meditation or chanting. O eternal Truth, all I have is innocent love and longing to dissolve in you.

tāvaka cintanam onninal hṛttaṭam
śōbha ēṭṭīṭaṇam kāruṇyāmbudhē
ajñāna-nāśakam ākum ā pādaṅgaḷ
hṛttāril ennum viḷaṅgīṭaṇē

Ocean of Compassion, make my heart effulgent with thoughts of you. May your lotus feet destroy my ignorance and shine forever in my heart.

ajñānattai pōkkum (Tamil)

ajñānattai pōkkum jñānāgniyē
anpum amaitiyum niṟaiya aruḷvāy
anaivaraiyum īśanāy kaṇḍu sēvikka
ammā kanintennai āśīrvatippāy

You are the fire of knowledge that burns away our ignorance. Bless me and fill me with love and peace. O Mother, be kind and bless me that I may see and serve everyone as God.

kaṇṇin imaipōla kāppavaḷ dēvi
unnōṭu irukka duḥkham ēn manamē?
nīkkamaṙa niṙaintirukkum paramātmāvai
ūkkamuṭan nī ninaintu ondriṭuvāy manamē

O mind, why this sorrow? You are with the goddess who protects like the eyelid protects the eye. O mind, blissfully remember the all-pervading, supreme consciousness and merge in it.

ānandam veḷiyil tēṭi alaiyāmal
un uḷḷil ānanda-rūpamadai uṇarntu
vivēka vairāgyam-enum jñānavāḷāl
paṫṫrai aṙuttu bhaktiyāl uyarvāy

Do not seek happiness outside. Realize the bliss within you. With the sword of knowledge, discrimination and dispassion, cut all attachments and progress with devotion.

akale allamma (Malayalam)

akale allamma en akatāril uṇḍu
akatāril uḷḷatō aṙiyēṇḍat-uṇḍu

My Mother is close, she is in my heart. I long to know the Mother within.

aṙiyān āyi uḷḷatum aṙivāyiṭṭ-uḷḷatum
aṙiyātt-ōraṙivāyi en akatāril uṇḍu

She is in my heart as knowledge and as that which is to be known, and as the knowledge that is, as yet, unknown.

aṙiyām ennura ceyvōr aṙiyātta amma
ātmārppaṇam ceyvōr aṙiyunna amma

She is the Mother who remains unknown to those who say they 'know' Her. She is the Mother who is only known to those who surrender to Her.

akatāril nityam niṙayunn-ōramma
sukṛtattāl amṛtatvam nalkunn-ōramma

She is the Mother who fills my heart, and she is the One who grants immortality to those who perform noble deeds.

nityam satyam cidātmakam amma
navyam bhavyam parātparam amma

Mother is eternal and she is the Truth. She is pure consciousness, ever new splendor and the most exalted of all.

akamadhikam (Malayalam)

akamadhikam azhalāl niṙaññu ammē
akatāril ittiri iṭam tarillē?
anudinam mṛti-bhayavum ēṙiṭunnu
anutāpam amba nī kaṇḍatillē

O Mother! My mind is full of sorrow. Won't you give me a place in the lotus of your heart? Each day, I fear death more. O Mother! Won't you see my distress?

oru nimiṣam eṅkilum vannīṭuvān
karuṇanīr-kaṭalē ninaykkukillē?
kālam kazhiyukil dēham patikkukil
kazhaliṇayil abhayam labhiccīṭumō?

Ocean of Compassion, won't you remember me and come to me for even a moment? When my time is over and my body falls away, will I gain refuge at your divine feet?

śuddham ākkū prēma-māriyāl mānasam
mugdhamām nin vadanam onnu kāṇān
nityam bhajicciṭām nin kṛpaykkāy
nityaśuddhē ennil aliv-ēkumō?

Purify my mind with the rain of your love, that I may see your lovely face. I shall worship you daily to receive your grace. O eternally pure one, won't you be tender-hearted towards me?

iha-lōka-lābham enikk-ēkolā
aham enna tāpam onnāṙīṭuvān
ahamaṫta mānasam siddham-āyeṅkilō
dēhātma-buddhi śamikkum allō

I do not want abundance in this world. Let my mind be free of the heat of ego and the delusion that I am the body.

akatāril amba nī maruvunnu

akatāril amba nī maruvunnu eṅkilum
aṙiyāte alayunnu ende cittam
nīrkkumiḷa ennapōl vannu pōkunnitā
bhakti-vairāgyaṅgaḷ hṛttil ammē

O Mother! You reside within me. Not knowing this, my heart still wanders. Devotion and detachment arise and subside in my heart like bubbles.

ātma-lōkattin vātāyanam allō
tyāga-pūrṇamām karmaṅgaḷ okkeyum

nin sēvayākunna pūjakaḷāl ende
ātma-bōdhatte uṇarttīṭaṇē

The door to the Self is the actions that we perform with renunciation. Awaken my awareness of the Self through the *seva* that I perform as your ceremonial worship.

anya-cintaykk-iṭam nalkiṭāt-en manam
divyamām rūpam smariccu nityam
ammayām saccidānandamām sindhuvil
aliyumāṙakaṇē ende janmam

Let only the thought of your divine form find a place in my heart. Let my life dissolve in my Mother, the ocean of existence, consciousness and bliss.

akataḷiril aṙivāy (Malayalam)

akataḷiril aṙivāy viḷaṅgunn-orambikē
nin nāma-rūpam en abhayamāy tīraṇē
nin mukha-kānti vazhiyunna hṛttilō
naṙutēn at-uṇṇunnor-anubhuti allayō

Mother, you shine as knowledge in a blossoming heart. Let your name and form be my refuge. My heart, filled with the radiance of your beautiful face, experiences nectarine bliss.

karuṇa-nīr tūkiyen mānasa-padmam
atamalamāy nin pādē arumayāy patiyaṇē
tava tiru-pādam patiyunna hṛtsūnam
dīptamāy pāṙinnu dīpamāy tīrunnu

May the lotus of my heart, filled with compassion, become pure, and fall with love at your feet. My heart bears the impression of your divine feet, and becomes effulgent, thus spreading its radiance over the world.

uyirin uṇarvāy vāzhum en janani nī
ūzhiyil vāzhum ī ñaṅgaḷe kākkaṇē
jagadambikē ninde puṇyamām nāmaṅgaḷ
avaniyil ennum muzhaṅgumāṙ ākaṇē

O Mother, you are the pure energy that rules over this universe. Please protect us who live in this world. Mother of the universe, may your glorious names resound forever in this world.

akatāril uṙavākum (Malayalam)

akatāril uṙavākum aṙivinde poruḷē
amṛtatva-sāramē atiśayapūramē
avikala-ramyē karuṇārdra-hṛdayē
akhilāṇḍa caitanya prēma-mūrtte

You are the essence of knowledge arising in my heart. You are immortal bliss, a wondrous festival. You are the pure beauty of a compassionate heart. You are the pure consciousness that pervades the universe, the form of love.

ākula-hṛttinde āmayam māṫṫū
āsura-bhāvaṅgaḷ vērōṭ-akaṫṫū
ā mahima-tannuṭe bhāvam pakartti
ānanda-sāgara-tīrē aṇaykkū...

Remove the miseries of my sorrowing heart, and uproot its evil tendencies. Awaken the greatness residing within, and bring me to the shore of your ocean of bliss.

imbam ēkum rāga-bhāvaṅgaḷ ēkū
indriyātītamām nirvṛti ēkū
ī bhuvi-tan śōka-mōhaṅgaḷ akaṫṫi
īṭuṫṫa janma-sāphalyam ēkū

Grant me the virtues of love and harmony. Grant me the bliss that transcends the senses and remove my sorrow and desire. As I live on this earth, make my life worthy of fulfillment!

akhila-carācaravum (Malayalam)

akhila-carācaravum nī mātram enn-aṙiññen
jīvitam pūjayāy māṙunna dinam ennō?
anubhava-tirakaḷe prasādamāy svīkaricc-
en manam tṛptamāy tīrunna dinam ennahō?

O Mother! When will worship become my way of life? When will I know that all beings are your manifestation? Will the day come when my mind is content and accepts all experiences as your *prasad?*

saccidānandābdhiyil veṙum oru hima-bindu
mātram ī 'aham' ennu amma tan tēn-mozhi
anubhavamāy vannu ammayām prēma-
sindhuvil 'ñān' layikkunn-oru dinam ennō?

When will I experience the truth of Amma's sweet words that we are only a dew drop in the ocean of existence-consciousness-bliss? Will the day come when "I" disappear in the ocean of your love?

ammē nin śrī-caraṇam mātram innen śaraṇam
ennen manakkāmbil uṙaccorī nin makaḷ
nin kaṭākṣattin anugraha-prabhāvattāl
ninnil layikkuvān tāmasam iniyentu?

O Mother! This daughter knows that your divine feet are her only refuge. Why do you delay to bless me with your glance and dissolve me in you?

akṣara-rūpiṇī amṛtēśvarī (Malayalam)

akṣara-rūpiṇī amṛtēśvarī
śubhrābja-nilayē nādāmbikē
ōmkāra-nāda taraṅgam uyartti nī
nṛttam āṭīṭumō en vāciyil

Immortal Goddess Sarasvati, origin of sound, seated on a pure white lotus. Will you awaken the *Omkara* within and be present in my words?

vāgdēvatē mama hṛttil vasicc-en
hṛdayam nin maṇivīṇa ākkīṭaṇē
ā maṇi-vīṇayil nī śruti mīṭṭumbōḷ
kanmaṣa-bhāram akanniṭunnu

O Goddess of speech, reside in my heart and make it your divine *veena*. When you play music on that veena, the burdens of my heart are lifted.

ātma-prakāśinī jñānāmbikē
uyirārnn-uṇarttuk-en ātmabōdham
ātmānandāmṛta-lahariyil ñān ammē
'nī tanne' ñān enn-aṙiññiṭaṭṭe

O Mother, source of all knowledge, light of the *atman*, awaken within me as awareness of the Self. In the blissful intoxication of the effulgent Self, let me know that you are my true essence.

alaññu valaññ-oru jīvane (Malayalam)

alaññu valaññ-oru jīvane kaṇḍ-uṭan
karma-pāśam aṙuttallō ammē
janmam atonn-ēki avatāravum pūṇḍu
bhavatāriṇi tāṅgāy vannuvallō

Mother saw us lost and wandering *jivas* and cut asunder our karmic bondage. She gave us life and incarnated as our support. In the form of Bhavatarini, she carries us across the ocean of birth and death.

ammē ī makkaḷ kṛtārttharāyi
ammē ī makkaḷ kṛtārttharāyi

O Mother, the lives of your children are fulfilled.

dharaṇiyil vīṇ-uṭan tala pokki en 'aham'
māyayām āzhiyil mallaṭiccu
amma tan cuṭu-muttam ēkiya śaktiyāl
amma tan prēmatte āśrayiccu

At birth, our ego raised its head and we struggled in the ocean of maya. Amma's loving kisses strengthened us, and we took refuge in her love.

ā kṣaṇam kēṭṭitā amma tan susvaram
'uḷḷil uṇḍ-amma, karutt-ēkiṭān'
cintanam ceyyukil hā! entor-ānandam
amma tan taṇalilāy oru jīvitam

We heard Mother say, "I am within you to give you strength." Think about how blissful is a lifetime in Mother's shade!

ala-tiṅgum-āzhiyil (Malayalam)

ala-tiṅgum-āzhiyil kuññala ñān ammē
nin pādapūjaykkāyi vembiṭunnu
ala utirkkum nura koṇḍu ñān
nin pādē pālabhiṣēkam naṭattum ammē

O Mother, in the abundant waves of the ocean, I am a little wavelet that longs to worship your feet. O Mother, I bathe your holy feet with the milk of the foam arising from the waves.

duḥkhitarkk-āśvāsa-vākkukaḷ ōti ñān
śuddhamām neyyabhiṣēkam ceyyum
klēśam sahippōrkku amma tan tēn mozhi
ōti ñān tēnabhiṣēkam ceyyum

Consoling words to suffering hearts are the ghee with which I bathe your feet. I wash your feet with the honey of your nectarine words that I whisper to those suffering hardship.

en manatāril udikkum vikārattāl
dadhyabhiṣēkam mudā ceytiṭum
en cuṭu śvāsamām paṭṭu-tuṇiyāl ñān
nin pādam ārdra-vihīnam ākkum

I joyfully bathe your feet with the curd of my heart's devotion. My heartfelt sighs are the silken cloth with which I dry your divine feet.

nīlāmbaratte kaṭam eṭutt-ammaykku
cēlēṙum nalloru cēla cārttum
muttum pavizhavum cērttu meneññu ñān
amma tan karṇṇābharaṇam ākkum

O Mother, borrowing the deep blue of the sky, I adorn you with a most radiant saree, and I bedeck you with earrings of pearl and coral.

tārāpathaṅgaḷe tāzhōṭṭu vanniṭū
amma tan kaṇṭhattil hāram ākām
āśakaḷ āyiram nāmaṅgaḷ āyinnu
arccana ceytu samarppikkaṭṭe

O stars, please come down and be the garland on my Mother's neck. O Mother, today I offer my countless aspirations as names in your worship.

ātma-prakāśamē aṇayāte ninniṭū
amma tan munnile dīpamāy
tava tiru munnile karppūra dīpamāy
māmaka janmam samarppikkaṭṭe

O light of the Self, stay steady as a bright lamp before me. O Mother, I offer my life to you as the burning camphor flame.

ambāṭi tannilē (Malayalam)

ambāṭi tannilē ponmaṇi paitalāy
gōkulam pālicca dēvā
pālkkaṭal nāthā mukil varṇṇā
paṅkajalōcanā kai tozhunnēn

O Lord, you sustain Gokula as its darling child. O dark-hued, lotus-eyed Lord of the milky ocean, I pray to you.

pāpikaḷ-ākum ī lōkarkk-ellām
pāpa vimōcanam nalkēṇamē
ī lōkattile ēzhakaḷkk-ennum
kāruṇyam ēkaṇē kārmukil varṇṇā

Please release all the people of this world from sin. Always be compassionate to the poor in this world, O dark-colored one!

piccakappūmāla cārttiyōnē
pītāmbaradhārī vēṇu nāthā
pullām kuzhal ūti vanniṭuka nī
pūtana nigraha pālaya mām

You wear the jasmine garland and the yellow robes, O Lord of the flute! Come to me, playing your flute. I take refuge in You, O slayer of Putana.

perumpāmbin mītē śayippavanē
pēmāriye taṭutta gōkula nāthā
enn-ātmāvile vēdana māṫṫi
nin pāda padmattil cērttiṭaṇē

You lay on top of the great snake and protected everyone from the rains in Gokula. Please remove the pain in my soul, and bring me to your lotus feet.

amma allāte ī pāriṭattil (Malayalam)

amma allāte ī pāriṭattil
āśrayam āruṇḍu prēma-mūrtē
antyam vare tirunāmam japikkuvān
anugrahikkū ammē anugrahikkū

O Mother, embodiment of divine love, who else in this world is our refuge? Please bless us that we may chant your divine name until the very end.

janmam muzhuvan tiraññu tiraññu ñān
oru nāḷ nin tiru mumbil etti
kāruṇyamōṭ-enne cērtt-aṇaccu – ende
mānava-janmam kṛtārttham ākki!

All my life I looked for you and, one day, I reached your divine presence. Drawing me close with your tender compassion, you blessed my human birth.

ārennu tān enna bōdham koṭuttu nī
prēma-dīpattāl nayicciṭunnu
mānuṣa-janmam dharicc-orammē – ninde
līlakaḷ āścaryam ennum ennum!

Bestowing the knowledge of who I am, you guide me with the lamp of love. O Mother, you have taken a human birth, and your divine plays are an eternal wonder!

'amma' enḍru solvatum (Tamil)

'amma' enḍru solvatum ōr arumandiramē
bandhaṅkaḷai viḍuvikkum aruḷ mandiramē
pēdai ivaḷ enḍrum untan kuzhantai amma
paṫtrudal vēṙondrum illai amma

'Amma' is a miraculous mantra that showers grace and frees us from worldly ties. This innocent one is always your child, O Amma. I have no other attachment.

sirupiḷḷai unaimaṙavā varam taruvāyē
cittamenum kōyililē kuṭiyiruppāyē
nēsattuḍan enaikkāttu aravaṇaippāyē
nīṅgāda un suḍarāy oḷiravaippāyē

Dwell in the temple of my heart, and grant this little child the boon never to forget you. Lovingly protect and embrace me, and make me shine as your eternal light.

ammā ennai aravaṇaippāyē
Mother, embrace me.
anbum yen annayum vēṙu illaiyē
anbē vaḍivāṇa tāyē amṙtēśvariyē
akilattai aravaṇaikkum akhilāṇḍēśvariyē
tiruppādam śaraṇaṭaindēn sarvēśvariyē

Love and my mother are not different. O love incarnate, O Mother, eternal Goddess of the Universe, you embrace the universe. Goddess of all, I surrender at your lotus feet.

ammā unnai śaraṇaṭaintēnē

O Mother, I surrender to you.

amma ennōrkkumbōḷ (Malayalam)

amma enn-ōrkkumbōḷ tuṭikkum en neñcakam
kaṇṭham iṭaṙunnu kaṇṇīr tuḷumbunnu
nin padāntē oru kīrttanam arccikkān
gītam ētonninnu pāṭiṭum ñān?

O Mother! When I remember you, my heart beats with longing, my voice trembles and tears fill my eyes. What song shall I offer as a hymn at your lotus feet?

kātaṅgaḷ dūre āṇenkilum ennuṭe
kātara-mānasam nī aṙiññu
māṙōṭ-aṇacc-ende nombaram āṫṫavē
mānasam toṭṭaṙiññ-īśvarane
mānasam toṭṭaṙiññ-īśvarane

You are miles away, yet you know my aching heart. You hugged me close and relieved my pain. My heart experienced God!

orāyiram pūkkaḷ niṙañña nin pūnkāvil
ī kāṭṭu-pūvinum iṭam taraṇē
śrīpādapūjā malarāyi tīruvān
karuṇā-kaṭākṣam nī coriyēṇamē
karuṇā-kaṭākṣam nī coriyēṇamē

O Mother! May this wildflower also grow in your garden, resplendent with thousands of flowers. Grace me with your lovely glance that I may become a flower offered at your lotus feet!

ammā enum sollukku (Tamil)

ammā enum sollukku mēl mandiram-uṇḍō
adaiviṭavum azhagāna sollum-uṇḍō
āyiram pērsolli sāttiraṅkaḷ tudikkum
ammā endru maṫṫum entan manam japikkum
manam japikkum

Is there a better mantra than the word 'Amma'? Is there a more beautiful word than that? The scriptures praise You with a thousand names, but my mind just chants 'Amma'!

karuṇayin kaṭale nī amṛtāmbike
atil oru tuḷiye nī vazhaṅkiṭaṇum
onrum aṙiyāda ennai ēmāṫṫrattōḍu
uppusuvai nīrinaye parugaceyyāde
ammā... ammā...

O Eternal Mother, Ocean of Compassion. Please grant me a drop of your love. Don't disappoint this ignorant child by making me consume the salt water (of maya). O Amma...

ārāda tuyaraṅkaḷai akaṫṫrum en tāye
nāmam japittum duḥkham enakkēno
enakkētu vantālum un nāmam japippēn
en vidhi endrendrum un kaiyyil ammā
ammā... ammā...

O my Mother! You alleviate even the worst sufferings. Then why this sorrow in spite of chanting your name? My destiny is forever in your hands, O Amma.

ammā kāḷi enakku maṭṭum (Tamil)

ammā kāḷi enakku maṭṭum endru ninaittiruntēn
pañcabhuta uṭaltanil maṭṭum kaṇḍu
makizhntiruntēn
alla alla endru nī solla paritavittēn atu ēn enavē

O Mother Kali, I thought you belonged to me alone. I enjoyed seeing your physical body made of five elements. When you said you are not limited to the body, I was desperate to know how it is so.

cintanai sey endre nīyum uṇartta
eppaṭi ammā ena viyantēn

uṇṇil 'ṅān' tane akaṫṫendrāy
cintayil teḷiyumē anta uṇmai

When you asked me to contemplate, I wondered how. You said, "I am within you. You will know this truth through contemplation."

aṙivin teḷivil bhēdam illaiyē
anpil ṅān nī ena illaiyē
nīkkamaṙa niṙaintiṭum poruḷ nīyē
ammā kāḷi anaittum nīyē

When Truth dawns within, there is no difference. Where there is love, there is no 'you' and 'me'. O Mother Kali, You are the all-pervading substratum of everything. You are everything.

aṙiyeceyvāy idai uṇaraceyvāy
aṙiyaceyvāy ammā uṇaraceyvāy

O Mother, help me to awaken and realize this Truth!

jai jai kāḷi ammā kāḷi
jai jai kāḷi śyāmē kāḷi

Victory to Mother Kali, the dark-hued one!

amma tan pādattil (Malayalam)

amma tan pādattil amarān koticcu ñān
urukum manassumāyi vann-aṇaññu
ōmalē ennamma ōtunna nēram en
akatāril aśru nīr dhāra peytu

With a mind tender with longing, I came to Mother, desiring to remain at Her holy feet. Hearing Her say, "My darling," my heart melted in a rain of tears.

amma tan kāruṇya pīyūṣa dhārayil
muṅgi kuḷiccu ñān dhanyanāyi
kōḷmayirkkoḷḷumā sāntvana vīcikaḷkk-
entoru mādhuryam enn-aṙiññu

I became blessed, immersed in the torrent of Mother's divine love. I experienced the sweetness of the soothing waves of the river of compassion.

kaṇmunnil minnum ī sundara-rūpam en
mānasattārilēkk-ennu cērum
hṛdayamām vīṇa tan tantriyil ñān oru
kīrttanamālyam koruttu melle

When will the beautiful, radiant form before my eyes shine within my heart? Softly, I wove a garland of song and played it on the veena of my heart.

ammaye pāṭi stuticcu ñān ānanda-
tundilanāy-ātma nirvṛtiyil
ammayām satyam en hṛtspandam-āyinnu
nirmala tattva prakāśamāyi

Singing Mother's glories, I became blissful in the ultimate freedom of the Self. The Truth that is Amma, the effulgence of the pure Absolute, became my very heartbeat.

amma tan prāṇan (Malayalam)

amma tan prāṇan pakarnnīṭum mantram
cittatte niścalam ākkiṭum mantram
hṛttinn-aṭittaṭṭil āzhnn-iṙaṅgi
ātma-caitanyam uṇarttum mantram

The mantra transfers Amma's divine energy to us and stills our mind. It reaches into the depths of our soul and awakens the glorious Self within.

janma-janmāntara-sukṛtam ī mantram
sañcita-pāpam akaṭṭum ī mantram
kavacamāy rakṣa ēkīṭum mantram
mukti-pradāyakam bīja-mantram

The mantra removes the accumulated burden of our sins. It is the fruit of many lives of great merit, and it is a protective shield. It is the seed mantra that grants liberation.

niṣāda-hṛttinde āsura-bhāvam
unmūlanam ceyyum puṇya-mantram
bhavarōga-duḥkha-vināśaka-mantram
vandē bhaya-haram guru-mantram

The mantra removes the wicked tendencies of the dark and asuric mind. It destroys the sorrows and disease of the external world. I pray the Guru mantra that destroys all fear.

puṇyam ī mantram guru-mantram mahā-mantram guru-mantram
dhanyam ī mantram bīja-mantram mahā-mantram guru-mantram

This great mantra, the Guru mantra, is the most potent and sacred.

ammā untan tiru (Tamil)

ammā untan tiru nāmamē
vāzhvil oḷi peṙa seyyum nāmamē
iruḷai nīkki aruḷai pozhindu
ānandam tantiṭum nāmamē

The name 'Amma' fills our life with light. The name 'Amma' dispels all darkness, grants refuge and fills us with bliss.

samsāra kaṭalai kaṭattiṭuvāy ammā
śaraṇaṭaintōrai kāttiṭuvāy
vēṇḍum varam aḷḷi tantiṭuvāy ammā
vidhiye māṫṫri nargati aruḷvāy

Mother, you take us across the ocean of transmigration. You save those who have taken refuge in you, and you bestow desired boons. Remove all obstacles and bring us to the noble path.

kārttikai tirunāḷil vanduttittāy ammā
dharmattai nilaināṭṭa avatarittāy
pārvayāl pāvaṅgaḷ anaittum nīkki
piṙavāvarattai aḷittiṭuvāy

Our Mother was born on the auspicious day of *Karthika*, incarnating to establish *dharma*. Mother's sidelong glance destroys all wrongdoings. She frees us from birth and death and bestows liberation.

ammayallē en (Malayalam)

ammayallē en ammayallē – ī
kuññin or-āśvāsam ammayallē

kuññu-manassile nombaraṅgaḷ – tāyē
oppi eṭukkān aṇayukillē?

Are you not my mother? Are you not the mother who consoles her little child? O Mother, will you not come close and dispel the grief of my child-like heart?

aṙiv-onnum-illātta paitaline
aṙivuḷḷor-amma kāttīṭukillē?
buddhiyum bōdhavum ēki ivaḷe
ninde kuññāy vaḷarān anugrahikkū

Will the all-knowing mother not protect her ignorant child? Imparting discernment and awareness, bless this little one to grow as your child.

kuññāy piṙannu ñān bhuvil ammē ninde
kuññāy vaḷarān maṙannu pōyi
prēma-bhakti-jñānam ēki ivaḷe
tṛppāda-padmattil cērkkukillē?

Mother, I was born as an infant on this earth, but I forgot to grow as your child. Grant me loving devotion and knowledge, and draw me close to your lotus feet.

ammaye kāṇān koticc-oru (Malayalam)

ammaye kāṇān koticc-oru kaṇṇande
vṛndāvanattilum amma etti
mātṛ-bhāvattōṭe mātāvu kaṇṇane
ā maṭittaṭṭil irutti annu

Little Krishna longed to see his mother, so she came to Vrindavan. With motherly love she placed Krishna on her lap.

mātṛ-snēhattinde mādhuryam ōrttatum
kaṇṇande kaṇṇunīr karakaviññu
amma tan cēla eṭuttiṭṭu kaṇṇande
kaṇṇunīr ellām tuṭaccu māṫṫi

Imbibing the sweetness of his mother's love, tears welled up in Krishna's eyes. Mother wiped away his tears with the end of her *saree.*

kaṇṇā karayallē kaṇṇanām uṇṇiykku
kaṇkuḷirkke amma veṇṇa tarām
kaṇṇan karaññīlā veṇṇa nukarnnīlā
ammayil tanne layiccu pōyi

Krishna, darling child, don't cry. Mother will give you fresh butter, a feast for your eyes. Krishna did not cry or eat the butter. He merged with his mother!

kaṇṇā... kaṇṇā... kaṇṇā... kaṇṇā...

ammē ādiparāśakti (Malayalam)

ammē ādiparāśakti
aṙiv-ētum illā paital ivaḷ
dīnata ēṙunna makkaḷōṭ-anyathā
bhāvam pularttuvān ākumō ammē...

O Mother, the primal supreme power! I am your daughter who lacks all knowledge, but you never consider your distressed children as separate from you.

prārabdha-bhāram tāṅgiṭuvān ākāte
cakitayāy stabdhayāy ninnu pōy ñān

ā prēma-gaṅgayām śrīpāda-tīrtthattil
ennum enne magna ākkiṭēṇam ammē

Unable to bear the burden of my accumulated karma, I stand here sad and helpless. O Mother, immerse me in the divine Ganga water that has bathed your holy feet.

ulakamām māyā-marīcikayil peṭṭu
ninne ñān oru nāḷum maṙannīṭollē
ōrō aṇuvilum nin prēmam tuṭikkēṇam
prāṇan poliyumbōzhum nin nāmam uruviṭēṇam

Let me never get trapped in the mirage of the world and forget you. Let your love pulsate in every atom, and let me chant your name as life leaves my body.

ammē aviṭutte savidhattil (Malayalam)

ammē aviṭutte savidhattil aṇayumbōḷ
aṙiyunnu nin divya mātṛ-bhāvam
ammē aviṭunnu māṙōṭ-aṇaykkumbōḷ
aṙiyunnu divyamām ātmabhāvam

O Mother, as I reach your abode, I experience you as the divine Mother. O Mother, as you embrace me, I experience you as the supreme Self.

satyamāyi ennum en hṛttil vasippū nī
ennatām satyam aṙiññiṭāte
enne veṭiññu nī dūre eṅgō maṙaññ-
ennu ninacc-ende uḷḷu tēṅgi

Not knowing the truth that you reside forever in my heart, I cry in anguish, believing that you abandoned me and are hiding far away.

viśrānti tēṭi alayunnu en manam
ammē tava divya līlābhuvil
tāvaka prēmābdhiyil aṇaccīṭuvān
kāruṇyam ēkumō viśvamātē

O Mother! My mind wanders in your divine playground in search of repose. Mother of this universe, please be compassionate and dissolve me in the ocean of your love.

kālaṅgaḷāyi ñān nēṭiya sarvavum
kālam kavarnnīṭum; ī tanuvum
kālattinum mīte mēvunnor-ammē nin
pādattil nityam namikkunnu ñān

Time will steal away everything I gain, including this body. O Mother who transcends time, I ever bow down at your divine feet.

ammē bhagavati kāḷi mahēśvari (Malayalam)

ammē bhagavati kāḷi mahēśvari
amṛtēśvari pādam kumbiṭunnēn
bhavarōga-śāntikkāy kēzhunnor-enne nī
bhava-nāśinī nī anugrahikkū

O Mother Kali, the supreme goddess Amriteswari, I bow down at your divine feet. I beg you to release me from all the sorrows of this illusory world. O destroyer of all delusion, bless me.

nin cintayil āṇḍu en manam ennum
prēmattin tantrikaḷ mīṭṭīṭaṇē

karmaṅgaḷ ōrōnnum antaraṅgattile
śrīpāda-pūjayāy tīrttīṭaṇē

May thoughts of you fill my mind and strum the musical notes of love. May my actions be a worship of your lotus feet placed within my heart.

nin naṙum-puñciri en manatārile
mōhāndhakāram akaṫṫīṭaṇē
nin mahā-maunam en antarātmāvine
bōdha-svarūpamāy tīrnnīṭaṇē

May your radiant smile illumine my mind and destroy the darkness of ignorance. May a constant stream of thoughts of you reveal the true Self within me.

ammē dayānidhē (Malayalam)

ammē dayānidhē ninnil aṇayān ñān
piṭayunnu nirjjala-mīna-samānam
sandīptamām nin mukhāmbhōruham sadā
ennil pozhiccīṭaṇē amṛtavarṣam

O Mother, merciful one, like a fish struggling to return to water, I long to reach you. May your radiant lotus face shower rays of ambrosial bliss upon me.

ammē... ammē... ammē... ammē...

O Mother!

prārabdha-bhāṇḍattin bhārattāl innende
mānasam māyā-prapañca-magnam
jīvannadhīśa nī tanne ennaṙikilum
smṛtipatham nin cāru-rūpaśūnyam

The burden of my previous actions has immersed my mind in this illusory world. You are the Goddess of my life, yet I forget your lovely form in the path I traverse.

nī ennilum ñān ninnilum eṅkilum
vidūram āṇinnum nin prēmalōkam
amṛtasmṛti ennum jīvanil ēki nī
aṭiyanum aruḷaṇē amṛta-padam

You are in me and I am in you, yet the world of your love seems so far away. May I remember you forever. Grant me refuge at your lotus feet!

ammē jaganmātē māyē (Malayalam)

ammē jaganmātē māyē
hṛttil viḷaṅguk-en bhāmē
iniyum tāmasam entē tāyē
ennuḷḷil nī niṙaññīṭān

O Mother, goddess of this universe, embodiment of brilliance, shine within me. Why do you delay to fill my heart with your presence, O Mother?

rāgādi-vairikaḷ antaraṅgam
svantam ākkān ennavaṇṇam ennum
nitya-sandarśakar āyiṭunnu
nīyillā nērattu nōkki ammē

Likes and dislikes and all dualities in my mind make my heart their home when you do not reside within me.

dhyāna-japādikaḷ ceyta nēram
telloru śānti labhiccirunnu

nin prēmam ennil niṙañña nēram
nī ennil āṇennu ñān aṙiññu

I gain a little peace when I meditate and chant. When love for you fills my heart, I find you within.

ennuḷḷil ennumā niṙavu nilkkān
entu ñān ceyyēṇḍat-ende tāyē
nin prēma-lahariyil nṛttam ceyyān
en manam ennum koticciṭunnu

What should I do, O Mother, for your light to inundate my heart always? My mind ever longs to dance in the bliss of your love.

ammē ñān aviṭutte (Malayalam)

ammē ñān aviṭutte svantam allē?
pinnentin-enne tazhaññiṭunnu?
ninnuṭe cārattu vann-aṇayān
etra nāḷāyi koticcu nilpu

O Mother, am I not your very own? Then why do you forsake me? For so many days I have longed to come close to you.

ni enne ōrkkumō innu tāyē?
viraha-tikkanalil ñān nīṙi jvalippū
snēhāmṛtattinde alayāyi vannende
manassil nī tūmaññin kuḷir ēkiṭū

O Mother, will you remember me today? I am burning in the fire of separation from you. Won't you come as a wave of ambrosial love and soothe my aching heart?

māyā-prapañcattil ninne tiraññ-ennāl
ennuḷḷil eṅgane nī vanniṭum?
ninnuṭe kara-sparśam neṙukayil patiññ-ennāl
ennuḷḷil nī uṇarnnīṭumallō

If I search for you in this illusory world, how will you enter my heart? If you bless me with the touch of your hand on my head, you will awaken within me.

nī ende cintayāy māṙīṭaṇē
nī ende karaṅgaḷāy varttikkaṇē
ōrōrō vākkilum ōrōrō nōkkilum
dēvi nī vannu niṙaññīṭaṇē... pinne
ninnil aliññu ñān nīyāyiṭum

May you be my every thought, may you act through my hands. O Devi, may you fill my every word and glance. I will dissolve in you and become you.

ammē ñān aviṭutte svantam allē?
ammē ñān aviṭutte svantam allē?

O Mother, am I not your very own?

ammē ninn-ōrmma tan (Malayalam)

ammē ninn-ōrmma tan ceppu tuṙannīṭave
nin prēma-taraṅgam en cuṫṫum parannu
en antaraṅgattin pontiri-nāḷam
nin prēma-jyōtiyil ujjvaliccu

O Mother, as I open the treasure chest of my memories of you, your love envelops me. The little lamp of my heart blazes up in the light of your love.

nin prēma-vanikayil oru bhṛṅgam-ennapōl
snēhāmṛtam nukarnn-ullasiccīṭave
mōha-jālaṅgaḷām nizhalil bhramiccu ñān
mōhita ākān ninacciṭollē

The nectar of your love intoxicates my heart, and I soar in your divine garden. Let me not stray into the shadows of desire and delusion.

ā divya-prēma-pravāham tazhukumbōḷ
amma tan smṛtiyil āzhtti enne
nin bōdha-niṟavilēkk-enne uṇarttuvān
hṛdaya-sūnam ninnil arppicciṭām

When the flow of your pure love caresses me, I become immersed in thoughts of you. I offer the flower of my heart at your feet, that I may awaken to the fullness of your knowledge.

ammē nin pādattil (Malayalam)

ammē nin pādattil vīṇu kiṭakkum ī
ēzhaye nōkkāttat-entē?
bhāricca vēdana tāṅguvān ākāte
kēṇu viḷikkunnu ninne, ammē

O Mother, why do you not look at this destitute who lies fallen at your feet? Unable to bear the burden of grief, O Mother, I cry out to you.

alivōṭe vāri puṇarnnu nī ennuṭe
akatārin-āśvāsam ēkū
nērāya pātayil nī nayikkū ennil
nērinde bōdham uṇarttū, ammē

Lovingly gather me in your arms and console my aching heart. O Mother, guide me along the correct path, and awaken true awareness within.

vyartha-svapnaṅgaḷe neytu kūṭṭīṭunna
cittatte taṭṭi uṇarttū
prēmatte hṛttil pakarū
martya jīvita sāphalyam ēkū

Let your divine touch awaken my mind that weaves countless, futile dreams. Fill my heart with your divine love, and let my life be fulfilled.

ammē nin tṛppāda-kamalattil (Malayalam)

ammē nin tṛppāda-kamalattil cēruvān
kōṭi janmaṅgaḷāy kāttirippū
samsāram ākum nin māyā-prapañcattin
etra nāḷ iniyum uzhalēṇḍū ñān

O Mother! I have waited millions of lives to unite with your lotus feet. How long must I wander in your illusory universe?

satyavum muktiyum nī enn-aṙiññiṭṭum
nitarām nin smṛti uṇarāttat-entē?
nin mukha-padmattil viṭarum ā naṙunilā-
puñciri kāṇmān ñān entu ceyvū?

I know you are the Truth and liberation. Why am I unable to remember you constantly? What must I do to receive your smile that resembles the soft, silver moonlight?

nistula-prēmamē! nin tiru līlakaḷ
kaṇḍu kōri taricc-enn-antaraṅgam
prēmāvatāramē! ninn-aṭittāratil
bhāva-samarpitam ende janmam

Your love is unequalled, and my heart is blissful watching your divine play. You are the incarnation of love. I offer my life at your lotus feet.

ammē śaraṇam amṛtēśvari śaraṇam (Malayalam)

ammē śaraṇam amṛtēśvari śaraṇam
dēvī śaraṇam paramēśvari śaraṇam

O Mother, immortal Goddess, I take refuge in you. O Devi, supreme Goddess, I take refuge in you!

yōgyata ētum illātt-ivaḷkk-ambikē
yōgyata ēkū nin putriyāyi
andhakārāvṛtam en manō-vanikayil
nanmozhi-muttināl prabha coriyū

O Mother! Make this worthless child worthy. Accept me as your own daughter. May your words enter as light into the dark forest of my mind.

kāmādi-vairikaḷ pēmāri peyyunna
māmaka mānasa-kānanattil
nistula-prēmattin vīcikaḷāl nī
pūrṇēnduvenna pōl teḷiccam ēkū

Desire, anger and other enemies rain down in the forest of my mind. Like the full moon, enlighten me with your pure love and shine your light upon my path.

māmaka janmam nin pūvāṭiyākkī – atil
viriyunna malarukaḷ mālyaṅgaḷ ākkīṭān
amṛta-kanaṅgaḷāy peytiṙaṅgi nī
ātma-harṣattāl vasantam ākkū

Let my life become your flower garden. Let the blossomed flowers become your garland. Rain down on me as drops of ambrosia. Let my mind blossom in the bliss of the true Self!

ammē śaraṇam dēvī śaraṇam (Malayalam)

ammē śaraṇam dēvī śaraṇam
śrīpādam mātram āṇ-ēkāśrayam
śaraṇam śaraṇam sadguru-caraṇam
tiru-kṛpa mātram āṇ-avalambam

O Mother, O Goddess, grant me shelter. Your divine feet are my only sanctuary. I take refuge at the feet of the *sadguru.* Your grace is my only support.

nirmala-hṛdayam āṇende lakṣyam
nirbhaya-cittam ākunnu lakṣyam
dharmam āṇ-ennuṭe mārgam ennum
guru-kṛpa guru-kṛpa ēkāśrayam

A pure heart and fearless mind are my goal. Dharma is ever my path, and the grace of the guru my sole refuge.

vāsanā-nāśam āṇ-ende lakṣyam
jñāna-prāpti ākunnu lakṣyam

arpaṇam āṇ-atinn-ēka mārgam
guru-kṛpa guru-kṛpa ēkāśrayam

Surrender is the only way to break free of all negativities and attain my goal of real knowledge. Guru's grace is my sole refuge.

amṛta-mahēśvari akhilāṇḍēśvari (Malayalam)

amṛta-mahēśvari akhilāṇḍēśvari
anavadhi śānti-sudātri

O Empress of ultimate reality, bearer of the nectar of immortality, you bestow everlasting peace.

aṭimalariṇa tozhum aṭiyanu nalkaṇam
amṛtānanda-padam

Do grant your servant the immortal bliss of your lotus feet.

śrīkari sumanōhari
hari-vidhivinutē śubhadē

Giver of auspiciousness, O charming one, you are worshipped by Vishnu and Brahma.

māmaka-janani mānasa hariṇi
mātaṅgi śyāmāṅgi

O Mother, you dissolve my mind. You are the Goddess of speech, music and knowledge, O dark-hued one.

bhūtalamātē tāvakapādē
sādaram-abhivandē

O Mother of the Earth, we bow with reverence at your sacred feet.

amṛtam śaraṇam amma (Telugu)

amṛtam śaraṇam amma entō madhuram amma
amṛtam śaraṇam amma entō madhuram amma

Mother is my only refuge, Mother is sweet immortal bliss.

ahānni anicce nī vātsalyam amṛtam
śuddha prēmanu nimbē nī kāruṇē amṛtam
kōpānni hariñce nī prēme amṛtam
nisvārtha manasicce nī sēve amṛtam

The immortal bliss of your affection removes my ego. The immortal bliss of your compassion fills me with pure love. The immortal bliss of your love dissolves my anger. The immortal bliss of your service bestows a selfless mind.

cittāni nilipe nī sannidhe amṛtam
citta-śuddhini cesē nī sahanam amṛtam
ānandam nimpē nī cūpe amṛtam
velugunu nimpē nī smarane amṛtam

The immortal bliss of your presence stills my mind. The immortal bliss of your patience purifies my mind. The immortal bliss of your sight fills me with joy. The immortal bliss of remembrance of you illuminates my life.

amṛtam śaraṇam amma entō madhuram amma
amṛtam amma madhuram amma

Mother is my only refuge, Mother is sweet immortal bliss.

amṛtavarṣiṇi gaṅgē (Malayalam)

amṛtavarṣiṇi gaṅgē
prēma-pravāhini gaṅgē
ajñāna-nāśini gaṅgē
duḥkha-vimōcini gaṅgē

O Ganga, flow of immortal nectar, river of divine love, you destroy ignorance and free us from suffering.

hṛdayēśvarī ammē jagadīśvarī
amṛtēśvarī ammē bhuvanēśvarī

O Mother, you are the Goddess of my heart, Goddess of the world, immortal Goddess of the Universe.

nin prēma-pravāhattāl ammē
ennile tāpam akaṫṫīṭaṇē
anavaratam nin amṛta-varṣattāl
ātmāvine tōṭṭ-uṇarttīṭaṇē

O Mother, dispel the sorrow of my mind in the flow of your love. Awaken my inner Self through your constant shower of nectar.

oru pāzh kusumam eṅkilum ñān
ammē nin padam aṇayān koticcū
kadanattāl katti kariyunnatin mumbē
kazhalaṭi cērttu rakṣiccīṭaṇē

O Mother, though I am a flower unworthy to be offered in worship, I long to reach your feet. Unite me with your feet and save me before the fire of sorrow consumes me.

ānandamē saccidānanda (Malayalam)

ānandamē... saccidānanda-svarūpiṇi ammē
aṇayū prāṇanil nitya-vasantamāy nī niṙayū
anantatē... viśva-caitanyamē en jīvanil
nī jñāna-dīpamāy teḷiyū

O Mother, embodiment of truth, consciousness and bliss! Come and be the eternal spring in my heart. O infinite one, you are the consciousness pervading the universe. Shine within me as the lamp of knowledge.

ēkāntam ākum en mauna-tīraṅgaḷe
kuḷiriḷam tennaläy nī toṭṭ-uṇarttavē
anubhūti-dhanyam ī nimiṣaṅgaḷ ammē
prēmārdram nī inn-en janma-puṇyam

You awakened the lonely and silent shores of my mind like a cool and gentle breeze. These moments are rich with blissful experiences and filled with your love.

aham enna bhāvavum bhēda-bhāvaṅgaḷum
akann-ātmabōdhattil uṇartīṭuvān
coriyēṇamē nin kṙpāvarṣam ennil nī
saphalam ākkīṭaṇē ende janmam

Let my ego and sense of duality disappear, and let me awaken to my true Self. O Mother, let your grace flow into me and fulfill my life.

ānandam uḷḷattil (Malayalam)

ānandam uḷḷattil uṇḍeṅkilum
ārāyunnilla nām antaraṅgē

Though supreme bliss is in our heart, we do not seek it within.

āyiram vātilil muṭṭunnu nām
ātmāvin vātil aṭacciṭunnu

We knock at a thousand doors but keep the door of the *Atman* closed.

āṛeyum āśrayikkunnu nammaḷ
ā paramēśane onnozhiye

We are willing to depend on anyone except the supreme Lord.

āvōḷam bhōgaṅgaḷ āsvadikkē
āntarayōgam taṭuttiṭunnu

Indulging the pleasures of the senses hinders our spiritual growth.

āśrama-jīvitam ēṙe iṣṭam
'ā' śramam āṇeṅkil vēṙe kaṣṭam

We like ashram life, but making a *shramam* ("that effort") is a different matter.

ārilum kuṫṫaṅgaḷ kāṇumbōzhum
ārānum kāṇunnō tande kuṫṫam

We keenly find fault with anyone, but do we see our own faults?

ācāryan ākuvān entu mōham
ācariccīṭuvān illa dāham

We desire to teach, but fail to practice what we teach.

āmnāyam colli-paṭhikkunnatō
ādyantamāya viśuddhi nēṭān

We chant Vedic mantras to gain ultimate purity.

āreyum taccutakarkkānuḷḷa
āyudham ākkēṇḍatalla vidya

Spiritual knowledge should not be used as a weapon to destroy another.

ānanda-dhāmam aṇaññiṭuvān
āgraham uḷḷil uṇḍāyiṭēṇam

We must yearn to reach the abode of bliss.

ā mahāśaktiyām amma uṇḍē
ātmārtthamāya vazhi kāṭṭuvān

O Mother, Supreme Goddess, you are here to show us the right path.

ānanda-nartaki ambikē (Malayalam)

ānanda-nartaki ambikē
ānanda-kallōlini
akhila-jagat-sṛṣṭikāriṇi
akhilarkkum āśrayam nin caraṇam

O Mother, blissful dancer, river of bliss! You are the creator of the entire world. Your feet are the refuge for all.

kāḷikē mahāmāyikē ambikē
kāḷikē mahāmōhini ambikē
kāḷikē bhavatāriṇi ambikē
kāḷikē avatāriṇi ambikē

O Mother Kali, divine incarnation, divine *maya,* great enchantress! O Mother Kali, take us across the ocean of transmigration.

cinmaya-rūpiṇi brahmarūpē
triguṇātmikē dēvi yōgēśvari
nī allāt-enikk-āruṇḍ-abhayam
nin pada-kamalam śaraṇam ennum

Your nature is consciousness. Your form is the absolute. You are the three gunas and the Goddess of union. I have no one other than you. Your lotus feet are forever my refuge.

prēma-svarūpiṇi amṛtānandam
nukarān vembunn-ivaḷ
ānanda-narttanam tuṭarū nī en
ātmāvām cētass-uṇarttū

Embodiment of divine love, this little one longs to taste immortal bliss. Continue your blissful dance and awaken within me as my true Self!

ānanda-naṭanam (Sanskrit)

ānanda-naṭanam anupama nṛttam
tāṇḍavam śiva tāṇḍavam
ananya naṭanam amṛta-svarūpam
tāṇḍavam śiva tāṇḍavam

The blissful dance, the incomparable dance, the dance of oneness, the dance of eternity, the *tandava* dance of Lord Shiva!

ḍama ḍama ḍama ḍama ḍamaruka-nādam
dhimi dhimi dhimi dhimi nūpura-tāḷam
tāṇḍavam śiva tāṇḍavam

'Dama dama', the sound of the damaru drum. 'Dhimi dhimi', the rhythmic jingling of anklets! The tandava dance of Lord Shiva!

ananta-naṭanam aghōra nāṭyam
tāṇḍavam śiva tāṇḍavam
acintya naṭanam ādima tāḷam
tāṇḍavam śiva tāṇḍavam

The infinite dance, the mighty dance, the tandava dance of Lord Shiva! The dance that transcends all thought, the primordial rhythm! The tandava dance of Lord Shiva!

amēya naṭanam apūrva nṛtyam
tāṇḍavam śiva tāṇḍavam
anādi naṭanam anādhi bhāvam
tāṇḍavam śiva tāṇḍavam

The pure dance, the unparalleled dance, the great tandava dance of Lord Shiva! The dance of eternal existence, the tandava dance of Lord Shiva!

añjana-kaṇṇane (Malayalam)

añjana-kaṇṇane anpōṭu kāṇuvān
antaraṅgattile mōham
kaṇḍiṭṭum kaṇḍillā-bhāvam naṭikkunnu
kaṇṇā ñān entini ceyyum?

My heart longs with love to see the dark-hued Lord. You see me, but you pretend that you don't. What shall I do now, O Krishna?

vṛndāvanattile pullilum kallilum
nin pāda padmam patiññu
gōpikaḷ gōpanmār ā puṇya-śālikaḷ
nin mēni kaṇḍu rasiccu

Your feet are imprinted in each blade of grass and each stone in Vrindavan. The gopas and gopis, people of great merit, saw your beautiful form and were transported to bliss.

oru nōkku kāṇuvān oru vākku kēḷkkuvān
paramātma-prēmam nukarān
oru mātra eṅkilum arikil nī varikillē
paritāpam āke akaṫṫān

I long to receive a single glance, to hear a single word, to imbibe your supreme love. Won't you come for even a moment and remove my despair?

aṙivillāppaitale (Malayalam)

aṙivillāppaitale aṭuttēkk-aṇaccappōḷ
ahantayāl akale ñān māṙi ninnu
atinuḷḷa śikṣayō dēvī ī akalam
aparādham poṙukkēṇam ammē

You drew this ignorant child close to you, but, in my ego, I moved away from you. Now you are far away. Is this my punishment? Please forgive me, O Devi

virahattāl vembunnen hṛdayam
iniyennu kāṇum ninne mama jananī
māyā-lōkattil alayum ī cittattil
sthira-bhakti ēki nī kṛpa coriyū
ammē kṛpa coriyū

My heart weeps with longing for you, O Mother! When will I see you again? My heart is wandering in this illusory world. O Mother! Shower your grace upon me, and grant me unshakeable devotion.

prapañcattin-ādhāram amma
en cintakaḷkkum sākṣi nīyē tāyē
śyāmē mahēśvari samsāra nāśini
nirmala-bhakti ēki nayiccīṭaṇe
ninnil layiccīṭaṇē

O Mother! You are the substratum of this universe. You witness all my thoughts and you destroy the cycle of birth and death. O Great Goddess, dark-hued One, grant me pure devotion and guide me. Let me dissolve in you!

aṙiyēṇḍat-aṙiyuvān (Malayalam)

aṙiyēṇḍat-aṙiyuvānuḷḷa mōham
aṙiyum varēyum nām kai-viṭāññāl
aṙivellām ninnuṭe uḷḷil āṇennu
guruvāy mozhiyāy aṙiññiṭum nām

Let us desire to know what should be known until we come to know the Truth. Then, the words of the Guru will make us realize that all knowledge is within us.

karmaṅgaḷ ellām nām śraddhayōṭe
gurupāda pūjayāy ceytiṭēṇam
aviṭutte vākkum nām kēṭṭiṭāññāl
ajñāna-valayil nām peṭṭu pōkum

We must perform all actions with faith, as worship of the Guru's divine feet. If we fail to listen to Her words, the trap of ignorance will catch us.

tatva-grahikkaṇam eṅkilō nām
jñāna-mārgam tanne kaikoḷḷaṇam

ātmalābham vēnameṅkil nammaḷ
ātma-samarppaṇam ceytiṭēṇam

We must follow the path of knowledge to understand the ultimate principle. If we want Self-realization, we must surrender our ego.

akhilavum ñān tanne ennaṙiññāl
ānandam kaivarum uḷḷilappōḷ
sarvacarācara vyāptan-ākum
īśvara-darśanam sādhyam ākum

When we understand that we are in everything, we will be filled with bliss. We will know that we pervade all beings, sentient and insentient, and we will see God in everything.

aṙiyunn-illen (Malayalam)

aṙiyunn-illen manassin bandham
mamatā-bandhanam aṙiyunnilla
salilōpari navanītam pōl
ātmāvine bōdhikkunnilla

My mind is unaware that attachments bind. It does not experience the unattached Self as like to butter that floats on water.

śruti ōtunnatu nīyajan ennu
jīvita-maraṇādikaḷ illennu
ennāl kāṇunn-iva ñān-ennil
mugdhan baddhan pōlāyī ñān

Scriptures proclaim that our true Self is unborn, having neither birth nor death. Yet I feel myself as subject to birth and death. I feel as if ignorant and bound.

ātma-jñānam dṛḍham-āyīṭukil
dagdham kāmāvidyā bījam
samyak mātṛ-svarūpam aṙiññāḷ
muktōham iti jñānam dṛḍhamām

When I become firm in knowledge of the Self, desire and ignorance will be like a burnt seed, unable to sprout. When we experience Oneness in the form of Mother, we become established in the knowledge that 'I am free.'

arṣabhārata samskṛti (Malayalam)

arṣabhārata samskṛti tan
ādimaddhyānta-poruḷē
ādi dēvi nin mahassil
āzhaṇē ñān vāzhaṇē

You are the everlasting essence of the Vedic culture of India. O Devi, the creator, let me dwell within your splendor.

ādi-dēvan tan kiraṇam
āzhiyil ninn-uyaravē
āzhnn-iṙaṅgi ennil ammē
ā nabhassin vaibhavam

As the rays of the Sun God rise from the ocean, the majesty of the resplendent sky enters deep within my heart.

ārttirambi ende uḷḷil
ā vacassin vaibhavam
ādi-dēvi nin padattil
āzhaṇē ñān vāzhaṇē

The wisdom of your words fills my mind like the waves of the ocean. O Devi, primordial Goddess, may I dive deep and dwell in you.

aruṇārkkabimbam (Malayalam)

aruṇārkka-bimbam sāgarattil aliyunna pōl
en manam ammē ninnil aliyān kotikkunnu
sandhyaykku kūṭ-aṇayān vembunna kiḷiye pōl
ninnil aṇayān ammē vembunn-en antaraṅgam

As the setting sun dissolves in the ocean, my mind longs to dissolve in you. As the bird yearns to reach its nest at dusk, my mind longs to merge in you.

nin divya-pātayil sañcariccīṭilum
vighnamāy tīrunn-en vāsanakaḷ
māya tan cuzhiyil akappeṭṭa ñānumē
ninnil ettīṭuvān kazhiyāte uzhalunnu

As I travel along your divine path, my *vasanas* (tendencies) become impediments. The whirlpool of illusion catches me and I cannot reach you.

en manō-mālinyam akatti en cittatte
ammē nin śrīkōvil ākkiṭaṇē...
ennile ninnil uṇarnn-ī janmam
tṛppāda-padmattil arppitam ākaṇē

O Mother, remove the impurities in my heart that I may enshrine you within. May I awaken to my true Self and offer my life at your divine feet.

āsaiyennum asuranvandu (Tamil)

āsaiyennum asuranvandu āṭṭivaikka toṭaṅkiviṭṭāl
ōsaiyinṭri en manamum ulagiyalil mūzhgum
ammā
adanāl unadaṭiyai azhagāna malaraṭiyai
appōdaikk-ippōdē piṭittu-koṇḍēn – ammā
appōdaikk-ippōdē piṭittu-koṇḍēn

O Mother, when the demon of desire makes me dance to its tune, my mind silently drowns in the material world. Then I cling to your beautiful lotus feet, O Mother!

kōpamenum koṭiyevanum kūrvēlāl tākkiviṭṭāl
pāvamtanai seydiṭavum pāzhum manam tuṇiyum
ammā
adanāl unadaṭiyai azhagāna malaraṭiyai
appōdaikk-ippōdē piṭittu-koṇḍēn – ammā
appōdaikk-ippōdē piṭittu-koṇḍēn

O Mother, when the devilish spear of anger attacks, my mind boldly sets out to commit terrible deeds. Then I cling to your beautiful lotus feet, O Mother!

kaḷavu enum kanniyumē kaṇjāṭai kāṭṭiviṭṭāl
vaḷainduviṭum buddhiyadu nērvazhiyai
maṙakkum ammā
adanāl unadaṭiyai azhagāna malaraṭiyai
appōdaikk-ippōdē piṭittu-koṇḍēn – ammā
appōdaikk-ippōdē piṭittu-koṇḍēn

The attitude of wrongdoing clouds my mind and I forget the right path. O Mother, in those moments, I cling to your beautiful lotus feet.

kālam kālamāga sērtta tīyavāsanai
dēvi undan pādampaṭṭra māyndupōgumē
kāma-nāśini kāḷi-bhairavi
jñāna-dāyini dēviśaṅkari

O Devi! All our negative tendencies, accumulated since ages, simply disappear when we cling to your feet. O Kali, Bhairavi, destroyer of desires! O Devi, Shankari, bestower of knowledge!

As I walk along (English)

As I walk along the path, many hands pull me off course.
Only your hands carry me and lead me to the goal.
As I walk along the path, many voices lead me astray.
Only your words keep me walking the right way.
As I walk along the path, shiny objects distract me.
Only your light shows my eyes what they ought to see.
As I walk along the path, I'm pricked by jealousy.
Only the sweet balm of your love heals me.
As I walk along the path, desires try to drown me.
Only your presence in my life saves me.

Amma you carry me (only you)
Amma you guide me (only you)

Amma you heal me (only you)
Amma you save me (only you)

atirillā kāruṇyam (Malayalam)

atirillā kāruṇyam nadiyāyi ozhukkunn-orammē
nin pādattil entu nalkum
mānasa-puṣpattāl arccana ceytīṭām
kaṇṇīr-kaṇaṅgaḷāl pūja ceyyām ammē
kaṇṇīr-kaṇaṅgaḷāl pūja ceyyām

O Mother! What can we offer at your feet? You flow as a river of boundless compassion. We will offer you mental worship and adore you with the flowers of our tears.

oru tiri hṛdayattil makkaḷ teḷikkumbōḷ
āyiram tiriyāy teḷiyunnu nī
amma tan vātsalyam kaṭalāy ozhukkumbōḷ
entivaḷ ceyyēṇḍū ende ammē ā
tṛppāda-sēvakkāy entu ceyyum?

When your children light a single lamp in their heart, You shine there with the brilliance of a thousand lamps. O Mother! Your compassion flows like the ocean. How should this daughter adore your divine feet?

onnumē aṙiyāte paitalāy vaḷarumī
makkaḷe ennum nī kāttīṭaṇē
aḷavillā kṛpayennum tūkīṭaṇē
tṛkkaram ēki nī nayiccīṭaṇē ā
tṛppāda-padmattil cērttīṭaṇē

Please take care of your children who grew up not knowing the Truth. Please shower your boundless compassion on us, take our hands and lead us to your divine feet!

ātmagāyakā (Malayalam)

ātmagāyakā muraḷīlōlā
en munnil varuvān amāntam entē?
kaḷiyāy innenne avaniyil īvidham
veṭiyuvatinn-ahō entu nyāyam?
ātmagāyakā... kṛṣṇā

O Player of the flute, music of my soul, why do you not come before me? Is it fair to abandon me in this world? Is it your divine play?

janmaṅgaḷ etra-mēl alaññu valaññālum
kātara-hṛdayayāy kāttirippū
mizhikaḷil prēmāśru-binduvumāy
mizhi-naṭṭirippū ninn-aruma-sakhī

I have traversed many lives and wander still, yearning to see you. Crying tears of love, I wait for you. Your dear friend gazes with longing, waiting to see you!

hṛdayattin nombaram ninniṣṭam ennāl
entiha ceyvatu ñān iniyum
māmaka janmam ninniccha mātram ennāl
maṫtentu vazhiyuḷḷū ivaḷkk-iniyum

If you enjoy the pain of my longing heart, what else can I do but long for you? Is this life of mine according to your will?

ātmāvil ānandam (Malayalam)

ātmāvil ānandam tēṭi alayunnōr-
abhayārtthi ñān ammē
satyattin ponmaṇi dīpam teḷikkū...
satya-svarūpiṇi ammē...

O Mother! I am a wandering refugee in search of the bliss of the *atman*. Please light the golden lamp of Truth, O Mother, embodiment of Truth.

ñān brahmam, ñān brahmam ennu collunnor
ñān brahmamāy-aṙiññīṭunnō?
tatvaṅgaḷ-okke kēṭṭaṙiññu...
tatvānuṣṭhānam etumilla

Do those who say "I am brahman" really know the Truth? They have heard the great spiritual truths, but have they ever experienced it?

bhaktiyum jñānavum ottu-cērnnāl
mithyayil onnum bhramikkayillā
ēkatvam tannil uṙacciṭātē...
ēkātma bhāvam varikayilla

If knowledge and devotion go hand-in-hand, we will not be deluded by this illusory world. Only when we stand firm in the knowledge of Oneness will we experience our oneness with the world!

vēdavum śāstravum vēda-vēdāntavum
nērvazhi kāṭṭuvān mātramallō
sarvātma-bhāvam vannīṭuvān...
sadguru-pādattil ēkāśrayam

The Vedas and scriptures only point to the right path. To experience the Oneness of the supreme Self, we must surrender to the Sadguru.

atulita-prēma-pravāhamē (Malayalam)

atulita-prēma-pravāhamē ammē nin
tṛkkazhal smarikkunnu avirāmam
en manam ānanda-sāndram...
ennil viṭarunnu śānti-puñjam

O Mother, river of incomparable love, the memory of your divine feet fills my mind with joy. Flowers of peace blossom within.

sarvajñayām amma kāṇmat eṅgum
ātma-caitanyam atonnu mātram
kāruṇya-pīyūṣa-varṣattāl
ende aparādham ellām poṙuttīṭaṇē

O all-knowing Mother, you see only pure consciousness everywhere. Please forgive all my mistakes in the ambrosial shower of your compassion.

dharmattin marmam aṙiññu nīṅgān
en mārgē dīpamāy jvaliccīṭēṇē
ā divya-dhāmattil aṇayān kazhiññāl
ī nara-janmam kṛtārttham ākum

Please shine as light on my path, that I may follow the way of dharma. This human life will be fulfilled when I reach your divine abode.

āyiram āyiram nadrikaḷ (Tamil)

āyiram āyiram nadrikaḷ ammā untan tiruvaṭiyil
ādiśakti annai nīyena aṙiyaseyda tiruvaruḷē

O Mother, unending grateful prostrations at your lotus feet. O Divine grace, you made me realize that you are the supreme Mother.

kaṇkaḷiraṇḍum kaṇṇīr utirkka
kaikaḷiraṇḍum tozhutu nirkka
kātukaḷ iraṇḍum unpukazh kēḷkka
kālkaḷ iraṇḍum unnai valamvaikka

My eyes shed tears, my palms join in prayer, my ears listen to your glories and my feet circumambulate you.

āzhiyil tuṙumbena alaintu tirintēn
ūzhiyil umayē unnai maṙantu
kālan varum nāḷe kāttunindrēn
kāḷī enai nī kāttīṭuvāy

O goddess Uma, I wander in the world like a rusted piece of iron, forgetting you in the quagmire of maya. Now I just wait for the Lord of death. O Kali protect me!

banta sonta paṫtil mūzhki
bhairavi unnai paṫtra maṙantēn
paṫtravadu un padamalartānē
paṇivuṭan unpadam paṇintēnē

Drowning in my attachments to kith and kin, O Bhairavi, I forgot to cling to you. Let my only attachment be to your lotus feet. I humbly bow down at your feet.

bhīmarūpi māruti (Marathi)

bhīmarūpi māruti prabhuśrī rām bhakta
mahārūdra dīnanāthā

rām dūtā rām bhaktā
rām dūtā rām bhaktā

O Hanuman of mighty form, devotee of Lord Ram, fierce one, protector of the needy, messenger of Ram!

jay jay hanumantā
jay jay māruti rāyā
rāma rāma rāma rāma rāma rāma rāmā

Victory to Hanuman!

vēdānsā sāru tsāṇi tō...
nāmācī ruci vāḍhvitō
jay jay rām dās hanumantā
rām dūtā rām bhaktā

He understood the essence of the Vedas and delighted in chanting the divine name. Victory to the servant of Ram, the messenger of Ram, the devotee of Ram!

jay jay hanumantā
jay jay māruti rāyā
rāma rāma rāma rāma rāma rāma rāmā

Victory to Hanuman!

sarvātmā rāmātsā prakāś
sītārām hṛdayī baisē
jay jay rām dās hanumantā
rām dūtā rām bhaktā

All beings are the light of Ram, Sita Ram, ever dwelling in the heart. Victory to the servant of Ram, the messenger of Ram, the devotee of Ram!

bhumiyekkāḷ kṣama (Malayalam)

bhumiyekkāḷ kṣama tyāgattin mātṛka
mātṛtva-sāram ennamma
cāravē vann-aṇaññu mahā-naukayāy
bhava-sāgarē ñān alaññīṭavē

My Mother is more patient than the Earth. The epitome of sacrifice, she is the essence of motherhood. As I drifted in the ocean of transmigration, she came to me as a divine boat.

kāla-cakrattin cuzhiyil amarāte
kāruṇya-hastam nīṭṭi amma
ajñānamām kūriruṭṭil alayāte
jñāna-dīpattāl nayicciṭunnu

Mother stretched out her compassionate hand and rescued me from the whirlpool of time. With the lamp of knowledge, she leads me, saving me from wandering in the darkness of ignorance.

amma tan vātsalya-madhu nukarum
janmam dhanyamāy entu ñān arppicciṭum
inn-enikk-ēkuvān onnumē illammē
enne nin tṛppādē arppicciṭām

I taste the tenderness of Mother's love, and my life is now blessed. What can I offer you? I have nothing to give you. O Mother, I surrender myself at your sacred feet.

candana manasuḷḷor-amma (Malayalam)

candana manasuḷḷor-amma nīla-
tāmara mizhiyuḷḷor-amma
cañcalam-ākum en manassil
cāru – candrikayāy-innu vannu

My Mother's heart is like fragrant, pure sandal. My Mother's eyes are like fresh lotus petals. She comes as the lovely moon and enlightens my fickle mind.

kaṭalōḷamuḷḷa nin kanivil
ñān aṙiyāte līnanāy pōyi
kāruṇya-rūpiṇi kāl-iṭaṙāte ñān
sānandam innum gamippu

I merged in the ocean of Her grace. O embodiment of compassion, my legs do not falter as I joyfully move forward.

kātaramāy-oren kaṇkaḷilēkk-amma
kāruṇyamōṭ-innu nōkki
karayuvān vembum en mizhiyiṇa tuṭacc-enne
kara-valayattil otukki
ā kara-valayattil otukki

Today, my Mother took me in Her arms and looked with compassion into my longing eyes. She wiped my tears and kept me safe in Her embrace!

ḍam ḍam ḍam ḍam (Hindi)

ḍam ḍam ḍam ḍam
ḍamaru bajāvē ḍamaru bajāvē
ḍamaru bajāvē naṭarājā ō...
naṭarājā ō... naṭarājā

O Nataraja! Play your two-headed drum that resonates with primal sounds,

ḍam ḍam ḍam ḍam
ḍam ḍam ḍam ḍam ḍam ḍam ḍam ḍam
naṭan karō jī śivajī jay jay
naṭan karō jī śivajī
naṭan rāj kī naṭan rāj kī naṭan rāj kī jay
naṭan rāj kī jay
bambam bhōlā nāth bhōlā
bambam bhōlā śivajī bhōlā

Play the *damaru* and dance, O Lord Shiva! Victory to the Lord of dance! Victory to the innocent Lord Shiva!

ḍam ḍam ḍam ḍam
ḍam ḍam ḍam ḍam ḍam ḍam ḍam ḍam
kailasa-vāsi digambarēśā
naṭan karō jī naṭarājā
naṭan rāj kī naṭan rāj kī naṭan rāj kī jay
naṭan rāj kī jay
bambam bhōlā nāth bhōlā
bambam bhōlā śivajī bhōlā

Our Lord Shiva, O simple, ascetic Lord who resides on Mount Kailasa. Victory to the Lord of the dance! Victory to the innocent Lord Shiva!

dayānidhiyē dayānadiyē (Tamil)

dayānidhiyē dayānadiyē
dayāpariyē dayaipurivāy

You are a treasure house of compassion, a river of love. Please show mercy to me.

uḷ manatil asaintāṭi varum mayilē
tēn amutenappāṭum isaikuyilē
ammā tāpattai nīkki aruḷiṭuvāy
daraṇiyil śāntiyai aḷikka vantāy

You are a peacock dancing in my mind, and a cuckoo singing with honey-like sweetness. O Mother, you have come to bring peace in this world. Please remove my sorrows and bless me.

māmarai ondrum teriyavillai
mātavam ētum puriyavillai
pāmaran endru pārkkavillai
pāvi ena nī vilakkavillai

I don't know scriptures and I have not performed austerities. I am ignorant and have committed many mistakes, but do not push me away.

mīn vizhiyāḷē, madhura mozhiyāḷē
maragata māmaṇiyē ānanta gītamē
aruḷ bhuvanēśvariyē, akhilāṇḍēśvariyē
vāgīśvariyē nī amṛtēśvariyē

O Mother, your eyes are fish-shaped and your speech is sweet. You are a precious gem, a blissful song. O Goddess of the world, Goddess of the universe, Goddess of speech, immortal Goddess!

dēva dēva mahādēva (Kannada)

dēva dēva mahādēva śiva
dēva dēva mahādēva śiva

O God of gods, great Lord Shiva!

trikarṇa triguṇa triśūla dhṛḍadi
sthāpisi kuḷite acala virāgi
manavemba jaṅgama basavananu kallāgi
sthāvaramāḍi kūḍiside

You sit, immovable in renunciation, firmly holding the divine trident. You turned the temperamental bull of the mind into stone, making it still.

ahaṃbhāvadi ninna avamānisida
prajāpatiya śirava maṇiside
mananī layanī smarahara he śiva
saccidānanda viṭhala priya

You severed the head of Prajapati who was blinded by his ego. You are the mind and its dissolution, and the destroyer of desire. Your nature is existence, consciousness and bliss, and you are dear to Vishnu.

śivāya namaḥ ōm śivāya namaḥ ōm
śivāya namaḥ ōm namaḥ śivāya

Prostrations to the Lord of auspiciousness!

dēvi dēvi dayāmayi (Malayalam)

dēvi dēvi dayāmayi tava-
pāda-pāmsuvil eṅkilum
cērttiṭēṇam anāratam mama
cañcalātmaka-mānasam

O compassionate Devi, make my fickle mind stay focused, even if only on the dust of your feet.

mānasatte ulacciṭum mada-
matsarādi gaṇaṅgaḷe
ennil ninnum eṭutt-akaṫti-
aṇaccu nī taṇal ākaṇē

The armies of pride, desire and other emotions shake my mind. Please remove them and grant me your shade.

ārum ārum aṙiññiṭāte en
vyadhita mānasa-kēsarē
tāvakāmṛta mantra mukharita
sāndra naṭanam atāṭumō?

Will you silently come and fill my grieving mind, as a mantra that resounds and dances within?

nin kṛpā-rasam en kaṭhōra-
manassil āzhnnu patikkukil
mānasam bata! māyayaṫt-
amṛtēśi ninnil layicciṭum

When your compassion flows into my hard mind, it will be freed of all illusion and merge in you, O Mother Amriteshvari.

dṛśya-prapañcam (Malayalam)

dṛśya-prapañcam itent-adbhutam! viśvanāthā
ninde līlayākum
viśva-saundaryatte varṇṇicciṭān ārālum
sādhikkayilla tanne
sūrya-candranmārum tārakaḷum uḷkkoḷḷum
ākāśa-gaṅgayāyum
atiloru ceṙugōḷam-ī bhumiyil anavadhi kāzhcakaḷ
kaṇḍiṭunnu!

O Vishwanatha! Lord of this Universe, wondrous is your divine play that manifests as this world — the sun, the moon, the stars in the sky, the heavenly *Ganga and this small planet earth*

vanya-mṛgaṅgaḷum pakṣikaḷum haritābha
vitaṙunna pūmaraṅgaḷ
pinneyum pūñcōla, parvataṅgaḷ okkeyum nin
kara-sparśamallō
ninnuṭe ceṙiyoru sṛṣṭiyākum sūryande nērkkonnu
nōkkiṭānāy
ceṙiya manuṣyarām ñaṅgaḷkk-ahō sādhikkayilla
parama-satyam

Wild animals and birds, green and flowering trees, flowing streams and great mountains — you create all by a mere touch of your hand. The truth is that we cannot look directly even at the brilliant sun you created.

antam illāttatām ākāśavum āzhiyum ninnuṭe karavirutu
avaye kaṇḍ-aṙiyuvān āyiṭāte ūzhiyil kēzhunnu pāvam-eṅgaḷ
ninnuṭe satkatha kēḷkkuvānum pāṭi stuticcu layikkuvānum
ninnuṭe māyakkēḷiyil ninnu mukti nēṭānum anugrahikkū!

The infinite sky and the vast oceans testify to your skill. We cannot fathom your greatness, and we cry in misery on this earth. Please bless us to hear your stories and merge in your songs. Bless us to gain liberation from your play of illusion.

viśvanāthā namō śivaśaṅkarā
viśvanāthā namō haraśaṅkarā
viśvanāthā namō abhayaṅkarā
viśvanāthā namō bhavatārakā

ēḍēḍu lōkāllō (Telugu)

ēḍēḍu lōkāllō ēmēmi jariginā
uṇḍālammā nī iccha mātram
jaragadu ēdī... nā kṛṣi tō mātram
jarupunu annī nī kṛpā kaṭākṣam

O Mother, whatever happens in all the fourteen worlds is your will only. Nothing happens just because of my effort. Everything is possible only by your grace.

triccina nōru mūyālaṇṭē
ettina cēyī diñcālaṇṭē
saripōdammā nā kṛṣi mātram
kāvāli sumi nī kṛpā kaṭākṣam

I need your grace even to close my mouth, or to lower my raised hand. My effort alone is not enough.

ahamkāramēmō himālayamanta
vairāgyamēmō sūdimonayanta
cēranu lakṣyamu nā kṛṣi tō mātram
cērccunu sumi nī kṛpā kaṭākṣam

It is impossible to reach the goal with my ego as big as the Himalayas and dispassion as tiny as the point of a needle. Only by your grace will I reach the goal.

kṛpa tō dorukunu kōranivannī
kṛpa tō dorakavu kōrinavannī
kṛpa tō perugunu bhakti virakti
kṛpa tō dorukunu jīvanmukti

By your grace, we receive things we did not asked for. By grace alone we don't get things we prayed for. With grace, devotion and dispassion increase. With grace, we attain salvation.

ēkam ēvam advitīyam (Sanskrit)

ēkam ēvam advitīyam amṛtānandam
parabrahmam
saguṇa-nirguṇam ātma-rūpam prēma-mūrtti
parātparam

O most supreme One, the one Truth without a second, immortal bliss, supreme absolute, with and without attributes, the true Self, embodiment of divine love!

parama-sannidhānam amba divyam adbhuta līlādhāmam
śaraṇam amba śaraṇam śaraṇam śaraṇam tava mṛduśyāma-caraṇam

O Mother, supreme presence, sacred wonder, abode of divine play, grant me refuge at your tender dark feet!

nityaśuddha-buddha-muktam kāruṇyāmṛta-paripūrṇam
śaraṇam amba śaraṇam śaraṇam viśuddha-śānti param-dhāmam

O Mother, eternal, ever pure, enlightened, ever free, perfectly full nectar of compassion, pure serenity, grant me refuge at your supreme abode.

dēhi mē niṣkāma-bhāvam dēhi mē nissaṅga-bhāvam
śaraṇam amba śaraṇam śaraṇam śaraṇam tava mṛdu-caraṇayugaḷam

O Mother, bless me with an attitude of selflessness and detachment. I seek refuge at your gentle feet!

sṛṣṭi-sthiti-laya-kāriṇi advaita-vidyā-pradāyini
śaraṇam amba śaraṇam śaraṇam śaraṇam tava mṛdubhavya-caraṇam

You are the cause of creation, sustenance and dissolution. You bestow the knowledge of non-duality. O Mother, I seek refuge at your soft feet!

ananta-kōṭi bhuvana-nāyaki ādyāśakti sadguru-
janani
śaraṇam amba śaraṇam śaraṇam śaraṇam tava
mṛdu-mañju-caraṇam

O Mother, you are the empress of infinite worlds, the primordial force, the mother *Sadguru.* I seek refuge at your adorable feet!

ēkānta-pathikayāy samsāra-tīrattu (Malayalam)

ēkānta-pathikayāy samsāra-tīrattu
eṅgō maṟañña en ammaye tēṭi
ammaye tēṭi ñān alayukayāy – en
ammaye tēṭi ñān alayukayāy

I travel alone on the shores of *samsara*, searching for my Mother. I wander in search of my Mother.

nīlavānile tūveḷḷa mēghaṅgaḷe
niṅgaḷ en amma tan cēla eṭuttō?
nīlavānile kārmēghaṅgaḷe
niṅgaḷ en amma tan niṟam cārttiyō?

O pure white clouds high up in the blue sky, are you wearing my Mother's saree? O dark clouds in the deep blue sky, have you put on my Mother's color?

kāṟala-mālayil teḷiñña saudāmini
en amma tan mauktikam aṇiññō?
viṇṇine trasippicca varṣāmbu muttukaḷē
amma tan harṣāśru niṅgaḷ nēṭiyō?

O Moon! Shining clear in the depth of the night, are you wearing my Mother's pearl? O raindrops that revive the earth, have you received my Mother's blissful tears?

bhūmiykku sāntvanam ēkum ī tennalē
amma tan snēham nī kaṭam eṭuttō
niśayuṭe saundarya pūrṇṇēnduvē
amma tan puñciri nī tūkiyō?

O gentle breeze that consoles the world, have you borrowed my Mother's love? O full moon, beauty of night, are you smiling like my Mother?

ellām prakṛti tan maṭittaṭṭil ēlpiccu
ennamma eṅgō maṙaññirippū
ēkānta pathikayāy alayum ī kuññinē
maṙanniṭāt-ennaṭuttu aṇaññīṭumō?

O Mother, you have given everything to the lap of Nature, and now hide far away. Will you remember this lonely traveler, your child, and come to me?

samsāram ākum ī tīccūḷayil peṭṭu
etra yugaṅgaḷ ñān ventu nīṙi
ellām sahicciṭām ninnil layicciṭān
ammē nin pādattil cērkkukennē

I have been caught in the furnace of *samsara* for many ages. I will bear anything to merge in your lotus feet!

ellām aṙiyunnuvenkilum (Malayalam)

ellām aṙiyunnuvenkilum kaṇṇanu
onnum aṙiyātta bhāvam – eppōzhum
onnum aṙiyātta bhāvam
ā naṙum-puñcirikk-uḷḷil oḷippikkum
gahanamām gītā-rahasyam – kaṇṇan
gahanamām gītā-rahasyam

Even though Kannan knows everything, he behaves as if he knows nothing. In his fresh and lovely smile, he hides the profound secrets of the *Gita.*

kurukṣētram ākumi jīvita bhūmiyil
pādam iṭari vīzhumbōḷ – martyan
pādam iṭari vīzhumbōḷ
antaraṅgattil guruvāy teḷiññ-avan
dharma-sāratte uṇarttum – munnil
karma-mārgam teḷiyikkum

When we falter and fall in the kurukshethra (battle-field) of life, Krishna manifests as the inner Guru, sings the essence of dharma, and illuminates the path of action.

sarva-dharmaṅgaḷum veṭiyumbōl martyan
śaraṇāgati aṭaññīṭumbōḷ – pūrṇa
śaraṇāgati aṭaññīṭumbōḷ
jīvante sārathiyāyiṭum mādhavan
viśva-prēmatte uṇarttum – uḷḷil
ātma-jñānam prakāśikkum

When we abandon all adharma and surrender completely, Madhavan becomes the charioteer of our life. He awakens love for the entire world and shines the light of knowledge of the Self within.

en amma ādiparāśakti (Tamil)

en amma ādiparāśakti ennai
māyā ulagattil paḍaittāḷē
kaṇṇāmūcci viḷayāḍalām enḍru
māyamāy punnagai purindāḷē

My Mother, Supreme Goddess, created me in this illusory world. With a mischievous smile, Mother said, "Let's play hide-and-seek!"

kavarntizhukkum māyā ulagattile
annayai tēḍa sonnāḷē
kaṇṇai kavarum poruṭkaḷ naḍuvē
en amma oḷindu koṇḍāḷē

In this enchanting world of maya, she told me to look for my mother. My mother remained hidden in the midst of alluring objects.

viḷayāḍa toḍankiya pinne nān
māyayil mayangi pōnēnē
tōnḍri maṙayum māyā ulagai
kaṇḍu bhayantu ninḍrēnē

As I started to play, I fell into a daze. I was scared seeing the illusory world appear and disappear.

bhayattil uṙaindu ninḍra nānum
ammāvai tēḍi alaindēnē
ennai maṙandu ammā...ammā...
ennai maṙandu ammā enḍrazhaittēn
adai kēṭṭu ōḍi vantaṇaittāḷē

I froze in fear, and wandered in search of my mother. I forgot myself and called out, "Amma, Amma!" Hearing my call, she ran to me and embraced me.

ammā ādiparāśakti

O Mother, Supreme Goddess!

en antaraṅgattil (Malayalam)

en antaraṅgattil āśa ēṙunnu
nin prēma-tīrtthattil āṙāṭiṭān
ā snēha-taṇalil vaḷarnnīṭuvān
anavadhi janmaṅgaḷ pūkiṭām ñān

My heart yearns to bathe in the river of your love. I will take many births if I can grow in the shade of your love.

veṇṇilāvōḷi ōlum-ā puñciri kāṇke
mati-maṙann-ennum ñān nilkkum ammē
nin apāṅga-vīkṣaṇam patiyukil enmanam
sānandam āṭum varṇṇa-mayūram allō

I forget myself in bliss in the resplendence of your radiant smile. My heart becomes a colorful, dancing peacock when your glance falls upon me.

prēmam niṙayum ā tēn-mozhikkāy ñān
kātōrtt-irikkām ennum ennum
nityamāy nin maṭittaṭṭil amaruvān
nin kṛpā-pātramāy tīrēṇamē ammē

I listen intently for your words filled with nectarine love. Make me worthy of your grace, that I may remain forever in your lap.

eṅkaḷ kuladaivam (Tamil)

eṅkaḷ kuladaivam ammā vēppilaikkāḷi
andham ellām paḍaittavaḷe ādiśakti
anbu vaḍivānavaḷe akhilāndha-nāyakiyē
kāppāṫṫra vandavaḷe kuṅkumakāri

O Mother, Goddess Kali, you hold neem leaves in your hand. Creator of the universe, you are the primordial power. You are love personified. You are the empress of the world. O Goddess, your wear *kumkum* (vermillion) and you have come to save us.

sīṙi varum siṅkattayum nañcuḍaya nāgattayum
unnarugil sēvakarāy aḍakki ninḍrāy
māṙivarum manakkuraṅgin maruḷaceyyum agantayinai
ennakatte kuḍi koṇḍu azhittiṭammā

You tamed the roaring lion and the poisonous snake and made them your attendants. Please reside in my heart and destroy the bewildering ego of my fickle monkey-mind.

sambantanin kural kēṭṭu jñāna pālai ūṭṭiviṭṭa
ambikayē ūzhvinaiyai aṙuppavaḷē – (jñāna)
cikkanavē un pāda-padmaṅgaḷai piḍittōmē
cittam tanai suttam seytu kāttiṭammā

O Goddess, you heard the cries of Thirujnana Sambandar (an ancient sage) and fed him your milk. You are the one who cuts asunder the effects of past karma. O Mother, we cling to your lotus feet. Please clean our minds and protect us.

ōm kāḷi... hrīm kāḷi... vēppilaikkāḷi...amma...

O Kali, you hold the neem leaves, O Mother

enna tavam seydēn (Tamil)

enna tavam seydēn amma
tāyāy guruvāy nī varavē
untan sannidhi aṭaintīṭinum
vīṇāy kālamum kazhittēnē

What penance have I done, O Amma, that you have come as my Mother and Guru? Even after reaching your abode, I have frivolously wasted time.

anbu mazhai nī pozhintiṭum pōtum
anbillai enakku suyanalamē
vēdattin nāyaki ponnoḷi vīsiṭa
vizhikaḷ mūṭinān iruḷinilē

Though you constantly shower love, I remain selfish and devoid of love. Even though, you, the goddess of Vedas, are enlightening us, I close my eyes and dwell in darkness.

tāyinai pōlavē sēy ivaḷ āgavē
ōraṭi nānum vaittiṭuvēn
tāmarai pādattil ennuyir sērntiṭa
tazhuvum kaikaḷāl kāttiṭammā

This child will take baby steps to become like you. O Mother, embrace me and protect me that my life may merge in your lotus feet.

ennile enne tirañña nēram (Malayalam)

ennile enne tirañña nēram
uḷḷilāy-onnu tirañña nēram
uṇmayāy-uḷḷil uṇḍ-eppozhum ñān
uḷḷatu kaṇḍ-aṅgu tṛptanāy ñān

As I searched for the 'I' within me, as I sought my true Self, I realized that 'I' am always within as the Truth. Thus, I became content.

ninnile nīyumāy-uṇma tanne
nērāya tattvam atonnu tanne
nēr-aṙiññīṭumbōḷ ōṭukilla
nēṭuvānāy pinne aṅgum iṅgum

The 'You' within you is the real Truth, the true principle. Knowing this, you will stop running here and there to attain it.

nēṭēṇḍat-etenn-aṙiññiṭēṇam
vīṇḍu-vicāravum vēṇḍa-vaṇṇam
nērāya mārgam cariccīṭukil
nērinde sārattil ettum ārum

We need to know what is to be gained and reflect upon it properly. Treading the right path, anyone can attain that supreme principle.

ennini kāṇum (Malayalam)

ennini kāṇum endammē
tāvaka cāratt-aṇaññiṭān mōham
tūmandahāsam viriyum mukhāmbujam
ennini kāṇum endammē

O my mother, when will I see you again? I long to come near you. When will I behold your smiling lotus face?

pōya kālangaḷil nī kaniññ-ēkiya
snēha-smaraṇakaḷ pīli nivartti
paṙayuvān avatill-ammē ennil
tira tallum hṛdaya-vikāram
ponnamma tan cāratt-aṇayān

The memories of your love awaken in my heart with the beauty of peacock feathers. Inexpressable feeling overwhelms my heart as I long to come near you.

kāruṇya-vāridhi prēmāmṛtam tūkum
snēha-tīrattil aṇayuvānāyi
prēmattin neyttiri-dīpam teḷicc-ennum
aṣṭa-maṅgalyam orukki
ponnamma tan cāratt-aṇayān

O Ocean of Compassion, I have lit the lamp of devotion that I may reach the shores of your love and come near you. I wait to perform your worship.

ennuṇṇi kaṇṇā (Malayalam)

ennuṇṇi kaṇṇā ponnuṇṇi kaṇṇā
kāyāmbū varṇṇā maṇivarṇṇā
ōṭi vā kaṇṇā kārmukil varṇṇā
cārattu vann-onnu nṛttam āṭu

My little Krishna, my darling Krishna, with the complexion of the *kay-ambu* flower! Come running, little Krishna, with the of rain-cloud hue, come close to me and dance!

hari kṛṣṇa kṛṣṇā jaya kṛṣṇā kṛṣṇā
hari kṛṣṇa kṛṣṇā jaya kṛṣṇā kṛṣṇā

Victory to Krishna!

amma-yaśōda tan ārōmalē
dēvaki-dēvi tan ponnuṇṇiyē
gōpijana-mana mōhananē nī
prēma-svarūpan allē
rādhika tan prēma-svarūpan allē
rādhika tan prēma-svarūpan allē

You are Mother Yashoda's darling, the precious child of Mother Devaki. You are the enchanter of the gopis' minds and the embodiment of Radhika's love. You are embodiment of love!

gōpikamāruṭe hṛdayam kavarnnu
vṛndāvanattil līlayāṭi nī
en hṛdayattilum narttanam āṭu
vṛndāvanam akkū vṛndāvanam
hṛdayam vṛndāvanam ākku
hṛdayam vṛndāvanam ākku

You stole the hearts of the gopis and enacted your divine play in Vrindavan. O Krishna, dance in my heart also, and make my heart your Vrindavan!

veṇṇa tarām pāl cōṙu tarām
ōṭōṭi vā ende citta cōrā
ponnin cilamb-iṭṭu ōṭa-kuzhal ūti
hṛdaya-kōvilil varu kṛṣṇā
hṛdaya-kōvilil varu kṛṣṇā
hṛdaya-kōvilil varu

Come running, little stealer of my heart. I will give you butter and rice pudding! Wearing golden anklets and playing your bamboo flute, come to the shrine of my heart, O Krishna!

en prabhuvin (Malayalam)

en prabhuvin pāda-smaraṇaykkāy-allāte
kaṇṇīr pozhikkuka illini ñān
ārdram ākillen nayanaṅgaḷ
duḥkhitarkk-āśvāsam ēkuvān allātini

I will cry no more tears except in remembrance of my Lord's feet. My eyes will become moist only in consoling the suffering.

svārttha-karmaṅgaḷe pulkiya pāṇikaḷ
svātma-lābhārtthamāy pūja ceyyum
alleṅkil ēzha-tan kaṇṇīr tuṭaykkunna
kaikaḷāy-en kaikaḷ māṙum innu

My hands used to work only for my selfish needs. Now they will perform worship to attain the Self and compassionately wipe away the tears of the suffering.

karayilla taḷarilla paribhavam pa?ayilla
pata?ātini ñān ā padam aṇayum
ini ende puñciri māyill-en cuṇḍil, nin
aṇayātta prēma-mantra-āśrayattāl

I will not cry, I will not falter, I will not complain. I will reach your divine feet with unwavering faith. A smile will never leave my face because your divine mantra will never leave my lips.

en prāṇa-vallabhan (Malayalam)

en prāṇa-vallabhan ārennu colluka
tāyē en māṅgalyam eprakāram
ē?um kutūhalāl mātāvinōṭāyi
mantriccu koñcalāy kuññu-mīra

"Tell me, who is the Lord of my life? Who will marry me?" the child, Meera, asked her mother with great curiosity and wonder.

āryē kiśōrikē nin varan-allayō
ārādhyan ākum ā śyāma-varṇṇan
hṛttil pratiṣṭhicc-avaḷ giridhāriye
māmuni nalkiya vigrahatte

"My darling child, your husband is the dark-hued one, worshipped by all." She enshrined, in her heart, the Lord who lifted the Govardhana mountain. She enshrined the idol gifted by the sage.

ūṇil u?akkattil uḷttārin uṇmayāy
tīrnnuvā kārvarṇṇan peṇkoṭikku
bhōjan varanāyi māran vasikkātta
mānasam mallāriyē variccu

As she slept and ate, in every moment of her life, the Lord became the Truth residing in the lotus of her heart. She was married to Bhoja, but her heart was wedded to the dark Lord, He who had vanquished Malla.

kāntan marikkilum śānti viṭāteyā
sādhvi gamiccu vrajam pūkuvān
vṛndāvanam pūki cintā-malarukaḷ
nandātmajan padē arppiccavaḷ

Though Krishna was no more on the physical plane, she went to Vrindavan with perfect peace in her heart. There she offered the flowers of her thoughts at the feet of the son of Nanda!

entē ammē en manam (Malayalam)

entē ammē en manam vāṭunnu
ennuḷḷil ennum viḷaṅgunna sattē
nin viḷi kēḷkkān kazhiyāttat-entē
ā prēma-nisvanam ñān maṙann-ennō?

O Mother, you ever shine within as my true essence. Why does my mind wilt? Why can I not hear your call? Did I forget the voice of your divine love?

ninnil ninn-en cittam oru mātra akalumbōḷ
nī aṙiyunn-ennu ñān aṙiññīṭilum
entin-enn-aṙiyāte en hṛdantam vṛthā
entinō vēṇḍi kaṇṇīr pozhikkunnu

I know you know when my mind strays away from you, even for a moment. Still my heart cries for something. I know not why.

śvāsa-niśvāsamāy prāṇanāy nī sadā
ennuḷḷil ennum vasicciṭunn-eṅkilum

eṅgu nī ammē nin vāsam eṅg-ammē
oru mātra darśanam nalkīṭuk-ammē

Though you dwell within me as my breath and my very life force, where are you, O Mother? Where do you dwell? O Mother, please grant me a glimpse of your form.

entini ceyyēṇḍat-ammē (Malayalam)

entini ceyyēṇḍat-ammē ñān ini
nin prēma mādhuri nukarān
entini ceyyaṇam ammē ñān ini
nin snēha-dhārayil aliyān?

O Mother, what must I do to taste the nectar of your love? What must I do to dissolve in the flow of your love?

niṣphala-karmaṅgaḷ ceyt-etra janmaṅgaḷ ñān
aṙiyāte tulaccu!
vēṇḍa vēṇḍ-ammē manam mayakkīṭunna lōka-
sukhaṅgaḷ vēṇḍ-ammā

How many lifetimes have I squandered in meaningless actions! O Mother, I no longer want worldly pleasures that delude my mind.

vēṇḍatu vēdana tīṇḍātta tāvaka prēmattin
pūntaṇal mātram
akatāril nin prēma mādhuryam illāykil vēdānta-
cintayum vyarttham

All I want is to rest in the cool shade of your love, where there is no pain. Even spiritual contemplation is meaningless if I don't feel the sweetness of your love within.

vaikarut-amba! nin prēma-pravāhattil onnu cērtt-
enne ozhukkū
nin kṛpa illātta ninnōṭu cērātta janmam it-
entināṇ-ammā?

O Mother, do not delay to carry me along on the flow of your love. What is the point of living without your grace and oneness with you?

tāvaka darśanam ēki nī ennile rāgādi vairikaḷ
pōkkū
ā pāda cintanam ceytu ceyt-ānanda dhāmamām
ninnil ettaṭṭe

Give me your darshan and drive away the enemies of my likes and dislikes. Let me meditate on your holy feet and reach the abode of bliss.

etra ṛtukkaḷ (Malayalam)

etra ṛtukkaḷ kaṭannu pōyi sakhi
kaṇḍill-iniyum ā prēma-svarūpanē
mōhana-nāda-taraṅgaṅgaḷ kēḷkkuvān
kātōrtt-irunnu ñān etrayō nāḷukaḷ

O my friend, many seasons have passed, but I have yet to see my Lord, the embodiment of love. I have waited so long to hear the enchanting melody of his flute.

vannuvallō mama nāthan manōharan
kaṇḍu ñān vaśyamām mōhana-rūpam
ānanda-tantriyil mānasam mīṭṭiya
rāga-layattil aliyāttat-entahō!

My beautiful Lord has come. I see his wondrous form. My mind sings blissful melodies, yet I am unable to lose myself in them.

mānasa-cōrā harē madhū-sūdanā
māyāmayā harē śyāmā manōharā

O dark one, stealer of the mind, slayer of the demon Madhu, supreme illusion, beautiful one.

muzhukaṭṭe ñān ā nāda-taraṅgattil
aliyaṭṭe ñān nin prēma-svarūpattil
śānti tan divya-svarūpamāy tīruvān
śāntam ākkīṭū en mānasam mādhavā

Let me merge in your music. Let me dissolve in your form of love. O Madhava, make my mind serene that I may merge in your divine form.

ettanai nāḷō (Tamil)

ettanai nāḷō ennakam vandiṭa
ēninda tāmadam kaṇṇā?
ittanai nāḷum ennakam vendiṭa
nīyaṙiyāttadō kaṇṇā?

When will you come and dwell in my heart? Why this delay, O Krishna? Have you not known my aching heart all these days, O Krishna?

vītimunai varai naṭanden
kālgaḷ tēyndu pōnatuvē
vizhiyil vazhiyum nīraittuṭaittu
kaikaḷ sōrndu pōnaduvē
varuvāyō kaṇṇā varuvāyō
varamāga unnai taruvāyō

My feet ache from walking in search of you. My hands are tired of wiping tears from my eyes. O Krishna, will you come and grant me the boon of your vision?

varuvānō? enṭru kēli
kēṭṭu seviyum nondadutē
varum vazhiyai pārttu pārttu
manamum taḷarndu pōnaduve
varuvāyō kaṇṇā varuvāyō
varamāga unnai taruvāyō

My ears are tired of hearing the mockery, "Will your Krishna come?" My heart sinks as I stare down the path of your arrival. Will you come O Krishna? Will you grant me the boon of your vision?

kaṇṇā mezhugai pōlē uruki
karaiyum munnē vanduviṭu
kaṇṇīr kaṭalil mūzhgi nānum
maṙaiyum munnē vanduviṭu

O Krishna, please come before I melt away like a candle. Please come before I drown in the ocean of my tears.

kaṇṇā... maṇivaṇṇā
kaṇṇā... kār mukhil vaṇṇā

O beautiful Krishna, the color of rain clouds!

eviṭe ānandam (Malayalam)

eviṭe ānandam bhūmiyil eviṭe ānandam
kadana-vāṭiyil viṭarumō sukham arutu pāzh-
mōham
manujā veṭiyu vyāmōham

Where is joy in this world, where is joy? Will happiness bloom in a garden of sorrow? It is a futile hope. O Man, give up your vain desires.

snēham enna padattin arttham tande sukham
ennō?
eṅkil svārtthamām tīccūḷayil jani vyarttham
āyīṭum
pakalum iravum paravaśam nī veṙute alayumbōḷ...
svantam ākkiya svapna-jālam arttha-śūnyaṅgaḷ

Does the word 'love' mean only your own joy? If so, your life will be wasted in the furnace of selfishness. As you wander day and night, aimless and exhausted,

your dreams become meaningless.
viphalamāy-orī śramam upēkṣicc-uṭane nī
manamē
sadā sakalavum svātmāvu tān ennaṙiyu nī vēgam
para-sukhattil karutal uḷḷoru hṛdaya-pāthōjan
taniye viṭarum surabhi eṅgum parilasiccīṭum

O Mind! Abandon your vain dreams now. Know that everything is your own Self. When the lotus of your heart cares for the supreme joy of all, it will blossom naturally and spread its fragrance all around.

gaṇa-nāyakanē (Sanskrit)

gaṇa-nāyakanē gaurī-sutanē
ēkākṣara śāśvata mantrakṛtē
bhūṣaṇanē bhuvanēśvaranē
skandāgraja sundara gānakṛtē

Lord Ganapati, leader of the ganas, son of mother Parvati, the form of the eternal mantra Om. Beautiful one, Lord of the world, elder brother of Skanda, the form of beautiful song.

jaya jaya gaṇapati vighna-vināyaka
jaya śubha-dāyaka jaya varadāyaka
śrita-jana-pālana śivapada-dāyaka
nityāya śuddhāya buddhāya tē namō namaḥ

Victory to Lord Ganapati, destroyer of obstacles. Victory to the bestower of auspiciousness and boons! You protect those who take refuge in you, and you grant the supreme state. Salutations to you, eternal one, pure one, supreme awareness!

pramathādhipanē paripūrṇanē
kalikanmaṣa-nāśaka kālapatē
bhava-sambhavanē abhayaṅkaranē
mṛtyuñjaya bhava-bhaya-nāśakanē

Lord of the attendants of Lord Shiva, perfect one, destroyer of the evils of kaliyuga, Lord of time! Son of Shiva, granter of fearlessness, conqueror of death, destroyer of the fear of transmigration!

dvai-māturanē agha-nāśakanē
jita-manmatha-vigraha kāntimatē

aparājitanē amṛtōtbhavanē
vara-siddhi-vināyakan avyayanē

One with two mothers, destroyer of sin, beautiful one who defeated the god of love. Undefeated one, fount of immortal bliss, Lord Ganapati, bestower of boons and destroyer of obstacles, eternal one!

gaṇapati bhagavānē (Malayalam)

gaṇapati bhagavānē vighna-vināśakanē
gajamukha sundaranē
śaraṇam taraṇē śivasutanē

O Lord Ganapati, destroyer of obstacles! You are the beautiful one with an elephant face. Please grant us refuge, O son of Shiva!

buddhi-pradāyakanē aṙiv-uṙavākaṇamē
aviratam en hṛttil
teḷiyaṇam nin padam
parama dayālō gaṇanāthā
gaṇapati bhagavānē vighna-vināśakanē

You grant intelligence and are a fountain of wisdom. O Leader of the *ganas*, most compassionate one, may your divine feet constantly shine in my heart. Lord Ganapati, destroyer of obstacles!

siddhi vināyakanē abhaya-pradāyakanē
nirvṛti pūkān varam aruḷīṭu
tava pada-śaraṇam maṅgaḷa-mūrtē

You bestow success and fearlessness. Grant a boon that we may reach the supreme goal of realization. O embodiment of auspiciousness, your feet are our refuge!

bāla gaṇapatē jay jay
varada gaṇapatē jay jay
vīra gaṇapatē jay jay
śakti ganapatē jay jay

Victory to the child Ganapati, to the bestower of boons! Victory to courageous Ganapati, to the most powerful one!

gaṇapatiyē unnai (Tamil)

gaṇapatiyē unnai vaṇaṅkugiṙōm
manadinil nīyum vīṭṭrituppāy
karppaga kaḷirē sorporuḷ suṭarē
porpadam kāṭṭi aruḷpurivāy

We worship you Lord Ganesha! Please reside in our hearts. O bestower of boons, lamp of knowledge, bless us and show us the way to your feet.

aṙaneṙi tannai tavaṙāmal
poruḷinai īṭṭa varam aruḷvāy
anmbuṭan pakirndu aḷippadilē
inbatte uṇaraceytiṭuvāy

Grant us the boon of a life established in goodness. Help us realize that true happiness is found in loving service to others.

vinaippayanālē piṙandu viṭṭōm
vizhalukku nīrena vāzhndu viṭṭōm
unai maṙavāmal vaṇaṅkiṭavē
uṙudiyāy vīṭu pēraṭaivōm

We are born due to past karmas, and have lived our lives in vain. If we remember to worship you, we are sure to reach the ultimate goal.

mūṣika-vāhana gaṇanāthā
mōdaka-hastā gaṇanāthā
cāmara-karṇṇā gaṇanāthā
vāmana-rūpā gaṇanāthā
gaṇanāthā hē gaṇanāthā
gauri-nandana gaṇanāthā
gaṇanāthā hē gaṇanāthā
gauri-nandana gaṇanāthā

O Ganesha whose vehicle is the mouse, who holds the modaka sweet in his hand! O Ganesha who has large ears, and is of short stature! O lord of the ganas, son of Parvati!

garbhattin nilaiyai (Tamil)

garbhattin nilaiyai viṭa manamumillayō
kāriruḷām uṙakkam teḷiya isaivumillayō
pēroḷiyil ulava nīyum tuṭikkavillayō
pēranbin aravaṇaippil tiḷaikkavillayō
mannuyirē uṇarndiṭu
mayakkamatai tuṙandiṭu

Don't you want to come out of your cocoon? Don't you want to awaken from the sleep of ignorance? Don't you yearn to reach the realm of supreme light? Don't you want to feel the ecstatic embrace of supreme love? O mankind, awaken. Cast off your delusion!

nēṫṫru kaṇḍadu inḍru illai vāzhvin nilaiyidē
kāṫṫril maṙaiyum pugaiyai pōndhru māyndu pōgumē

sēṫṫril muḷaitta semmalar pōl manamum malaravē
teḷinda nīril nilavu pōla azhagum oḷirumē
mannuyirē uṇarndiṭu
mayakkamatai tuṙantiṭu

What you saw yesterday is gone today. This is the law of life. Everything disappears like smoke vanishing in the air. When the mind blossoms like a lotus in murky waters, beauty shines forth like the moon's reflection on rippleless water. O mankind, awaken. Cast off your delusion!

nāḷum tēyndu kālam kaṭantu maṙainditum munnē
nāmeṭutta piṙavi iṅku muṭindiṭum munnē
naṙcceyalkaḷ bhaktiyuṭan nāmum seyyavē
ettisayum niṙaiyum kāḷi kāttu nirppōḷē
mannuyirē uṇarndiṭu
mayakkamatai tuṙantiṭu

Perform good deeds with devotion before it is too late and your life on Earth ends. Then the all-pervading Kali will protect you. O mankind, awaken. Cast off your delusion!

gatakāla-smaraṇakaḷ (Malayalam)

gatakāla-smaraṇakaḷ satyam ennōrttu ñān
bhāviye bhāvana ceytu taḷarnnu
aṙiyēṇḍat-aṙiyāte alayunnu ñān ammē
aṙiyēṇḍat-aṙiyuvān kēzhunnu ñān

Dwelling on the past and dreaming about the future, I have become weary. I wander, not knowing what I should know. O Mother, I cry to know the Truth.

aṙiyēṇḍappōl ninne aṙiyuvānāy ammē
entu ñān ceyyēṇam aṙivīl enikkahō
ammē dayāmayī uḷppū viṭaruvān
nī tanne śaraṇam enn-aṙiyunnu ñān

O Mother what should I do to know you as the supreme Truth? O Mother, compassionate one, let my heart blossom. I know you are my only refuge.

bandhanam ākunna bandhaṅgaḷ illāte
vāzhuvān nin kṛpa aṙivāy pozhikku nī
ammē kṛpāmayī ātma-santṛptanāy
ennile enne aṙiyān kaniyu nī

Please shower your grace as knowledge that I may live free of the entanglement of attachment. O Mother, most compassionate one, may I know my true Self and rest content.

gaurī manōharī durgē (Sanskrit)

gaurī manōharī
durgē bhavānī
kālakāla hara
priyē mōhinī

O Mother Parvati, most captivating Goddess, Mother Durga, Bhavani, beloved of Lord Shiva, enchantress of all.

umē bhairavī
triśūla dhāriṇī
dēvī kārtyāyanī
parvata-nandinī

O Mother Uma, Bhairavi who wields the trident, Goddess Parvati, Kartyayani, daughter of the mountain.

śyāmē dayāmayī
śrīśaila vāsinī
trilōka pālinī
rājarājēśvarī

O dark one, compassionate Mother who dwells in Sri Shaila, protector of the three worlds, empress of all.

ānanda-rūpiṇi
ānanda-dāyinī
ātma-svarūpiṇī
ātma-prakāśinī

O Mother, you are the embodiment and giver of bliss. You are the nature of the Self, the light of the Absolute.

gōḍ tū ga āyī (Marathi)

gōḍa tū ga ā'ī... kiti gōḍa gōḍa ā'i
gōḍa tū ga ā'ī... kiti gōḍa gōḍa āi

How adorable you are, O Goddess Amba!

gōḍa tujhē, rūp kitī gōḍa hē svarūp
bhāvāta gōḍavā maunāta gōḍavā ambā mātā gōḍa
bōlaṇē cālanē vāganē hasanē sarva madhura
madhura madhura
manō bhāvē japuṇi nāma hō'ūyā madhura
madhura madhura

Your appearance is pleasing, your true nature is blissful and your silence is enticing. The way you walk, talk and laugh — everything about you is gracious. Let us chant your divine name with the right attitude. Then, we will be transformed into such sweetness.

gōḍa tujhī mūrti kitī, gōḍa tujhī kīrti
darśani gōḍavā, prasādi gōḍavā dēvī mātā gōḍa
bhajana vādana kīrtaan nartana sarva madhura
madhura madhura
nisaṅga bhāve karūṇi sēvā hō'ūyā madhura
madhura madhura

O, Devi, your form is sweet and your glory is enchanting. Your darshan, your prasad, everything about you is sweet. Your hymns, your musical instruments and your dance — all are so captivating. Let us do selfless service and become sweet like the divine Mother.

gōḍa tujhē svapna kitī, gōḍa tyācē smaraṇa
kṛpēt gōḍavā kaṭākṣi gōḍavā kāḷi mātā gōḍa
caraṇa śaraṇa tāraṇa haraṇa sarva madhura
madhura madhura
prēma bhāve gāuni sarva hō'ūyā madhura
madhura madhura

How mesmerizing is our dream of you, O Mother Kali! Remembering these dreams enraptures us. Your grace and your glance are enchanting. When we take refuge at your Holy Feet, you dispel our sorrows and take us across the ocean of samsara. Let us sing to Mother Kali with love and merge in the sweetness.

gōḍa tū ga āyī, prēma āmhām dē'ī, nāndō viśva-śāntī
nāndō viśva-śāntī

O Mother, you are so fascinating. Please fill us with unconditional love and fill this world with peace and happiness.

ā'ī rēṇuka... mangaḷa-rūpiṇi
ā'ī kāḷika... manalaya-kāriṇi
tuḷajā-bhavāni... madhura-bhāṣiṇi
ā'ī śivāni... duḥkha-nivāriṇi
ā'ī rakhumāyi... hṛdaya-nivāsini
ā'ī ambābāyi... ānanda-dāyini

gōpālā gōpālā nām (Hindi)

gōpālā gōpālā nām gātē jā
gōvindā gōvindā lētē nām jā
sundar ati sundar hai nand kā lālā
naṭkhaṭ aur catur hai yaśōdā kā bāl

Sing the name of Gopala, sing the name of Govinda. Nanda and Yashoda's son is exceedingly beautiful, and he is also mischievous and clever.

muraḷī sē chēḍhē gōpāl madhur tān
us nād amṛt mēṅ ḍūbā brahmāṇḍ
curātā hai gōpiyōṅ kē gṛhōṅ sē sadā
dahī mākhan aur unkē citt bhī gōpāl

He plays sweet notes on his flute, and the entire cosmos is submerged in that ambrosial sound. He steals curd and butter from the gopis' houses, and he also steals their minds.

śarāratōṅ sē bharā hai khēl śyām kā
galī galī phirtā vō saṅg gvāl bāl

kabhī phōḍē maṭki tō kabhī ahaṅkār
phir bhī thā vō sabkī āṅkhōṁ kā tārā

The pastimes of the dark Krishna are filled with mischief. He wanders through the lanes of Vrindavan along with cowherd boys. Sometimes he breaks pots, sometimes he breaks their ego. He remains the apple of their eye.

rūp ḍhang uskā hai baḍā salōnā
śyām raṅg kōmaḷāṅg sabkō bhātā
bējōḍ prēm vō nibhāyē sabkē sāth
mukh pē thā sabkē bas ik nām gōpāl

His form and ways are most captivating, and his dark complexion and delicate body endear everyone. He had a relationship of incomparable love with all, so everyone had the name Gopal on their lips.

gōpālā gōpālā gōvindā gōvindā

gōpāl sundar (Hindi)

gōpāl sundar gōpī manmōhan
rādhā mādhav kṛṣṇā
man kē jamunā taṭpē ānā
ākē tū bansī bajānā

O beautiful Gopala, enchanter of the gopis, beloved of Radha, come play your flute on the banks of the Yamuna river of my mind!

mōhanēvālē māyā mōhan
mōhak darś dikhā jā
jhalak tērī pānē kō tarsē
vyākul man aur naynā

O Mayamohan, you captivate everyone. Please grant me the vision of your enchanting form. My mind and eyes pine for a glimpse of you.

gōvindā harī gōvindā gōkulanāthā gōvindā
rādhā vallabh gōvindā rās vihārī gōvindā

O Govinda, Hari, the Lord of Gokul! Beloved Lord of Radha, Lord Krishna who delights in the Rasa dance!

mēl yē sāri man ki miṭākē
banāō isē ik darpaṇ
jahāṅ mēṅ dēkhūṅ pratipal tērā
rūp binā kōyī aḍcan

Remove the impurities from my mind. Make it clear like a mirror where I can see your form directly, at every moment.

man yē sadā nirantar tujhmē
ramā rahē vrajnandan
man kē kusumit kuñj mēṅ nit din
viharnē āō mōhan

O young boy of Vraj, may my mind constantly rejoice in thoughts of you. Most enchanting one, come and stroll in the flower garden of my mind.

gōvinda gōpāla mādhava (Tamil)

gōvinda gōpāla mādhava jaya jaya
gōvinda gōpāla mādhava jaya jaya
gōvinda gōpāla mādhava jaya jaya
gōvinda gōpāla jay jay

Victory to Govinda, Gopala, Madhava!

rādhaiyai pōlē azhaittiṭumbōdu
yādavan tāḷil samarppaṇattōṭu
māsugaḷ nīṅki tudittiṭum pōdu
mādhavan taruvān dariśanamē

When we call out to him like Radha, with complete surrender at His holy feet; and, when we pray with a pure mind, Lord Madhava will grant us his vision.

kōdaiyai pōlē ninaindiṭum pōdu
ninaivinil neñcam urugiṭum pōdu
mālaiyum sūṭa tavam seyyumbōdu
mālavan taruvān dariśanamē

When we think of Him like Andal [a South Indian saint]; when our hearts melt in His thoughts; when we perform austerities to attain Him, the Lord will grant us His vision.

mīrāvai pōlē pāṭīṭumbōdu
mīḷāda tuyaril vāṭiṭumbōdu
yāvaiyum tuṙakka tuṇindiṭumbōdu
māyavan taruvān dariśanamē

When we sing to Him like Meera, and when we wilt in our deepest sorrows, and when we have the courage to renounce everything, the Lord will grant us his vision.

rādhe śyām rādhe śyām
rādhe śyām rādhe śyām

O Shyam, beloved of Radha!

harasalendu (Kannada)

harasalendu kanasinalli nīnu bandeyā?
mugilininda bhuvige nīnu iḷidu bandeyā?
maguva baḷige bantu nīnu muddu garedayā?
iruḷinalli baḷalu venage beḷaku tanteyā?

Did you come in my dream to bless me? Did you descend from the clouds above to this earth? Did you love and caress your child? Did you bring light to me who am suffering in darkness?

svapnadalle hṛdaya-doḷage pūje paḍedeyā?
nānu gaida pāpagaḷa kṣamisi hōdeyā?
candranante sadā beḷagu nanna manadali
vandisuve pādadhūḷi prasāda nīḍu nī

In the dream itself, you received my worship, didn't you? And then, you forgave my sins. Shine like moon always in my mind. I bow to you-please bestow the sacred blessing of the dust of your feet.

kaṇṇu eraḍu ninna kaṇḍu dhanyavādavu
kaigaḷ eraḍu pāda muṭṭi dhanyavādavu
mahime kēḷi kivigaḷ eraḍu dhanyavādavu
ninna paḍeda janmavenna dhanyavāyitu

My eyes are gratified and fulfilled by having seen you. My hands are gratified and fulfilled by having touched your holy feet. Listening to your glories, my ears have become blessed. Having you in my life, my life has become blessed.

hari hari hari vāsudēva (Tamil)

hari hari hari vāsudēva hari
pāṇḍuraṅga hari viṭhal hari
tantiram yēdum indri mayakkum sundaranāmam
hari hari

Lord Hari, son of Vasudeva! Lord Panduranga, Vithala! The beautiful name of Hari is itself enough to captivate the mind.

pāmaranum avan pādam piṭittu
oru taram azhaittāl hari
sādhusaṅgam tandu mēnmai aḷittu
yōganilai koṇḍu sellum paṭi

If even an ignorant person once utters the name 'Hari', while holding on to the Lord's feet, that will grant him the company of saints. He will progress spiritually and attain the state of Oneness with the Lord.

mōna tavasigaḷin idaya
kamalattil miḷirum oḷi
tāḷam isainditṭa gānam pāṭiyē
tāvi gudittazhaippōm hari

Hari is the divine light shining in the heart of great sages who perform severe penance. Let us sing 'Hari, Hari!' with rhythm and sweet devotion, and dance in bliss.

nāṭi taḷarndavan kūṭa iruppavan - hari hari hari hari
vōṭum mazhalaigaḷōṭu kaḷippavan - hari hari hari hari
vāṭum ceṭikaḷin vērukku nīravan - hari hari hari hari
kūṭikkalanduyir tannil vasippavan - hari hari hari
hari

Hari is close to those who are weary, having lost their strength. Hari, the blissful one, joyfully plays along with little children. Hari is water for the roots of withered plants. Hari dwells within all living beings.

hē santōsī mā (Odiya)

hē santōsī mā bhabatāriṇī mā
matē tōro pākhērē rokhīdē ō mā

O Santoshi, you take us across the ocean of transmigration. Keep me near you, O Mother!

tōro bisayarē bhābi mātē nida lāgūni
kēbē tatē mūṅ dēkhī pāribi dēbī mā
ākāsoro tārā rē tate mū khōjūchī
mōra hṛdayorē sadā tū bāsa karo mā

I lose sleep longing to see you again, O Devi. I search for you in the stars in the sky. Please reside in my heart always, O Mother.

ekā basīkī māgō tumo kathā bhābūchī
tumari darsanā māna poḍūchī ō kāḷī mā
tū mora hatha dhori bākū mū cāhūñchi
mōro jībana ku dhanyā baneide ō mā

When I am alone, I remember you and your darshan, O Mother Kali. Please hold my hand and bless my life, O Mother.

hṛdaya bāgiḷa (Kannada)

hṛdaya bāgiḷa teredu ninagāgi kādiruvē
baruveyā oḷagē śiva omme
baruveyā oḷagē śiva omme

Opening the doors of my heart, I am waiting for you. Will you come in at least once, O Shiva?

hagaḷiraḷu ninnade nāmāmṛta smaraṇē
kanasu-nanasallu nī kāśināthā
ādiyu nīne antyavu nīne
tumbiruve elleḍe ī jagadi nīne

Day and night, I remember your nectarous name. Dreaming, waking, there is only you, O Lord of Kashi. You are the beginning, you are the end. This entire world is pervaded by you.

śiva śiva śambhō śaśi śēkharā
hara hara śambhō harikēśā

O Auspicious Lord Shiva, adorned with the Moon!

nīlakaṇṭhane ninna mahimeyā hōgaḷuve
ninna daruśanā bhāgya nīḍu namagē
bhava bandhanavu enna kāḍutiḍe avirata
mukti kāṇade bandiruve ninneḍegē

O blue-throated one, I delight in singing your praises. Grant us the fortune of your vision! The bonds of worldliness ever haunt me. Not finding freedom, I have finally come to you

bhaktarā bandhu kāruṇya sindhu
daya tōri bā prabhuve hṛdayadoḷagē
ninna nambiha namage karuṇisu acalā
śraddhe bhakti ninna caraṇagaḷali

O friend of the devotees, compassionate one, be merciful and come to my heart! Be kind to us who place our faith in you. Bless us with unwavering devotion to your feet!

hṛdayam uruki (Malayalam)

hṛdayam uruki ñān tapiccitumbōḷ
kadanattin vēnalil kariyunna nēram
tiru mizhi ennil paticcīṭavē
amṛta-mazha ennil kuḷirma ēki

Sorrow melts my grieving heart, and I wither in the summer heat of yearning. Then, your divine glance falls upon me, and ambrosial rain cools my heart.

janma-janmāntara karma-bandhaṅgaḷāl
ninne mar̊annu naṭann-orenne
tṛkkaram nīṭṭi tannōṭ-aṇacc-amma
ar̊iyāte tēṅgi pōy-en hṛdantam

The entanglements of many previous lives made me wander alone and forget you. O Mother! You reached out and drew me close, and my heart weeps in gratitude!

nissvārttha-karmaṅgaḷ ceytiṭānāy
uḷprēraṇa nalku ammē
tṛppāda-padmattil arccanā-puṣpamāy
arcciccitaṭṭe ī marttya-janmam

O Mother! You inspire us from within to perform selfless deeds. I offer my life as a flower of worship at your divine feet!

hṛdaya-sandēśam (Malayalam)

hṛdaya-sandēśam en kaṇṇande tṛppādē
arccanā-puṣpamāyi vīṇiṭumbōḷ

mana-murukīṭunnu tanu taḷarnnīṭunnu
kaṇṇā nī enne maṙanniṭallē

My heart's message falls as flowers of worship at the feet of my Krishna. My mind and body are grief-stricken. Krishna, please remember me.

prēma-gaṅgayāy ozhukunna vēṇu-gānam
hṛdayattil ennō āzhnnu pōyī
kaṇṇunīr muttāl orukkiya mālyam
svīkariccīṭumō nī mukil-varṇṇā
svīkariccīṭumō nī mukil-varṇṇā

Your flute music flowed as a Ganga of love and entered deep into my heart. O Krishna, dark-hued one, please accept this garland made from the beads of my tears?

kēḷkkunnuvō nī en maunamām tēṅgalukaḷ
kāṇunnuvō en niṙamizhikaḷ
janmaṅgaḷ ini etra uṇḍeṅkilum tava
tṛppāda-smaraṇayil ozhukīṭaṇē
tṛppāda-smaraṇayil ozhukīṭaṇē

Do you hear my silent cry? Do you see my tear-filled eyes? I may have many more lives, but please fill them with the memory of your lotus feet.

iruḷil dharayilāy-āzhnnu (Malayalam)

iruḷil, dharayilāy-āzhnnu kiṭann-oru
pazhvittu tāntamāy tēṅgi...
tirukara-sparśattin prēmāmśu-dhārayāy

cētass-uṇarnnu tuṭiccu, atil
nal-naṙu-nāmb-aṅkuriccu

Crying and exhausted, the seed lay lost in earth's darkness. At the loving touch of your divine hands, it awoke and rose up from the earth.

tvat-kṛpā-varṣattāl kisalayam-āditya-
kiraṇattilēkk-udgamiccu
vātsalya-vēliyāl rakṣa ēkīyatil
jīvarasam nī niṙaccu

In the shower of your grace, the tender shoot grew up to greet the sun. The fence of your tenderness protected this sapling and filled it with life.

pērttum kṛtajñatā-bhārattāl śākhakaḷ
tāṇu, taṇal ēki nilkke
nāḷe nin tēn phalam lōkattinde tanne
sadguru-vākyam śraviccu
nalkal-āṇēṫṫam udāttam ennuḷḷorā
sadguru-vākyam śraviccu

Now the branches of the tree bow down in gratitude and give shade to many. It heard the words of the *sadguru*: "Tomorrow your nectarine fruits will feed the world." She said, "Giving is the noblest ideal."

jīva-taru atin janma-sāyujyam ōrtt-
ānanda-bāṣpam utirttu
ūrddhvastham avyayam aśvattha-mūlamām
śrīpāda-padmam namiccu

The tree shed tears of joy as its life became fulfilled. She bowed to the divine feet, the supreme Self, the origin of the imperishable ashvatha tree descending from the heavens.

iruḷārnna jīvita-vīthiyil (Malayalam)

iruḷārnna jīvita-vīthiyil ennum nī
kanivārnnu pāliccirunna satyam
aṙiyave en-manam ārdramāy tīrunnu
aḷavaṫṫa nin kṛpa ōrttu nityam

O Mother! in the dark path of my life, you compassionately guard the Truth. When I realize your love, my mind becomes tender, knowing your grace towards me!

vīṇum uruṇḍum piṭaññum ñān – nīṅgavē
ōrō cuvaṭilum nī tuṇaccu
vīṇiṭum vīthiyil tāṅgi nirtti enne
nērvazhi kāṭṭi anugrahiccu

As I stumbled and fell and tried to get up, you helped me take each step. You kept me on the right path and blessed me so that I did not stray.

nēti nēti ennat-ārāññu ñān innu
nērāya nin tiru munnil etti
nērāya ninne aṙiyuvānāy in
nērāyi enne anugrahikku

Now, I have reached your sacred presence and I know that you are the Truth. Bless me to know you as the absolute Truth reached by constant self-inquiry.

īśvaran ārāṇ-enn (Malayalam)

īśvaran ārāṇ-enn-aṙiyāte eṅkilum
īśvara-nāmam sadā japiccu
ētō viśvāsamām śrīkōvilil
ennuṭe ammaye kāttirunnu

Though I didn't know God, I chanted God's name constantly. I waited for Mother in the shrine of my faith.

pūjakaḷ arppiccum tēṅgi karaññum en
ammaye mātram ñān ōrttirunnu
oru mātra kāṇān kazhiññilla eṅkilum
prārtthanā-vēḷayil dhanyanāy ñān

I offered worship and cried with longing, thinking only of my Mother. Though I was unable to see Her for a moment, in my prayers I was blessed.

oru nāḷ amma tan tiru divya-darśanam
en mauna-nombaram akaṫṫiyallo
jīvita-yātrayil kḷēśaṅgaḷ tīrkkunna
sāntvanam nalki anugrahiccu!

One day the divine vision of Mother dispelled my silent grief. Mother blessed and consoled me, putting an end to all afflictions on the journey of life.

satyam āṇīśvaran jñānam āṇīśvaran
nityamāyi nilkkum prakāśam āṇīśvaran
jīvita pātayil satya-dharmaṅgaḷām
mārga-dīpamāy nin prakāśam

God is Truth, God is Knowledge, God is eternal Light. Truth and dharma are your effulgence that lights up the path of life.

jagadambikē hṛdayāmbikē (Malayalam)

jagadambikē hṛdayāmbikē
jagadambikē dēvī amṛtāmbikē

Mother of the Universe, Mother of my heart, Devi, my immortal Mother!

vazhi aṙiyāte vann-ettiya jīvanu
nin kṛpā-varṣam abhayam ēki
arhata yātonnum ill-ennākilum
artthikkunnu ñān nin prēma-bhaktikkāy

Your grace granted refuge to this jiva who was lost and wandering. I am not deserving, yet I beg for loving devotion to you.

cañcalamām en hṛttil irunnum
puñciri tūki nērvazhi kāṭṭum
nin tṛppādamām lakṣyam pūkān
ennil kaniyān tāmasam arutē

Smiling, you reside in my fickle heart and show me the right path. Now, show your compassion so that I may reach your lotus feet.

mārgavum lakṣyavum nī tanne ammē
mārga-vighnam nīkkum śaktiyum nīyē
ātma-kṛpayāy ennil niṙayū
jñānamṛtam tūki ninnōṭu cērkkū

O Mother! You are both the way and the goal. You are the strength that removes all the obstacles on the way. Fill my heart as grace for my own true Self. Grant me knowledge of immortality and hold me close to you.

jagajjananī (Tamil)

jagajjananī unnai śaraṇaṭaintōm
jagadōdhāriṇī darisanam tā
jagamennum māyai valaiyaṙuttu
jagadīśvarī nī sutantiṙam tā

O Mother of the Universe! We take refuge in you. Grant us your darshan, O Goddess of the Universe. Free us from the bondage of maya!

aḷavē illā prapañcattinai
aṙintiṭa aṙivum tēṭutammā
niṙaivē illā poruḷinpam
ninaittē manamum ōṭutammā

O Mother, my intellect seeks ways to understand the vast world, and my mind runs after worldly pleasures which never give satisfaction.

āsaiyai toṭarntu seyalkaḷammā
atilvarum inpam tunpam ammā
ulakattin sukhattil āsaiyinai
umayē taḷaiyāy aṙuttiṭammā

Desires lead to actions. So-called pleasure from actions results in sorrow, O Mother! O Uma! Please cut away my desire for worldly pleasures.

jagajjananī iruḷ akaṫṫriṭammā
jagadīśvarī viḷakkēṫṫriṭammā

jagatkāraṇī tuyar pōkkiṭammā
jagadōddhāriṇī kāttiṭammā

O Mother of the Universe, please remove the darkness, and light the lamp. O Mother, who created the universe, please remove our sorrows and protect us.

jagavella nīnē (Kannada)

jagavella nīnē jagadīśvari
daṙuśana nīḍu amṛtēśvarī – ninna

You pervade the whole universe, O Supreme Empress. Do grant me your vision, eternal Goddess!

andhakāradi alēdāḍuttiruvē
kaṇṇugaḷ-iddū nā kāṇadiruvē
ī viraha-vēdanē sahisallārē
nī surisu bēganē amṛta-dhārē

I wander, lost in darkness. Though I have eyes, I do not see. Unbearable is this agony of separation. O Mother, please shower me with your flow of immortal nectar.

māyā jagadinda enna rakṣisū
bhakti-mārgadali munnaḍēsū
śaraṇāgati nīḍi ī jīva naukeyanu
bhava-sāgara-dinda nī dāṭṭisū

Protect me from this illusory world and lead me on the path of devotion. Grant me complete surrender. O Mother, take my boat across the ocean of transmigration.

kaṇgaḷalli ninna rūpa sadā beḷagali
kivigaḷalli ninna kīrtti tumbi-kkōḷḷali
usiru ninna nāmava nitya japisali
hṛdayadalli ninna caraṇa kamala araḷali

May your form ever shine in my eyes, may your glory ever fill my ears. May every breath of mine chant your sacred name. May the lotus of your sacred feet blossom within my heart.

amṛtēśvarī jagadīśvarī

O Eternal Goddess, Goddess of the Universe!

janimṛti-cakrattin (Malayalam)

janimṛti-cakrattin poruḷ aṙiyāte
iruḷ ārnna jīvita-pātayil ñān
nēr-aṙiyāte poy pōya nāḷ onnil
kaṇḍu ñān kāruṇya-rūpamām ammaye

I knew not the meaning of samsara (the cycle of birth and death) and walked the dark path of ignorance. One day, I saw the compassionate form of my Mother.

mātṛ-vātsalyattāl vāri puṇarnn-amma
śānti tan pāta teḷiccor-ā nāḷ
ātma-viśvāsamām neyttiri nāḷavum
uḷḷil teḷicc-enne dhanya ākki

My Mother embraced me lovingly and shed light on the path of peace. She lit the lamp of Self-confidence within me and gave meaning to my life.

jīvande mārgavum jīvita-lakṣyavum
īśvara-prēmattāl pūrṇam ākum
vismariccīṭāte nīṣṭhayōṭ-ennum ī
pātē carikkān anugrahikkū

The path of life and its ultimate goal become complete in God's love. Bless me to remember this truth so that I may travel the path of love.

janmātaḥ maraṇāntam (Sanskrit)

janmātaḥ maraṇāntam nistāra-bījam ajñātvā
kṣīṇitāḥ niśāvanē niravadhi manujāti
bhramitāḥ lōkāraṇyē nistulānandam aprāpya
manujā! tvam śiṣṭa-kālē mahā-mantram
jamjapyatām

From birth to death we wander, exhausted, in the dark forest of life. We know not how to cross over the ocean of *samsara*. O Man! You have yet to attain immaculate bliss. In the time remaining to you, chant the great mantra.

ōm namaḥ śivāya mantram amṛta-sundara-
mantram

The mantra, 'om namah shivaya', the immortal, beautiful mantra!

vāsanānām mahāsindhau nimagnaḥ cētapitvam
vyasanasya bhayam āstu niśśaṅka-manasvī dhīra!
vicārēṇa vismaryatām viśaraṇa vikarmāṇi
vismayēna samsmarayatām nitya-śūddha-
mugdha-mantram

O man of courage and steadiness! Do not let fear distress you even if you are drowning in the ocean of your negativities. Renounce all bad actions, and constantly remember this great, very pure and enchanting mantra.

sadvijñāna-pradāyakam guru-vākya suśravaṇāt
cidākāśam mārjāyatē pratīyatē samyag-jñānam
nirguṇa-nirupādhika brahma-tattvam samyag-jñātum
saraḷa-sundarōpāyam ādiguru mahāmantram

The Guru's words grant knowledge. When we focus on them, our heart becomes pure, and true knowledge dawns. The mantra of the supreme Guru, Lord Shiva, is the sweet and simple way to the knowledge of the attributeless, absolute principle.

ōm namaḥ śivāya mantram madhurasusvādu mantram
amṛta-sundara mantram nityānanda dāyakam

The mantra, 'om namah shivaya', the sweet mantra, the immortal, beautiful mantra bestows eternal bliss!

jay jay bōlō (Hindi)

jay jay bōlō bam bam bōlō
jay bōlō bhōlē-nāth kī
amarnāth jay viśvanāth jay
jay jay śiv bhagavān kī

Chant 'Victory, victory!' Chant 'Victory' to the innocent Lord Shiva! Victory to the Lord of immortality, to the Lord of the Universe! Victory to Lord Shiva!

sirpē jñān ki gaṅgā sōhē mātēpē kālkā candramā
kar mē ḍamaru 'om' dhvani kā, triśūl tīn guṇōṅ kā
bhasm sadā jō tan pē malē vō, pratīk naśvaratā kā
tūtō anādi tūhē anant, tū jag kā ādhār śivā
ḍamaru bājē mṛdaṅg bājē
dhumukkiṭṭatakk dhumukkiṭṭata dhumukkiṭṭata

The Ganga, adorning your head represents knowledge, and the crescent moon on your forehead represents time. In your hand, you hold the *damaru* (drum), representing the primordial sound 'om'. Your trident represents the three *gunas*. The ash that you smear on your body represents impermanence. You are beginningless and endless. O Shiva, you are the substratum of the world.

śiv kē nām kā ānandāmṛt manuvā tū nit pīyē jā
satya anāmay sundar niścal, śubh śiv pad kō pāyēgā
kaluṣit man kō pāvan karlē śiv śiv jāp sē tū sadā
tan tō śav hē śiv kē binā, śiv kē śaraṇāgat hōjā
ḍamaru bājē mṛdaṅg bājē
dhumukkiṭṭatakk dhumukkiṭṭata dhumukkiṭṭata

O Man, keep drinking the blissful nectar of the name of Lord Shiva. You will attain the state of Shiva, which is Truth, taintless, beautiful, still and auspicious. Purify your impure mind by always chanting 'Shiva, Shiva'. Without Shiva, the body is a mere corpse. Take refuge in Lord Shiva!

jay jay śaṅkar hara hara śaṅkar jay jay satya śaṅkarā
jay jay śaṅkar hara hara śaṅkar jay jay śiv śiv śaṅkarā

jay jay śaṅkar hara hara śaṅkar jay jay sundar
śaṅkarā
jay jay śaṅkar hara hara śaṅkar
jay jay śaṅkar hara hara śaṅkar

Victory to Lord Shiva! Victory to the supreme Truth! Victory to Lord Shiva, victory to Hara! Victory to beautiful Lord Shiva!

jay maṅgaḷ janani (Hindi)

jay maṅgaḷ janani dēvi durgē mā
śubh kāriṇi varadē śaṅkari bhadrē
simhavāhini mahiṣāsura-marddini
jagakāriṇi pālini nāśini bhavatāriṇi

Victory to the divine Mother, Goddess Durga, bestower of auspiciousness, granter of boons, the lovely consort of Lord Shiva. The Goddess who rides a lion, slayer of the demon Mahishasura, creator, sustainer and destroyer of the world, takes us across the ocean of transmigration!

dil mēṅ liyē āśā āyē ham dvār tērē
daras kē pyāsē hamrē nainā matvārē
jñān aur bhakti kā man mēṅ dīp jalāō mā
vintī sunlō hamrī jagjayyā durgē mā

We have come to your door with hope in our hearts, and with eyes longing and thirsting for your darshan. Kindly light the lamp of knowledge and devotion in our mind. Please hear our prayer, O victorious Mother Durga!

pār utārō bhavsāgar sē ambē mā
himagiri-nandini hai pāvanī tū jag-jananī

śubh aur maṅgaḷ kī rāh hamē dikhlāō
karuṇā bharī dṛṣṭi sē śītaḷ kar dēnā mā

O Mother, daughter of Mountain Himavan, pure one, mother of the universe, please take us across the ocean of transmigration. Show us the path of auspiciousness and well-being. Soothe us with your compassionate glance.

jay jay mā jay jay mā jay jay mā jay jay mā
jay jay mā jay jay mā jay jay mā jay jay mā

Victory to the Mother!

jaya jaya śaṅkara hara hara (Tamil)

jaya jaya śaṅkara hara hara śaṅkara jaya jaya paramēśvarane
hara hara śaṅkara jaya jaya śaṅkara hara hara karuṇākarane

Victory to Shankara, the supreme Lord! Victory to Shankara, the compassionate one!

vānmakaḷ gaṅgai varum vazhi tannil āṇavam koṇḍāḷē
niḷmuṭi ennum siṙayinil adanai nīkkiya guru nīyē
āṇuṭan peṇṇum oruvarukkoruvar pūrakam endhrāyē
āgamapporuḷē umaiyoru bhāgan āgiyē nindhrāyē

When the Ganga flowed with ego, you, the Guru, bound her in your hair and removed her ego. O supreme Lord, you showed that men and women are equal by giving your half to Parvati.

pāṙkaṭal viṣamāy uyirkaḷukkellām pēriṭar vandālē
pōṫṫriṭum iṙaiyē abhayamaḷittu kāttiṭuvāy nīyē
pārvati kēṭka guruvin gītai pāṅkuṭan sonnāyē
pāridan guruvē makkaḷai kākka tāyena vandāyē

When the milky ocean was churned and the deadly poison came up, you consumed it to protect the world. At Parvati's request, you enlightened her through the Guru Gita. You are the supreme Guru. You have come as our Mother to protect us.

jaya jaya śaṅkara – hara hara śaṅkara

Victory to Shankara!

jīvitamām van vipinatil (Malayalam)

jīvitamām van vipinattil
maṇṇil āṙāṭi madiccu-naṭann-oru
manam ākum mattēbhatte
kṛpayālē nin arikil aṇaccu

O Mother!, my mind roamed in this forest of life like a wild elephant throwing dirt all over itself. But your compassion brought me to you.

nin snēhamām pon-śṛṅkhalayil orukkān
etramēl kḷēśaṅgaḷ nī sahiccu
vātsalyamām amṛt-ūṭṭi nī enne
karuṇayāl śikṣaṇam ēki nayiccu

You went through great hardship to string me in the garland of your love. You fed me the nectar of tender love and disciplined me with compassion.

alaṅkāramāy nin guṇam cārtti nin

tiṭambēṭṭān ammē anugrahikkū
janimṛti-cakramām nakrattil ninnu nī
kara ēṭṭi ninnōṭu cērttīṭaṇē

O Mother! Bless me to be caparisoned with your goodness and to hold your golden image aloft. Save me from the wheel of birth and death, and make me one with you!

jō amma jōjō (Telugu)

jō amma jōjō jōjō jōjō
jagadamba jōjō nidurappō
ammā lālī... jōjō lālī...

O Sweet Mother, lullaby to you... Mother of universe lullaby to you... please sleep now, Mother, lullaby to you.

nī jagamanta niduriñcinadammā
nī biḍḍalandarū bajjuṇḍinārammā
hariharulu saitam paruṇḍināru
kṣaṇamaina mā kōsam pavvaḷimppavammā
ammā lālī... jōjō lālī

All of your creation is sleeping now, and all of your children have fallen asleep. Even Vishnu (the sustainer) and Shiva (the destroyer) have gone to sleep. For our sake, at least for a minute, please sleep. O Mother, lullaby to you...

jōlapāḍi māku jñānamiccināvu
ceyya paṭṭi mammūnaḍippiñci nāvvu
biḍḍalanu kāpāḍi alasipōtivammā
niduriñcani nīvū niduriñcālammā
ammā ammā lālī... jōjō lālī

By singing us cradle songs, you gave us knowledge of Self. Holding our hand, you led us to walk along the path. You protected your children, O Mother, and now you are tired. O Mother, who never sleeps even a moment, please sleep! O Mother, lullaby to you.

nidranu kanipeṭṭē velugē nīvammā
hṛdillō uṇḍēṭi sākṣivi ammā
amṛtānandamai unna ō ammā
manassu uyyālalō nidurapō
ammā lālī... jōjō lālī

You are the light that witnesses sleep. You dwell in our hearts as eternal consciousness. You are eternal bliss that has manifested as our Mother. Please make our ever-swinging mind your cradle, and sleep. O Mother, lullaby to you.

jōgoto jononī (Odiya)

jogoto jononī mātā durgā bhovānī
kṛpā koro kṛpāmoyī bhokti-prodāyīnī

O Goddess Durga, Mother of the universe, compassionate one, please shower your grace and bestow devotion.

jāhā mu pāūci mātā jahā mu dēkhūchi
sobū rē pochore mātā saṅkēto āsuchi
bujhi no pāri yē monō bhromito heyūchi
soṅsāro bondhonore mā choṭo poṭo heūcchi

Whatever I receive and see in life happens because of causes I do not understand. My confused, restless mind wanders in the world of samsara.

bipodo āsīle mātā bisvāso rohunī
tumo binā mono moro sthira hi rohūnī
tumo anubhobo mātā dhorito pārūni
jñāno diyo prēmo diyo śokti prodāyinī

During troubled times, I lose my faith. My mind is disturbed without your presence. I have many experiences but cannot apply them when situations arise. O Mother, please give me knowledge, love and strength.

guhārī suṇogō mātā duḥkha nivāriṇi
prēmō bhokti diyo mote mukti prodāyinī
bisvāso bondhono re mā diyo mote bāndhī
ē bhobo sāgoru mātā diyo mote mukti

O Mother, healer of sorrows, please hear my prayer. Give me love, devotion and eternal bliss. Bind me in deep faith in you. Free me from the bondage of the world and from the cycle of birth and death.

mā... mā... mā... mā...

kālacakravu (Kannada)

kālacakravu sariyutide nirantara
kelavē dinagaḷa ī payaṇa
hari nāmava japisi naliyōṇa
guru pādava dhyānisi bhajisōṇa

Human life is a short journey. The wheel of time does not stop for anyone. Let us happily remember God and meditate on the Guru's holy feet.

kastūri tannoḷagē hudugiddaru
mṛga huḍukuvudu kānanadi
hariyu hṛdayadi vāsipanendu
aṙiyade aleyuve samsāradi

The musk-deer searches the forest for the enchanting scent, unaware that it emanates from its own body. Similarly, unaware of God's presence within, you are lost in samsāra (cycle of births and deaths).

gōvindā gōpālā
murahara giridhara muraḷi manōhara
sujñāna nīḍuvā śrī pādagaḷa
śaraṇu paḍedare paramānanda
andhakārava nīguvudu
jīvana dāriya beḷuguvudu

If one surrenders to those holy feet that grant knowledge, one attains supreme happiness. The darkness of ignorance will be removed. The path of life will be illumined.

kālamām yātrayil (Malayalam)

kālamām yātrayil vazhi teṫṫi pōyappōḷ
kara kāṇākkaṭalil alayēṇḍi vannappōḷ
oru nūṙu sūrya-kiraṇattin prabhayāl
tava pāda-padmam kaṇḍu
hṛttil snēhāmṛtam niṙaññu

I lost my way in the journey of time and swam in despair, not seeing the ocean's shore. Then, I saw your lotus feet, more brilliant than a hundred suns, and my heart filled with the nectar of love.

oru nōkku kāṇān ennuḷḷam piṭayavē
oru vākku kēḷkkān kātōrtt-irikkavē
akatāril paninīrin malar-maṇam paratti
tava mātṛ-vātsalyam coriññu
manam prēmāmṛtattin aliññu

As I yearned for the vision of you and listened intently for a word from you, a divine fragrance filled my heart. You showered me with your tender love, and my heart merged in the ambrosia of your love.

tava snēha-mādhuryam nukarumbōḷ aṙiññilla
prāṇande śvāsamāy māṙum
hṛttil jīvande nāḷamāy cērum
aṙiyāte ninnil ninn-akalān iṭayāyāl
tirike viḷikkaṇē dēvi
nin kanivē enikk-abhayam

I did not know, when I imbibed the sweetness of your love, that you would become my life breath. You are the inner flame that enlivens my heart. If I unknowingly stray away from you, O Devi, please call me back. Your compassion is my sole refuge!

kālaṅgaḷ etra kazhiññīṭum (Malayalam)

kālaṅgaḷ etra kazhiññīṭum eṅkilum
ñān ennum amma tan kuññu-makaḷ
kātaṅgaḷ etra akale āṇeṅkilum
ñān ennum amma tan cārē tanne
ñān ennum amma tan cārē tanne

Time will pass, but I will always remain your little daughter. I am miles away from you, but I always remain near my Amma. I am always near my Amma.

māṫṫaṅgaḷ ēṙunn-en manuja-janmattil
māṫṫam illāttat-onnu mātram en amma
ennuṭe prēmavum bhaktiyum ninnōṭu
mātram ennuḷḷil aṙiyunn-en amma
mātram ennuḷḷil aṙiyunn-en amma

Many changes happen in my life, but my Amma is the one changeless Truth. You know that my love and devotion are for you alone, O Amma. You dwell within me and know.

ammaykku makkaḷ ī lōkam eṅgum
oru muttāy enneyum certtīṭēṇē
anya-mōhaṅgaḷ illende uḷḷil
eṅkil ī jīvitam dhanyamāyi
eṅkil ī jīvitam dhanyamāyi

The world is full of your children. Make me a pearl among them and hold me near. I have no other desire. My life will be fulfilled if I become one of the pearls that you hold near you.

kāḷi kāḷi kāḷi kāḷi triśūlī (Tamil)

kāḷi kāḷi kāḷi kāḷi triśūlī
kāḷi mahāmāyi karuṇāmayi nī
kāḷi mahākāḷi tripura-sundariyē
āyī mahāmāyī amṛta-varṣiṇiyē

O Kali, holding the trident, supreme illusion, you are the embodiment of compassion! O great Kali, tripura sundari, divine illusion, O Mother, you shower the nectar of immortality!

kāruṇyatiṅkaḷē kaṭaikkaṇ pāramma
malarpadam sērttu kāttaruḷvāy amma
manam pōkum pōkkilē enai nī viṭāte
un anpināle eppōtum tāṅkiṭuvāy

You are the full moon of compassion. Please cast a side-long glance in my direction. Grant me refuge at your lotus feet and protect me. Do not let me yield to the whims and fancies of my mind. Always protect me with your tender love.

nittiyamē sattiyamē sundaravum nīyamma
nin pāda salankai oḷi ōmkāram muzhunkatamma
unnaiyē ninaittiruntēn ninaittapaṭi vārum ammā
nī tannai nānendru uṇarttiṭuvāyamma

O Mother, you are Truth, auspiciousness and everlasting beauty. The anklets adorning your feet reverberate with the sacred syllable om. I think of you constantly, O Mother. Come to me in the way I visualize you. Help me to realize that you are my true Self.

kāḷi kāḷi ōm bhadrakāḷī (Malayalam)

kāḷi kāḷi ōm bhadrakāḷī
kāḷi kāḷi ōm mahākāḷī
vāḷum śūlam ēnti lāsya-nṛttam āṭum kāḷī
kāḷum hṛttin āmayaṅgaḷ pōkkuk-en karāḷī

O Kali! You dance enchantingly with the sword and the trident in your hands. My Mother, please remove the impurities from my yearning heart!

dharma-rakṣa ēkuvān avataricca ambikē
sadguruvāy bhūtalē virājamāna dēvikē
kāḷī... bhadrakāḷī... kāḷī... mahākāḷī

O Ambika! You incarnated in this world to protect *dharma*, and you exult in this universe as the great *Sadguru*.

parama-prēma-rūpiṇī nirantaram bhajikkuvān
śuddha-bhakti ēki nityam kāttukoḷka caṇḍikē
kāḷī... bhadrakāḷī... kāḷī... mahākāḷī

You are supreme love. Please protect me and grant me pure devotion to you. I pray to you unfailingly.

kāḷi ninde diya-rūpam kaṇḍu mōham-ārnnor- en
kaṇṇil ninnum dhārayāy ozhukiṭaṭṭe kaṇṇunīr
kāḷī... bhadrakāḷī... kāḷī... mahākāḷī

O Kali! When I see your divine form, I fall in love with you. Let my tears of adoration flow continuously.

śvēta-vastra-dhāriṇī jagajjanani pūjitē
aharnniśam mām pāhi dēvī kṛpā-vāridhē
kāḷī... bhadrakāḷī... kāḷī... mahākāḷī

O Devi, dressed in white, you are worshipped as the mother of this universe. Ocean of compassion, protect me, without fail, every moment of my life!

kāḷi nin kaikaḷil (Malayalam)

kāḷi nin kaikaḷil cērnnorā nāḷ
kaṇcimmi ninnu veṇ tārakaṅgaḷ
kātaranām ende mugdha-svapnam

kaṇḍorā tārakaḷ conna pōle

Kali, the stars sparkled in the skies the day you embraced me. They had witnessed the beautiful dreams of my yearning mind. It was as if the stars spoke to me.

ninde vyathakaḷum ninde yatnaṅgaḷum
ninnātma-nombaram tan kanalum
kālaṅgaḷ tāṇḍiya ninde yātra
ōrmakaḷil innum niṙaññu nilppū

Your sorrow and your striving, the burning ache in your heart, the long journey that took you to Her, all that is still fresh in our memory.

innu nī tīram-aṇayunna nēram ī
tārāpathaṅgaḷ ānanda-sāndram
kālaṅgaḷ ponnupōl kāttu nin paitale
kāḷikē tirike ēkunnu ñaṅgaḷ

Today you have reached the shore, and the stars shine in an ocean of bliss. O Kalika, we have taken great care of your child and today we return him to you.

nīyā paramporuḷ pon makanallayō
vāzhka nī muktanāy kālam ciram
amma tān ninnuṇma amma tān ninnamma
amma tan paitalāy velka nityam

You are the son of the supreme Truth. Live your life in the knowledge of the Absolute. Mother is your existence. Mother is your very own. Remain as mother’s darling child forever.

kaḷḷam kāṇikkīlum (Malayalam)

kaḷḷam kāṇikkīlum kaḷḷiyallā kāḷi
kālattin kāpaṭyam ēśātt-avaḷ
kāla-kālan tava kālkkal allō sadā
kāḷikā-dēvī kapāla-hastē

Kali plays pranks on us, yet She remains eternally pure and free of all deceit. Shiva, the destroyer of death, is at your feet, O Devi Kalika, you who hold a human skull in your hand.

kaṇṇinum kaṇṇāyi kaṇḍirippū dēvi
kātinum kātāyi kēṭṭirippū
kaitava-śōṣaṇam kaikkoṇḍ-anīśa nī
kātyāyani śivē rākṣasaghnī
kāla-sarpattinde damśanam ēṫṫivan
kālapurikk-aṅgu pōyiṭāte
kāttiṭān kelpezhum ambikē śrīkarī
kādambarī-priyē rakṣākarī
kāla-cakrattil kuṭuṅgi amarunna
kōlaṅgaḷkk-āśrayam āyirikkū

O Devi you reside within as the eye of the eye. You hear everything as the ear of the ear. You are the goddess who destroys all deceit, O Katayani, O Goddess Shivā. You destroy demons. Let not the serpent of time bite me and send me to death's abode. O Mother! You are the one who will save me. You are the abode of all auspiciousness, the protector, who loves the kadambari flower. Remain as the refuge for all who are caught in the wheel of time.

mannitil maṇṇāyi māṙiṭunnu dēham
māṫṫam illāttatām māṫṫamāyi

mānasam prāṇanōṭ-ottu gamikkumbōḷ
mālakaṫṫū mama mānasaghnī
mannilum viṇṇilum cuṫṫi naṭann-ivan
mātṛ-jaṭharattil ettiṭāte
mātṛ-caraṇa-yugaṅgaḷ smaricc-ende
mānasam māyil layicciṭēṇē
mōhavala neyta māya tan māntrikam
māyāmayi tanne nīkkīṭaṇē

The body returns to the earth, and the eternal Self travels upward along with the vital energy. Free me of all sorrow, O destroyer of the mind! Let me not wander on the earth or up in the sky, and return again to the womb of a mother. Let me always remember my Mother's feet. Let my mind dissolve in you. O Mother! You weave the magic web of illusion. Will you not release me from all illusion?

kanaka cilambum (Malayalam)

kanaka cilambum vaiḍūrya mukkuttiyum aṇiññu
madhupānamattayāy nilkkunnor-ammē
tanka prabhayōṭe ennakatāril nī vāzhunnat-
aṙiyātē
ninne tēṭi ñān puṙamē alayunnu

My ever-blissful Mother is adorned with golden anklets and a sparkling nose-ring. Unaware that you dwell in my heart as a golden effulgence, I searched for you outside.

nin tiru mandahāsattāl innen
manassile kārmēgham vazhi māṙunnu
uḷḷil uṇḍeṅkilum aṙiyān kazhiyāte
en manam tēṅgunnu ammē

Today your divine smile dispels the dark clouds in my mind. Though you are within, my heart weeps, unable to know you.

nīṙunnor-en manam aṙiyunnu nī mātram
tava pāda sarasīruhē en praṇāmam
nin kṛpā kaṭākṣattāl ennum
ñān aṙiññiṭaṭṭe ammē nin spandanam

You alone know the aching of my heart. I bow down before your divine lotus feet. Through your side-long glance of grace, may I feel your presence, O Mother.

kānhā kahāṅ hō (Hindi)

kānhā! kahāṅ hō tum
kahāṅ kahāṅ nahi ḍhūṇḍhā mainē tumhēṅ ō kānhā
ābhi jāō kānhā... mēre pās āō kanhā
kānhā! kahā hō tum

Where are you, O Krishna? I have looked everywhere for you. Please come to me this moment.

khuṣiyōṅ kō ḍhūṇḍhā maine bāhrī jagat mēṅ
tum nē dikhāyā hai vō bhītar ki sampadā
kānhā ō... mēre pās āō
kānhā ō kānhā mēre pās jaldi āō
mēre dil mēṅ nācō

I looked for happiness in the outside world, but you showed me that That Wealth is within me. Come to me quickly, dear Krishna, and dance in my heart.

tēri bāṅsurī ki dhun sē jhūm uṭhē sabkā man
sukhsāgar mēṅ jaisē dūb jāyē tan man
mēre pās āō kānhā
kānhā ō kānhā mēre pās jaldi āō
mēre dil mēṅ nācō

The tune emanating from your flute makes everyone rejoice as if body and soul are submerged in an ocean of happiness. Come quickly, dear Krishna, and dance in my heart.

mēri bhūlēṅ bhūl jānā, dūr mujhē na karnā
prēm dēkar śakti dēkar pār lagā dēnā
kānhā ō... mēre pās āō
kānhā ō kānhā mēre pās jaldi āō
mēre dil mēṅ nācō

Forget my mistakes. Do not keep me far from you. Give me love and strength, and take me across the ocean of transmigration. Come quickly, dear Krishna, and dance in my heart.

kaṇṇane kāṇān koticcu (Malayalam)

kaṇṇane kāṇān koticcinnu gōpikaḷ
kaṇṇunīrāṭṭil kuḷicciṭunnu
kaṇṇande vērpāṭil ēvarum khinnarāy
kaṇṇā nī ennini vannu cērum?

Longing to see Krishna, the gopis bathe in the stream of their tears, saddened by the departure of their Lord. "O Krishna, when will you come back to us?"

kaṇṇande āgamam kāttu kāttu
vṛndāvanam nidraviṭṭu paṇḍē
gōkkaḷum mēyāte ninnu pōyi
pāṭān maṙannu pōy pūṅkuyilum

Vrindavan sleeps no more as it waits for Krishna. The cows forget to graze, the birds forget to sing.

saṅkaṭam tīrāte kāḷindiyum
kaṇṇane ōrttu karaññu pōyi
vannilla centāmarākṣan-innum
vṛndāvanam duḥkha sāndramāyi

Unable to bear her sorrow, Kalindi cries as she remembers him. The lotus-eyed Lord has not yet returned. Vrindavan is an ocean of sorrow.

kālam itēṙe kaṭannu pōyi
kaṇḍilla kaṇṇande āgamavum
vṛndāvanattinde kaṇṇunīr dhārakaḷ
maṫṫoru kāḷindiyāy-ozhuki

Time passes and Krishna has not yet come. Tears stream down from Vrindavan, flowing as another Kalindi river.

kaṇṇane ōrttōrttu (Malayalam)

kaṇṇane ōrttōrttu kēzhum ī rādhayum
kaṇṇane-pōl prēma-rūpamāyi
rādha tan bhāvanā śuddhiyil kaṇṇande
sarva-bhāvaṅgaḷum siddhamāyi

Thinking of Krishna and yearning for Krishna, Radha became Krishna, the embodiment of love. In her purity, Radha acquired all the divine moods of Krishna.

prēmārdra hṛdayattil ennum śraviccitām
kaṇṇan pozhikkum ā vēṇu gānam
kaṇṇane viṭṭavaḷkk-illa maṫtonnumē
kāṇunnu kaṇṇande rūpam eṅgum

In her heart tender with love for the Lord, she constantly heard the melody of his flute. There is no one but Krishna for her. She sees his form everywhere, in everything.

kaṇṇande kayyile vēṇu pōle
rādhayum kaṇṇande bhāgamāyi
kaṇṇande bhaktiyāl unmattayāy
viśvam maṫannaṅgu ninnu rādha

Like the flute Krishna held in hands, Radha also became a part of the Lord. She became blissful in his love, and stood there, forgetful of the world.

rādha tan bhāvam pakarnnu ninnu
kaṇṇane pōlavaḷ puñciriccu
ānanda-magnarāy gōpikaḷum
rādhayōṭ-ottavar nṛttam āṭi

She merged with Krishna and smiled his bewitching smile. All the gopis lost themselves in joy and danced in rapture with Radha.

kaṇṇan varum enna (Malayalam)

kaṇṇan varum enna cintayil ñān
veṇṇayum pālum orukki vaccu
kaṇṇan varunnēram āṭuvānāy
ūññālu keṭṭi ñān kāttirippū

Believing that Krishna will come, I set aside milk and butter for him. I made a swing and waited for Krishna to come and swing on it.

kaṇṇande koñcum mozhi enikku
kēṭṭu kēṭṭ-unmattayāyiṭēṇam
ōṭakkuzhal viḷi onnu kēṭṭāl
ellām maṙannu ñān nṛttam āṭum

I will become blissful hearing Krishna's baby talk. Hearing Krishna's flute, I will dance and forget the world.

melle varunnuṇḍu kaṇṇanuṇṇi
vāri puṇarnn-umma nalkiṭaṭṭe
kaṇṇanu veṇṇayum pālum ēki
ūññālil āṭṭi rasicciṭaṭṭe

Krishna is coming towards me slowly. Let me enfold him in my arms and hug him tight. Let me feed him with milk and butter and enjoy watching him in the swing.

uṇṇī nī eṅgōṭṭum pōyiṭallē
ninne piriññiṭān vayy-enikku
nī piriññ-eṅgānum pōyi ennāl
vayy-enikk-ā vyatha tāṅgiṭāṇāy

Krishna, do not leave me. I cannot bear separation from you. My agony will be unbearable if you leave me and go away.

kaṇṇaṭaccīṭumbōḷ (Malayalam)

kaṇṇ-aṭaccīṭumbōḷ kāṇunnu ñān ammē
ninde manōhara-rūpam
kātōrtt-irikkumbōḷ kēḷkkunnu ñān ammē
ninde manōhara-gānam

I close my eyes and see your beautiful form, O Mother. I listen intently and hear your beautiful songs.

ñān onn-uṙaṅgumbōḷ ñān aṙiyunnu nin
sāntvanamām kara-sparśam
ñān uṇarumbōḷ ñān ānandam koḷḷunnu
ammē nin darśanam nēṭān

I slide into sleep at your soothing touch. My heart fills with joy when I wake up to receive your divine darshan.

ñān aliyunn-ammē ninnil aliyunnu
ñānum nīyum atonnāyi māṙunnu
ñān enna bhāvam at-illāte āvunnu
nī enna satyam at-onnāyi tīrunnu

I merge in you, O Mother, and we become One. I lose my sense of "I" and merge in your Truth.

aviṭutte apāra kṛpā-tirēkattāl
tattvam atent-ennu ñān inn-aṙiyunnu
etticcīṭunnu nī en jīvane ammē
tat-tvam-asi pada-lakṣya-svarūpattil

Your infinite compassion has given me knowledge of the ultimate principle. O Mother, merge this *jiva* in the supreme Self, the goal of the great dictum, "You are That".

kaṇṇīr-ppūkkaḷāl (Malayalam)

kaṇṇīr-ppūkkaḷāl kaḷam-orukki ninne
kāttirikkunn-itā ēkayāyi
kālocca melle en arikattu kēḷkkumbōḷ
kātōrtt-irippū ñān dhanyayāyi

I made a floral decoration from the flowers of my tears, and I wait for you all alone. With a sense of fulfillment, I faintly hear the sound of your feet.

aṙiyātta vīthiyil alaññīṭavē tellu
aṙivāy uḷḷil nī aṇayū
nēṭiyat-onnumē nityamalla – ātma
satyattin pātayil vyarttham ellām

When I wander unknown paths, please come to me as knowledge. Make me realize that all gains are ephemeral and of no value in the path of Truth.

kāṇunnat-onninde mūrta-bhāvam – aka
kaṇṇil teḷiyum amūrta-bhāvam
uṇma tan nērkaṇḍa tattva-bōdham – en
akatāril uṇaraṭṭe ātma-bhāvam

With my inner eye, I see the embodiment of the supreme Self, the formless supreme consciousness. I have seen the ultimate Truth with my own eyes. Let me become established in the Oneness of the Self!

kaṇṇunīr tōrātta sandhyakaḷ (Malayalam)

kaṇṇunīr tōrātta sandhyakaḷ ī janmam
kaṇṇāy-en mizhi-munnil onn-aṇayū
iruḷ mūṭi nilkkum ī jīvita-vīthiyil
veṇṇilāvāy nī vazhi kāṭṭiṭū

The passing days are an endless flow of tears. O Krishna! Please come as moonlight on the dark path of my life and show me the way.

gatakāla-jīvita nāṭaka vēdiyil
pala vēṣam āṭi timirttu allō
eṅkilum svāntattil viśrānti vannīla
vidhiyuṭe viḷayāṭṭam ī vidhamō

I have played my part in the drama of many previous lives, yet I never found peace. Is it fate's cruel play?

grīṣmamāy eriyunna ende ī hṛdayattil
sāntvana-tīrtthamāy vann-aṇayū
dīnata ārnnorī māmaka cittatte
kāruṇya-nētrattāl onn-uzhiyū

My heart burns like the scorching summer heat. Come to me like soothing rains. Please glance with compassion into my sorrowful heart.

sāphalyam aṙiyāte rāppakal nīḷavē
kātaram en mizhi kāḷindiyāy
ennini kaṇṇā ñān nin prēma-sāgarē
vann-ulayicciṭum onnāy tīrum?

As the days and nights pass by, tears flow from my eyes like the river Kalindi. O Krishna! When will I merge with you in the ocean of your love?

kāṇpatu āyiram (Tamil)

kāṇpatu āyiram iṅgē – atai
kāṭṭiḍum nijamatu onḍrē
nān atai tēḍuvateṅgē? – vazhi
yāriḍam kēṭpatu nanḍrē?

My mind perceives countless forms, yet in Truth the seer is only one. Where shall I find that Truth? Who will guide me?

āṅgoru aruḷenum oḷiyē – atu
kāṭṭumō nijamatan mukamē?
īṅkatu kāṭṭiṭum dinamē – atai
kāṇumō pētaiyen manamē?

The light of grace shines at a distance. Will it reveal Truth's face at last? If that moment comes, will my clouded mind even see it?

etuvum maṙaiykkātiruntāl – nām
eṅkeṅkum kāṇpatu nijamē
ellām manadāl tuṙantāl – atu
onḍṛutān maṙai nīṅgum vazhiyē

When all obstructions vanish, Truth is seen everywhere. The mind finds its way to Truth when it renounces what is not.

kār nīla kaṭarkarayil (Tamil)

kār nīla kaṭarkarayil kāḷīśvari
piravi kaṭalai kaṭakka udavum paramēśvari
tunba kaṭalin muzhukum emai durgēśvari
inba kaṭalin āzhtta vantāy laḷitēśvari
kāḷīśvari paramēśvari durgēśvari ammā
laḷitēśvari

O Kali, you reside on shores of the dark blue ocean. O Goddess, you help us cross the ocean of birth and death! O Durga, we are drowning in the ocean of sorrow. O Lalita, you have come to plunge us into the ocean of bliss. O mother Kali, Supreme Goddess, Durga, Lalita!

ucchantalayil tāmarayil kamalāṭcci
niccalamāy vīṭrirukkum nī sāṭcci
paccai paṭṭu puṭavay azhakil mīnāṭcci
iccai ellām pūrtti seyyum kāmāṭcci
kamalāṭcci ō nī sāṭcci mīnāṭcci ammā kāmāṭcci

O Kamakshi, you reside peacefully, as the witness, in the lotus at the top of our head (*sahasrara chakra*). O Meenakshi, you are beautiful, wearing a green silk saree. You fulfil all our desires. O Mother Kamakshi, Meenakshi, you are the divine witness!

jñāna vazhiyai vāzhntu kāṫṫum jñānāmbikai
bhakti vazhiyai pāṭi kāṫṫum parvatāmbikai
karma vazhiyai seytu kāṫṫum karppakāmbikai
dharma vazhiyil naṭatti cellum dharmāmbikai
jñānāmbikai ō parvatāmbikai
karppākāmbikai ammā dharmāmbikai

O Jnanambika, you live the path of jnana. O Parvatambika, you show us the path of devotion. O Karpakambika, you show us the path of action. O Dharmambika, you lead us in the path of dharma. O Mother, Jnanambika, Parvatambika, Karpakambika, Dharmambika!

muttukkellām muttē ammā māṙiyammā
vittaikkellām vittai nīyē pēcciyammā
porumaikkellām uraiviṭamē ponnammā
sirumaitanam poruttaruḷum cellammā
māṙiyammā ō pēcciyammā ponnammā enkal cellammā

O Mariyamma, you are the gem of gems. O Pechiyamma, you are the master of all arts. O Mother, you are the storehouse of patience. O darling Mother, you bear with all our shortcomings. O darling mother, Mariyamma!

ōm śakti ōm śakti ōm śakti ōm
ōm śakti ōm śakti ōm śakti ōm

kāruṇya-gaṅgayām (Malayalam)

kāruṇya-gaṅgayām ammaye tēṭunna
kātarayām kuññ-aruvi ñān ambikē
ārtt-ozhukīṭum ī hṛnnīr it-ennuṭe
śōka-mōhattāl kalaṅgi enn-ambikē

O Mother, I am a little wandering rivulet eagerly searching for you, the divine Ganga of love. A torrent of tears flows from my sorrowful heart filled with desire.

azhalinde vēnalil urukunnu ñān
tazhukunna śānti tan ala utirttīṭaṇē

gati pinniṭunn-orī vīthikaḷ okkeyum
pada-tīram aṇayān uḷḷ-āyam āyīṭaṇē

I am melting in the heat of sorrow. Arise within me as a soothing wave of peace. Let all the roads I travel lead me to your sacred feet.

mahita-mahārṇavam tannil paticc-ende
taḷarum ī janmam puḷakitam ākaṇē
coriyaṇē nin kṛpa atināyi nityavum
aliyaṇē jīvan ā snēhamām sāgarē

I have fallen into the ocean of samsara. Rejuvenate my tired soul, and shower your grace forever that I may merge into the ocean of your love.

kāruṇya-kaṭalākum ammē (Malayalam)

kāruṇya-kaṭal ākum ammē ennil
nin kṛpa tūvukayillē...
nin tiru snēham illeṅkil ñān
vāṭi taḷarnnu pōyīṭum

O ocean of compassion, please shower your grace upon me. Without your divine love, I am withering away.

ceppil mutt-enna pōle karaḷil
cērtt-aṇaccīṭunnu ninne
nī enne kai-veṭiññ-ennāl vyartham
āyīṭum ennuṭe janmam

I hold you in my heart like the pearl within its shell. If you abandon me, my life will be in vain.

ellām nī enna satyam ñān
aṙiyunna nāḷ ennu tāyē?
atināyiṭṭ-innu ñān ellām nin
padatāril arppicciṭunnu...

O Mother, when will I ever know that you are everything? I offer myself at your lotus feet that I may know this Truth.

kaṭalil nadi enna pōle ninnil
cēraṇam ñān ende tāyē
ninnil aliññīṭum eṅkil ahō!
ñān illa nī tanne ākum

O Mother, as the river merges into the ocean, may I merge in you. Then, I will cease to be, and you alone will remain.

kāruṇya-kaṭal (Malayalam)

kāruṇya-kaṭal-ākum ammē ninde
tīratt-orikkal ñān vannu ninnu
jñānamō bhaktiyō ētumillā
ñānum ā kaṭalile ōḷamāyi

O Mother, ocean of compassion! I stand on your shore. I have neither knowledge or devotion, yet I am a wave in your ocean.

bhavatāpa-taptamām man-mānasam
nin prēmam tēṭiyat-entu-koṇḍu?
pūrva janmārjita puṇyattālō?
ākasmikam mātram ennākumō?

My mind burns in the heat of this world of transmigration. How did I come to seek your love? Is it merit gained from previous lives? Or did mere chance lead me to you?

kāluṣyam ēṙeyuḷḷ-en hṛdantam
ammaykku cērum vasatiyāṇō?
pāzh-kuṭilām antaraṅgam tava
tṛppāda-sparśanam tēṭiṭunnu

Many emotions disturb my heart. Is it a fit abode for you? O Mother! my heart longs to touch your divine feet!

kāṫṫinde īṇattil (Malayalam)

kāṫṫinde īṇattil kātōrttirunnu ñān
yamuna tan tīrattil ēkākiyāy
niśāgandhiyōṭ-ottu ñānum ī rātriyil
tēṭukayāṇ-ende priya tōzhane

Sitting alone on the banks of the Yamuna, I listen intently to the rhythm of the breeze. On this lovely night, I seek my beloved. Fragrant night-blooming jasmine waits with me.

paurṇamikk-entitra cantam innu
kaṇṇan varum ennu nī aṙiññō?
rākkiḷi-kūṭṭamē niṅgaḷ inn-īṇattil
prēmānurāgam pozhippat-entē

The radiant moon is so lovely tonight. Did you hear that Krishna is coming? O nightingales, why are you singing love songs tonight?

rāvinum inn-oru nāṇam kuṇukkam
āreyō kāttirikkunna pōle
cillakaḷ talatāzhtti pūmazha peyyunnu
nirvṛtiyil muṅgi rāvunīḷe

The night seems to wait shyly, expecting someone. The branches bend low and shower flowers on the ground. The night is immersed in bliss.

vēṇugānam muzhaṅgīṭunnu nīḷe
kōri taricu nilkkunnu rādha
kaṇṇande āgamam vaiki ennākilum
svapnaṅgaḷ okkeyum pūvaṇiññu

A flute melody fills the air, and Radha's thrilled heart stands still. Krishna tarried, but now he has arrived, and all her dreams burst into flowers!

kōṭi-divākara-prabha (Malayalam)

kōṭi-divākara-prabha vitaṙum
tējōmayi āṇ-en sadguru
parama-tattvattin nitānta-rūpam
kāruṇya-mūrttiyām tējaḥ-svarūpam
kāruṇya-mūrttiyām tējaḥ-svarūpam

My Sadguru is the radiant one who shines with the brilliance of crores of suns. She is the supreme, the Absolute, the resplendent form of compassion.

arkka-candrādikaḷkk-udayam nalkiya
viśva-janani āṇen sadguru
ārṣa-samskārattin param poruḷē ammē
sadgati ēkuka ennil ennum

My Sadguru is the Universal Mother who illumines the sun, moon and stars. O Mother, supreme essence of the Vedic culture, always keep me on the right path.

anādi-caritam vāzhtti-stutikkum
nāda-bindu-kalātītē
anupama-sāra-sarvasvamē ammē
aṭiyanil uṇarttū satyāvabōdham

Your story is praised since beginningless time. You are the essence of sound, the flawless one. O Mother, incomparable essence of all, awaken the awareness of Truth in me.

kōṭisūrya prabhēyuḷḷa (Kannada)

kōṭisūrya prabhēyuḷḷa
jagajyōti dēvi nīnu
narara bāḷanu hasanu goḷisuva
advitīya jananī advitīya jananī

Devi, you are the light of the world, shining with the effulgence of a million suns. You are the Mother without a second, who makes human lives easy.

māyā mōhada balegē siluki
bhava-sāgaradī nā toḷalidē
ninna nāmava biḍadē japisuvā
sadbhaktiya nīḍammā sadbhaktiya nīṭammā

I flounder in the ocean of transmigration, ensnared in the net of maya. Please grant me true devotion, that I may constantly chant your name.

dharaṇi-yāḷuva varadāyiniyē
dayētōrī salahammā
vairāgyava ni mūḍisi manakē
jñānadarivā uṇisammā jñānadarivā uṇisammā

O Devi, you rule over the world and graciously grant boons. Please watch over me. Make dispassion arise within, and please feed me with knowledge, O Mother.

laḷitāmbikē amṛtāmbikē
vimalāmbikē vijayāmbikē

O Divine Mother, eternal Mother, most pure Mother, victorious Mother!

kṛpa tūki cāre aṇaccu (Malayalam)

kṛpa tūki cāre aṇacc-aṭuppicc-amma
mānasam samsāra-sāgare alayavē
prēma-varṣattāl uḷḷam kuḷirppiccu
prēma-pravāhattil āzhtti enne

Mother gathered me close with infinite compassion as I wandered in the ocean of the world. Her love healed my aching heart, and I was immersed in the flow of Her love!

kāla-pravāhattin nīrccuzhiyil
kāl iṭaṙāte tuṇaccu ammā
tāṅgāy taṇalāy abhayakaram ēki
vāri puṇarnn-enne cērtt-aṇaccu

She guided me away from the whirlpool of time. Her arms became my refuge and support as She held me close to Her.

dīnadayāmāyi tava kṛpa atu mātram
ēzhayām ī jīvann-ādhāramāy
tval-kṛpā-varṣattāl samśuddham-ākki nī
tṛppāda-padmattil cērttīṭaṇē

You are the the substratum of my life and the Goddess who has compassion for the distressed. Shower your purifying grace on me and merge me into your lotus feet!

kṛpaykkāyi bhajippū (Malayalam)

kṛpaykkāyi bhajippū ñān jananī
mama jananī mama jananī
kṛpaykkāyi bhajippū ñān mama jananī
mama jananī mama jananī

I worship you to receive your grace, my Mother!

ambē pāhi pāhi pāhi
pāhi pāhi pāhi mām

O Mother, protect me!

ennuḷḷinn-uḷḷil uṇarum ī
mōhattin neṭu vīrppukaḷil
coriyaṇē daya kṛpānidhē
ninnil ninnum ñān akalāt-irikkān

Desires arise within me, O treasure-house of compassion. Please shower your grace that I may always feel close to you.

kaivazhikaḷ palat-aṅgu tāṇḍi
sāgaram tēṭunna nadi ennapōl
vazhi aṟiyāte en manam
tēṭunnu tava caraṇa-yugaḷam

As a river seeking the ocean flows into many small creeks and rivulets, my mind wanders in search of your divine feet, not knowing the way to you.

kṛṣṇā harē kṛṣṇā harē (Malayalam)

kṛṣṇā harē... kṛṣṇā harē
manamōhanā... hṛdayēśvarā

Victory to Krishna, enchanter of the mind, Lord of our heart.

mazha-mukilvarṇṇā muraḷī-dharā
pītāmbara-dhara mōhana-vadanā
māyā-mōhana mānasa-cōrā
śyāmā manōharā rādhēśvarā

Dark-hued one, divine flute-player, clad in yellow silk, with a bewitching face! Divine enchanter, stealer of the mind, dark one, beautiful one, Radha's lord!

āpad-bāndhavā anātha-rakṣakā
gītā-nāyaka sarvēśvarā
pāpa-vināśakā pāṇḍava-tōzhā
bhaktajana-priya jagadīśvarā

Eternal friend in times of danger, saviour of the helpless, Lord of the Gita, God of all! Destroyer of evil, friend of the Pandavas, beloved of the devotees, Lord of the world!

kṛṣṇā harē... kṛṣṇā mukundā...
kṛṣṇā harē... kṛṣṇā murārē...

Victory to Krishna, giver of liberation, enemy of the demon Mura!

kūriruḷ tiṅgumi (Malayalam)

kūriruḷ tiṅgumi ende hṛttil
nī prēma-dīpamāy aṇayuk-ammē
takarunnu cittam taḷarunnu tanuvum
maruvunnu ñān innum ēkayāyi

O Mother! My heart is heavy with darkness. Shine the lamp of love in my heart. My mind and body are desolate as I live here all alone!

nīrada-śyāma kaḷēbare ninnuṭe
nīḷ mizhitumbāl talōṭiṭumbōḷ
nirmalam ākaṭṭe ende cittam śyāmē
nin tiru madhuramām smaraṇayālē

O dark-hued one! may the caress of your lovely eyes purify my mind. Let me remain absorbed in sweet memories of you.

nirupama śānti niṙaññ-ezhum ninnuṭe
niṙavuṫṫa lāvaṇya kāntiyālē
tikavuṫṫat-ākkaṇe ende hṛttum śyāmē
teḷivuṫṫa bōdha-svarūpamāyi

May the radiance of your peerless beauty free my heart of all blemish. O lovely one, dark as a rain cloud, awaken within me as pure awareness!

kṣaṇikam ī jīvitam (Malayalam)

kṣaṇikam ī jīvitam enn-aṙiññālum
kṣaṇa-nēram ī bōdham uḷḷil illa
kaṇ-munnil etra pēr maṇ-maṙaññ-ennālum
ñān marikkil-enna tōnnal uḷḷil

Life is momentary, yet we are not aware of it even for a moment. Many have been buried before our eyes, yet we forget that we ourselves will also die

malsaricc-ōṭunnu mānavar nām
pērum praśastiyum kai-varikkān
veṭṭi piṭiccatum taṭṭi paṙiccatum
taṭṭi teṙippikkum kāla-cakram

We race to gain name and fame, and we conquer and take by force; but the inexorable wheel of time will bring us to our end.

jalarēkha pōle ī svapnam ellām
nimiṣārddham aṅgatu nērttu pōkum
onnitōrtt-uṇaruka tannilēkku
janimṛti duḥkham ataṅgu māyum

All our dreams are like a line drawn on water. They vanish in a second. Know this, and awaken to your true Self. Then, the sorrow of life and death will disappear.

kuvalaya-mizhikaḷ (Malayalam)

kuvalaya-mizhikaḷ aṭaññu kāṫṫil
kuṙu-nira āṭi ulaññu

kaṭa-mizhi iṇakaḷil kadanam niṙaññ-oru
kaṇṇīr kaṇaṅgaḷ tuḷumbi

Her blue lotus-eyes closed gently in the breeze that caressed the dark curly hair. Tears of longing fell from her eyes.

kaṇṇande kālin cilambin nādam
kātōrttu ninnavaḷ tēṅgī
kāṇā-maṙayatt-alaññ-oru kaṇṇukaḷ
kātaramāyi maṭaṅgi

She cried as she listened for the sound of Krishna's anklets. Her eyes vainly searched, in the far distance, for her Lord.

mōhana-rūpande māṙil mēvum
mālayāy tīrān kotikkum...
kṛṣṇa-tuḷasī katirukaḷ pōl avaḷ
kṛṣṇanēyum kāttirunnu

She waited for Krishna like a garland of tender tulasi leaves that yearns to adorn the Lord.

śyāmande cintayil viṅgī-bhāram
tāṅgān arutāte rādhā...
kāḷindī tīratt-alaññ-alaññ-ā maṇṇin
māṙil taḷarnnavaḷ vīṇu

Filled with thoughts of her dark Lord, her heart became heavy with his absence. Unable to bear her grief, Radha wandered the shores of the Kalindi river and finally fell to the lap of mother Earth.

mahādēvi (Malayalam)

mahādēvi mahādēvi mahādēvi tozhunnēn
aṭimalariṇa raṇḍum kai-kūppi tozhunnēn
azhak-ēṙum bhagavatiye kaṇi-kaṇḍu tozhunnēn
kēśādi-pādam sadā manatāril tozhunnēn

O Great goddess, I worship you. I worship your divine lotus feet. I see and worship the lovely form of Bhagavati when I open my eyes at the break of dawn. Let your form, from head to toe, shine in my blossoming heart.

kārkuntal-azhalōlum tirumuṭi tozhunnēn
vārtiṅkaḷ prabha coriyum mukha-padmam tozhunnēn
tilakattāl śōbhikkum tiruneṫṫi tozhunnēn
kāruṇyam tuḷumbunna tirumizhikaḷ tozhunnēn

I worship your beautiful, long, dark and curly hair. I worship your lovely lotus face, radiant as the silver moon. I worship your divine brow that shines with a sandal-paste mark. I worship your divine eyes that brim with compassion.

mukkutti aṇiññoru nāsika tozhunnēn
sūrya-candranmār viḷaṅgum karṇṇaṅgaḷ tozhunnēn
niṙakānti tiṅgum tūmandahāsam tozhunnēn
ātmaprabha coriyum pūppuñciri tozhunnēn

I worship your nose that wears a brilliant nose ring. I worship your ears wearing the sun and moon as earrings. I worship your peerless beauty and tender smile that overflows with the bliss of the Self.

centoṇḍi-pazham vellum adharaṅgaḷ tozhunnēn
mullappū-niṙam ōlum dantaṅgaḷ tozhunnēn
madhura-gītam pozhiyum kaṇṭham-atu
tozhunnēn
makkaḷe cērtt-aṇaykkum vakṣassu tozhunnēn

I worship your lovely lips, and your teeth that are the color of jasmine flowers. I worship your throat that flows with sweet melodies. I worship you who hold your children close to your bosom.

makkaḷe tārāṭṭum tṛkkaraṅgaḷ tozhunnēn
ākāśam pōl viśālam maṭittaṭṭu tozhunnēn
graha-dōṣam tīrkkunna jānukkaḷ tozhunnēn
bhaktarkk-ānandam ēkum tiru naṭanam
tozhunnēn

I worship your divine hands that caress your children. I worship your divine lap, as expansive as the sky. I worship your lovely knees that destroy the evil effects of planets. I worship your divine dance that delights devotees.

satya-dharmamāy viḷaṅgum cēvaṭikaḷ tozhunnēn
bhaktakōṭi namikkum daśa-nakham tozhunnēn
aṭimuṭi paramēśi dēviye tozhunnēn
pādādi kēśam nityam tozhuttiṭānāyi tīraṇē

I worship your feet that shine resplendent as Truth and virtue. I worship your toenails that millions of devotees bow down to. I worship your lovely form, the supreme Goddess, from your divine feet to your lovely hair. May I worship your divine form every day of my life.

mahādēvi mahākāḷi (Kannada)

mahādēvi mahākāḷi mahāmāyē mahēśvari
mahābuddhi mahāsiddhi mahāvidyē namō'stutē

Salutations to the great Goddess, great Kali, divine illusion, supreme Goddess, divine intelligence, ultimate goal, supreme knowledge.

sarvajñē sarvaśaktē sarvamaṅgaḷē, sarvēśvari
anugrahisu nammanu amṛtēśvari namō'stutē

All-knowing, all-powerful, all-auspicious Goddess! Goddess of all, eternal Goddess, our salutations to you. Please bless us!

ādiśakti parāśakti ananta-rūpiṇi ānanda-kāriṇi
kṛpetōrū namage amṛtēśvari namō'stutē

Primordial power, supreme power of infinite forms, bestower of bliss, immortal Goddess, our salutations to you. Please shower your grace on us!

sāvitri gāyatri amba sarasvati tripūrasundari
kāpāḍu nammanu amṛtēśvari namō'stutē

Mother, you are Savitri and Gayatri. Goddess Saraswati, beautiful one of the three cities, immortal Goddess, our salutations to you. Please protect us!

sadgati-pradāyini sarva-mantra-svarūpiṇi
bhavapārumāṭu nammanu amṛtēśvari namō'stutē

You guide us along noble paths and are the embodiment of all mantras. Immortal Goddess, our salutations to you. Please save us from the ocean of transmigration!

kāḷi mā kāḷi mā kāḷi mā kāḷi mā

O Mother Kali!

mahiṣāsura-marddini mahā-pātaka (Sanskrit)

mahiṣāsura-marddini mahā-pātaka-nāśini
praṇatārtti vināśini praṇavābdhi vihāriṇi
malayācala-vāsini mamatā-mada-nāśini
saccinmaya-rūpiṇi śaraṇagata-pālini

O Mother! Slayer of the demon Mahishasura, you revel in the ocean of consciousness represented by the syllable Om! You dwell in the Malaya mountain, and destroy attachment and pride. Embodiment of consciousness, protector of those who take refuge in you!

pāhi mām jagadīśvari dēhi mē karuṇāmṛtam

O Goddess of the world, protect me! Grant me the nectar of your compassion!

jñānāmṛta-dāyini jani-duḥkha-vināśini
karuṇāmṛta-varṣiṇi kalikanmaṣa-nāśini
vēdāmṛta-rūpiṇi varadē abhayaṅkari
caraṇāmbujam ambe tē śaraṇam mama santatam

You grant eternal knowledge and destroy the suffering of transmigration. You shower us with your infinite mercy and destroy the evils of this dark age. You are the nectar of the eternal Vedas. You bless us and make us fearless. O Mother, your lotus feet are forever my refuge.

mā kā mantr-jap (Hindi)

mā kā mantr-jap rē man
prēm mantr jap rē man

O mind, chant the mantra, 'ma'. Chant the mantra of love.

bhakti na jānu jñān na jānu
phir bhi ās hai man mēṅ mā
āvō mērē dil mēṅ mā
man mandir mēṅ bas jāvō

I know nothing of devotion or knowledge. Still, my heart hopes. Come, O Mother, and reside in the temple of my heart forever.

prēm bhakti kā sudhā pilāvō
bhav sāgar sē pār karō mā
mōh jāl sē hame chuḍāvō
mērē dil mēṅ nācō mā

Feed me the nectar of love and devotion and help me cross this ocean of transmigration. Free me from the net of attachments and dance in my heart, O Mother!

jñān bhakti kā dīp jalākē
śuddh bōdh kā uday karākē
param śānti mēṅ līn karāvō
mērā jīvan dhanya banādō

Lighting the lamp of knowledge and devotion, awaken pure awareness in me. Immerse me in supreme peace and make my life fruitful and worthy.

makkaḷa dēvane (Kannada)

makkaḷa dēvane muddu kṛṣṇa
tekkegē bārō nammappa kṛṣṇa
ākaḷa salahida gōvaḷa kṛṣṇa
bēṇṇeya kadda bāla kṛṣṇa

Come to my arms, darling Krishna, darling God of children. Gopala Krishna, protector of cows. Little Krishna, butter thief!

gōpiya kāḍida tuṇṭa kṛṣṇa
beṭṭavanettida diṭṭa kṛṣṇa
kāḷiṅgamardana vesagida kṛṣṇa
kamsa-samhāri śūra kṛṣṇa

Naughty Krishna, you teased the gopis. Mighty Krishna, you lifted the mountain. Valiant Krishna, you slew Kalingathe surpent. You are the brave Krishna who conquered Kamsa.

bhaktajanarā bhaṇṭa śrīkṛṣṇa
sarvajña viśvarūpa kṛṣṇa
kōḷalanuduta muraḷīkṛṣṇa
sumēdaḷa baḷi bārō śrīkṛṣṇa

Sri Krishna, servant of all devotees. Omniscient, all-pervading Krishna. O Murali Krishna, play your flute and come to Sumedha!

sumadhura kṛṣṇa sakalara kṛṣṇa

Adorable Krishna, everyone's Krishna!

manamē... hē manamē (Malayalam)

manamē... hē manamē manamē... hē manamē
iniyum entinī paritāpam
aṟiyuka nī ī janana-maraṇaṅgaḷ
dēhiyil alleṭō dēha-mātram

O mind, why are you still in distress? Know that birth and death belong only to the body and not to the indwelling soul.

nīṫṫil iṙaṅgiya lavaṇa-kaṇattin
rūpavum bhāvavum pōy-maṙayum
nīronnu vaṫṫiyālō tanirūpattil
kāṇuka illatrē saindhavatte

The salt rock loses its shape and identity when it sinks into the ocean. It will never regain its original form even if the water dries up.

ēkatva-bōdham prakāśikkum jīvanum
nāma-rūpam veṙum ārōpaṇam
vyaktitva-bōdham naśikkum ā jīvanō
saccidānanda-svarūpam ākum

Name and form are mere superimpositions on the jivan who is the pure light of consciousness. When the sense of 'I' disappears, the jivan discovers its true nature is existence, consciousness and bliss (satchidananda).

advaita-śāstraṅgaḷ ghōṣiccīṭunnatum
māṫṫam illāttor-ā satyamallō
tattvattin-uḷḷil viḷaṅgum ā vaibhavam
satyamām amma tan tat-svarūpam

O Mother, you are the changeless Truth proclaimed by Advaita. You shine as the glorious embodiment of Truth, the principle of non-duality.

maṇamilla madhuvilla (Malayalam)

maṇamilla madhuvilla vana-sūnam ñān ammē
neṭunāḷ ninakkāyi kāttirippū
onnē enikkoru āśayuḷḷu – tava
pūjā-malarāyi tīrnniṭēṇam – ā

tr̥ppāda-padmattil cērnniṭēṇam

O Mother, I'm a wild flower devoid of fragrance or nectar. I've waited so long for you to come. Please fulfil my desire and make me an offering at your holy feet..

annapānādikaḷ illāte nidrā-
vihīnayāy ammē ñān kāttirippū
vāṭāte taḷarāte veyil ēṭṭu kariyāte
ātmārppaṇattināyi kāttirippū... ammē
pūjā-malarāy nī cērkkukillē?

O Mother, I have forgone food, drink and sleep waiting for you to come. Let me not wilt or get scorched by the sun so that I can surrender to you. O Mother, won't you let me be a flower worshipping you?

ammē... ammē... ñān ninde ponnōmal sūnuvallē

O Mother, am I not your darling child?

onn-ende cārē nī vannīṭumō
en manō-vēdana kaṇḍīṭumō?
tr̥kkara-valliyāl onn-enne tazhukukil
ende ī janmam sudhanyam-allō... ammē
ñānum nin malaraṭi cērum-allō

Won't you come close and see my anguish for yourself? If you caress me with your holy hand, my life will be blessed. I will merge In your feet.

pizhayentu ceytu ñān ambikē neṭunāḷāy
padamalar cērāttī kāṭṭu-puṣpam?
innu varum amma ippōḷ varum enna
āśayōṭe ñān kāttirippū... ammē
ājīvanāntam ñān kāttirikkām

O Mother, what mistake have I done that you keep this wild flower away from you? I am waiting for you to come today, now. O Mother, I am prepared to wait for my whole life.

mānattu mārivil (Malayalam)

mānattu mārivil aliyunnatu pōle
kāḷikē nin makkaḷ-ākum ñaṅgaḷ
madhuramām tāvaka prēma-madhuvuṇḍu
manam aliññ-illāte āyiṭaṇe

O Kali, may your children drink the honey of your love and dissolve in you as the rainbow dissolves into the sky.

āzhiyil āzhunn-orādityan ura ceyvū
amṛtābdhi tannil aṅg-āzhū kuññē
vāridhiyil tira vilayam ākum pōle
aliyānāy vembunna tira ñān ammē

The sun sinks into the ocean and says, "O child, dive deep into the ocean of immortality." O Mother, I am a wave that longs to merge in you as the waves merge back into the ocean.

āditya dēvane hṛdayattil ēṫṫunn-
oru kuññu maññu kaṇam pōle
nin prabha ennilum vilasitam ākuvān
amalamāy tīraṇē antaraṅgam

Like the dew drop enshrines the sun god in her heart, may my heart become pure, that your brilliance may shine within.

man laṅkā par (Hindi)

man laṅkā par rāvaṇ rāj
dhīmī thī sītā ki āvāz
lōbh mōh kitnē dikhlāyē
birah ghāv prabhu hī bhar pāyē

The mind as Lanka is being ruled by ego as Ravana. The faint voice of the inner self as Sita is heard from there. The voice says, 'No matter how much you try to allure me, the pain of longing can only be cured by my Lord.'

kahē rāmā rāmā rām rām
kaṇ kaṇ ban jāye tav dhām
'Ram Ram Ram' she calls out, and prays that he
may pervade every atom of her being.
kāñcan mṛg kē mōh ne ghērā
rām sē biccaḍ gayī yē sītā
rām rām kehkē pukāre
nām smaraṇ sētu ban jāyē

The golden deer, representing the distractions of the world, has separated Sita from Ram. Now her intent calls for her Lord have taken the form of a bridge.

viṣaya vāsanā sē ṭakkṙāyē
guru sahāy bin hār hī jāyē
pūrṇ samarpaṇ tab raṅg lāyē
tab hī guru tārak kehlāyē

When we confront our inner weaknesses, without the guru's grace we are bound to fail. Complete surrender brings success, that's why the Guru is called the Savior.

manmōhan kē pyārē (Hindi)

manmōhan kē pyārē kaisē bane ham sārē
pūchē bhōlī rādhā sē vraj kē jan sārē
rādhā bōlī man kē gaharāyi sē āyē nām
har dam bōlō rādhē śyām
har kṣaṇ bōlō kṛṣṇa nām

The people of Vraj asked the innocent Radha: "How do we all become dear to Krishna, the enchanter of the mind?" Radha said, "Chant his name deep in your heart." Chant 'Radhe Shyam' every instant. Chant the name of Krishna every moment.

bhalē hī vō mākhan cōr jiskē dhun pē nācē mōr
apnē antaryāmī vō, tīn lōk kē svāmī vō
unkā prēm pānē kō rāg-dvēṣ kō chōḍ dō
rādhā bōlī man kē gaharāyi sē āyē nām
har dam bōlō rādhē śyām
har kṣaṇ bōlō kṛṣṇa nām

Though he steals butter like a thief, and peacocks dance to his tune, he dwells in our hearts and is the Lord of the three worlds. To win his love, renounce attachment and aversion. Radha said, "Chant his name deep in your heart." Chant 'Radhe Shyam' every instant. Chant the name of Krishna every moment.

karuṇā kā bhāv hō, sabkē pratī prēm hō
sukh-dukh kā pal jō āyē samatvatā kā bhāv hō
man karm har vāk bhī kṛṣṇa nām sē lipt hō
rādhā bōlī man kē gaharāyi sē āyē nām
har dam bōlō rādhē śyām
har kṣaṇ bōlō kṛṣṇa nām

Have compassion and love for everyone. When moments of happiness and sorrow come, be equanimous. Let your mind, actions and speech be immersed in the name of Lord Krishna. Radha said, "Chant his name deep in your heart." Chant 'Radhe Shyam' every instant. Chant the name of Krishna every moment.

man samjhē (Hindi)

man samjhē sab khēl tumhārā
jhūṭhē jag kā sab sac mānē
aisā māyā-jāl pasārā
man samjhē sab khēl tumhārā

My mind has recognized your play that makes us mistake the unreal world to be real. O Lord, what a net of illusion you have spread over us! My mind has recognized your play.

gupt tumhīṅ hō prakaṭ tumhīṅ hō
bhāṣā tum hī, maun tumhīṅ hō
kyā-kyā nyārē rūp sajāyē
khud sirajan, khud sirajanhārā

You alone are the unmanifest as well as the manifest. You alone are both speech and silence. What an array of forms you present, being yourself the creation as well as the creator!

āṅkh-micōlī bahut khilāī
māyā-jāl mēṅ mati bharmāī
thakā-hārā maiṅ śaraṇ mēṅ lē lō
nirbal jan kā tū hī sahārā

Enough of this game of hide and seek, O Lord, you confused me in your net of illusion. Now, please grant refuge to this weary supplicant. You alone are the support for the weak and destitute!

man samjhē sab khēl tumhārā... khēl tumhārā
man samjhē... man samjhē...

My mind has recognized your play...

man tujhme rahē (Hindi)

man tujhme rahē bas magan magan
din rāt rahē bas ēk lagan

May my mind always be absorbed in you. Day and night, may I long for you.

kaise tujhē pāūṅ
tujh mēṅ bas jāūṅ
ḍhūṇḍhūṅ maiṅ tujhkō
yā khud khō jāūṅ

How can I reach you? How can I merge in you? May I lose myself in search of you.

kaise maiṅ manāūṅ
sāvallkō rijhāūṅ
āṅsū kī laḍiyāṅ
din rāt pirōūṅ

How can I please you? O Beloved, how can I cajole you? Day and night, I string garlands of tears for you.

kisē hāl sunāūṅ
yē dard batāūṅ
jaisē jalbin machlī
yūṅ taḍpat jāūṅ

To whom can I tell my sorrow? How do I express this pain? I am writhing in pain like a fish out of water.

māривillin ēzhu varṇaṅgaḷil (Malayalam)

mārivillin ēzhu varṇaṅgaḷil
amma tan rūpam viṭarnnu
śōṇima ārnnoru sandhya tan ceñcāyam
amma tan sindūram allē

Mother's form blossomed as the colors of the rainbow. The crimson of the setting sun is the vermilion mark on Mother's forehead.

nīla-vāniṭattil nakṣatra-śōbha en
amma tan nāsābharaṇam allē
kāḷima ōlunna niśayuṭe cāruta
amma tan kārkuntalābha allē

The brilliance of the stars in the deep night sky is the sparkle of Mother's nose ring. The dark beauty of the night is the shine of Her dark hair.

ī prapañcattin nitya-caitanyam en
amma tan prēma-prabhāvam allē
ā prēma-dhārayil āmagnayāyi ñān
amma tan hṛdayamāy tīrnniṭaṇē

The eternal energy of the universe is the resplendence of Mother's love. Immersed in Her love, may I merge in Her heart.

mā tērē prēm mēṅ (Hindi)

mā tērē prēm mēṅ magan hōkar
duniyā kē bandhan tōṭ kar
āyī huṅ tērē dvār par lēkar
darśan kī abhilāṣā mayyā

Absorbed in your love, I have broken all ties with the world. Thus, I reached your doorstep hoping for your divine vision, O Mother!

mayyā ō dēvī mayyā
Mother, O divine Mother!
tūhī mērā sahārā mayyā
kāḷī ban kar chalī ānā mayyā
tērē bin jhūṭhā hai sansār
jhūṭhē riśtē sārē jhūṭhā parivār

O Mother, you are my sole refuge. Come running to me as Mother Kali! Only you are real in this world. Unreal are all relationships and family.

sun lē mērī pukār tū mayyā
kahī dūb na jāyē mērī nayyā
araj mērī yē sunlē mayyā
karkē kṛpā duḥkh har le mayyā

Please hear my call, O Mother. Do not let my boat sink! Hear my humble prayer, O Mother. Bless me and free me from sorrow!

kṛpā karō mā rakṣā karō
dūr karō mā jag kī māyā

O Mother, shower your grace and protect me. Dispel the illusion called 'world'!

mathuraykku pōyiṭṭu (Malayalam)

mathuraykku pōyiṭṭu nāḷ-ēṙayāy-allō
madhu-sūdanan kaṇṇan mōhana-varṇṇan
maṭaṅgi vannīṭuvān mizhinīr tuṭaykkuvān
mādhavan entē maṭiccituṇnu

It has been so long since the dark-hued Krishna, destroyer of the demon Madhu, left for Mathura. Why does Madhava tarry there? Why does he delay to return and wipe the tears from my eyes?

kṛṣṇa-murārē kṛṣṇa-murārē kṛṣṇa-murārē
kṛṣṇa-murārē kṛṣṇa-murārē kṛṣṇa-murārē

O Krishna, who destroyed the demon Mura.

nin virahāgni śaraṅgaḷ orāyiram
uḷḷu tuḷaññu taṙaññu
kṛṣṇa... kṛṣṇa...
cambaka sūna sugandha parāgampōl
āgatam āvuka saundaryamē

Great sorrow and longing pierce my heart like a thousand arrows. Krishna, O Krishna! O beautiful one, come to me like a gentle breeze bearing the fragrance of the champaka flower.

eriññu-tāzhum tārakamāy mizhi
kuzhaññu vīzhum mumbē
kṛṣṇa... kṛṣṇa...
karaḷin iṭavazhi nizhal mūṭum mumbē
ēkuka nin karuṇamṛta rupam

Before my eyes fade like a falling star, Krishna, O Krishna! Before the path darkens that leads to my Self, grant me the vision of your compassionate, immortal form.

mātṛ-vātsalyamām (Malayalam)

mātṛ-vātsalyamām nin mahā-naukayil
ammē ī jīvan-iṭam taraṇē
ēkāśrayam ākum amma veṭiññ-ennāl
jīvitam vyartham aṙiññīṭaṇē

O Mother, please grant me a place in the great ship of your love. If you, my sole refuge, abandon me, my life will be futile.

tṛkkaṇ-kaṭākṣaṅgaḷ ēṫṫ-ende jīvanum
pūttu taḷirtt-ullasiccīṭaṇē
nin mahā-vaibhavam ennum aṙiññu ñān
janmam kṛtārtham enn-aṙiññīṭaṇē

Let my life blossom and dance as your divine glances fall on me. Let me know your glory that my life may be fulfilled.

tūmandahāsattāl enne tazhukumbōḷ
madhura-anubhūtiyil manam ārdramāy
cintaykk-agamyē! nin centāraṭikaḷe
cintanam ceyyān anugrahikkū

As your pure and gentle smile caresses me, my mind becomes fervent and experiences sweet bliss. O Mother, thought cannot reach you! Bless me to meditate constantly on your lotus feet!

māyāpūrita-tāpattāl (Malayalam)

māyāpūrita-tāpattāl tapikkavē
āgamicc-ammayām pīyūṣa-dhārayāy
vaśya-madhuramām tēnmozhi tūkiyā
puṇya-pūrattāl tazhuki enne

I burned in the fire of delusion, and Mother came to me as a river of ambrosia. She caressed me with Her loving words that are sweet as honey.

andhakārattin-orantyam kuṙikkuvān
aṙivināl akamalar punitam ākkīṭuvān
akhilēśi nin tiru kṛpa tūkīṭilum
atināyi pātrī-bhavikkumō ñān?

You shower your grace to end my darkness and make my heart bright and effulgent with knowledge. Will I ever be fit to receive your grace?

acirēṇa amma tan amaratva-padabhuvil
azhal ozhiññ-ettumō ēzhayām ī makaḷ
ā kṛpā-pātramāy tīruvān ennuṭe
antaraṅgattine samśuddham ākkaṇē!

Won't your poor daughter swiftly reach your holy feet? Please purify my heart that I may be fit to receive your grace.

mērī pyāri mā (Hindi)

mērī pyāri mā... ō sundar mayyā
tēre darśan se man mērā khil gayā ammā
darśan nē tēre miṭā diyā duḥkh kō
khuṣiyōṅ se man mērā bhar gayā ammā

My darling Mother, my beautiful Mother, my heart blossoms with your darshan. You removed my sorrows and filled my heart with happiness.

bhavasāgar nē ghēr liyā thā
har pal maiṅ yē soc rahā thā
kaun bacāyēgā mujhkō?
mā kī āṅkhōṅ ne diyā mujhe viśvās
kī mā hamēśā hai mēre sāth mēre pās

The ocean of samsara trapped me, even though, every moment, I thought, “Who will rescue me?” Mother’s eyes gave me faith that she would always be close to me.

kitnē janmōṅ se bhaṭak rahā thā
cintāōṅ mē ulajh gayā thā
hōgā kyā nahī patā thā
mā ke caraṇōṅ mēṅ mil gayi mukti
janam kā lakṣya mēre pūra hō gayā

How many lifetimes have I wandered, lost and entangled in worries. Fearful about the future, Mother saved me and gave me refuge at her feet. The purpose of my life is now fulfilled.

mizhikaḷ en (Malayalam)

mizhikaḷ en mozhikaḷāy kaṇṇunīr tūkiyō?
mizhiyilūṭ-ozhuki en smṛtiyuṭe nombaram
paṙayuvān āvātta vyatha ende mizhikaḷil
ennennum tōrātta kaṇṇīr pravāhamāyi

Do my eyes speak to you as they shed tears? The pain of remembrance flows from my eyes. My searing, inexpressible pain flows as unending tears from my eyes.

duritaṅgaḷ pēṙi nirartthamāyi nīṅgumbōḷ
nukarunnu navajīvan ammayil mātram
pakalil en ninavāyi iruḷil en kanavāyi
eriyum en hṛdayattil nīruṙavāyi

My sorrowful life is bereft of all meaning. Only from my Mother do I gain new life and hope. I contemplate on you in the morning. At night you enliven my dreams. You are healing waters that soothe the scorching pain in my heart.

vijanamām vīthiyil peyt-ozhiññ-ennuṭe
viphalamām cintā pravāhaṅgaḷ ellām
gati aṙiyātt-oren jīvita-yātrayil
vazhi-viḷakk-enna pōl amma iṅg-etti

The stream of my futile thoughts rained down on deserted streets. I had no goal as I journeyed through my life. O Mother, you came as a radiant guiding light.

mizhinīr ozhukki (Malayalam)

mizhinīr ozhukki ñān kāttu nilpū
ammē nin mandahāsam innonnu kāṇān
kālaṅgaḷ ēṟeyāy kāttu nilpū
ammē kaṇṇīrumāyi ñān kāttu nilpū

O Mother! With tears streaming down my cheeks, I wait to see your smiling face. O Mother! I have waited for so long. With tears I wait for you.

prēma-sāgaram ambikē
nin cāratt-aṇayān ñān koticcu
veṇtiṅkaḷ prabhayōlum vadanam kāṇān
vembunna manamōṭe kāttu nilpū

O Ambika, ocean of love! I yearn to be near you. My aching heart waits to see your face, radiant as the silver moon.

kāruṇya-vāridhe jagadambikē
tavapāda pūjakkāyi ñān koticu
paninīr malarin itaḷpōle
tṛppādam aṇayān kāttu nilpū

You are the ocean of compassion, the Mother of this universe. I yearn to fall at your feet in worship as fragrant petals of a delicate rose.

ammē mahēśvari jagadambikē
ādiparāśakti kaitozhunnēn

O Mother! Great Goddess, Mother of the Universe, primordial power, I pray to you with deep reverence.

mizhiyiṇa onnaṅgu (Malayalam)

mizhiyiṇa onnaṅgu pūṭṭiyāl teḷiyunnu
vairūpyam ārnnorā citraṅgaḷ-uḷḷatil
hṛdayattin-aṭittaṭṭil maṟaññ-irikkunnuvō
sadgurō nin tiru caraṇāravindaṅgaḷ

When I close my eyes, distorted pictures arise in my mind. O Satguru! Do your divine feet hide in the depths of my heart?

tṛppāda-darśana-saubhāgyam mōhiccu
ūḷiyiṭṭ-uḷḷilēkk-āzhnn-iṟaṅgīṭavē
duṣṭarām rāgādi-vairikaḷ śaktiyāy
pinnilēkk-āññu valikkunnu nirddayam

As I dive deep within, I long for a glimpse of your divine feet. Then the cruel forces of anger and desire pull me back.

anargaḷam ozhukīṭum guruvin kṛpaykku
pātram āyīṭuvān sādhikkilō, spaṣṭam
ōṭi akalum en vāsanā-jālaṅgaḷ
teḷiññīṭum-uḷḷattil śrīpāda-padmam

With the grace of the Guru flowing ceaselessly towards me, all my negative tendencies will run away and hide. Then your divine feet will shine in my heart!

mṛta-prāyamāyor-en (Malayalam)

mṛta-prāyamāyor-en bōdha-maṇḍalattinu
mṛta-sañjīvani ennum amma
oru tari veṭṭattin-uzhaṟum enn-uḷcciratil
amma tan nētraṅgaḷ ponnoḷiyāy

O Mother, you are the life-giving herb that awakens my awareness. Within me a lamp was longing to be lit, and your eyes became its radiance.

nin mṛdu-hāsa-nilāv-uṇṇuvān en
jīva-cakōram paṙann-uyarnnu
manam oru parṇa-śālayākki atiloru
pīṭhattil ammaye pratiṣṭhippū ñān

The bird of my life flew high to drink the moonlight of your smile. I enshrined Mother in the temple of my heart.

tanuvum manavum ammayil arppiccu
aśruvāl padatār kazhukiṭām ñān
jñānauṣadhattāl bhava-rōgam śamippikka
antaraṅgē niṙadīpamāy jvalikka

O Mother, I offer my body and mind to you as I bathe your sacred feet with my tears. Please destroy the disease of samsara with the medicine of knowledge. Let my heart blaze forth in your light.

muḷu muḷugi (Kannada)

muḷu muḷugi ēḷ kāgē
ēddamel hār kāgē
muḷugēddu hāriddu ōnde kāgē
adu jīva kāgē

Many crows (jivas) appear to dive into the ocean of samsara, but in reality, it is but one jiva traveling through countless births.

hala janma muḷu muḷugi biḍugaḍēyu bekāgi
hārittu muktigāgi namma śrīharigē śaraṇāgi

After taking birth and death again and again over many lifetimes, finally the jiva gets fed-up and desires eternal freedom. Then, he takes refuge in Lord Sri Hari.

tānōnde uṇṇade tannēlla baḷagava
kāv kāv ēndū kūgittu kāgē
idda ōkkaṇṇu kāṇade mudi indu
mankāgi kuḷitittu ōnṭi kāgē

As a crow caws to call all its relatives, not wanting to eat alone, the jiva involves others in fulfilling his selfish desires. Not using its eye of viveka, the crow sits dazed and confused, not knowing what to do next.

hindaṇā janmagaḷa nēppāgi kōragittu
saccidānanda viṭhṭhalanna nēnēsittu
tīrtha-kṣetradi bhaktarunḍ-ēlēya hēkkittu
muktiphala dōrakidant-āytu jīvakkē
muktiphala dōrakidant-āytu

Recalling his bad deeds done in the past lives, the jiva grieves and repents. Now he remembers Lord Vithala, the source of true bliss. In the company of saints and devotees, the jiva engages in satsang and finally attains ultimate freedom.

hari hari gōvinda śaranu
hari hari gōvinda śaranu śaranu

Seek refuge at the sacred feet of the Lord Sri Hari.

nāgēśvara nārāyaṇa-sēvita (Kannada)

nāgēśvara nārāyaṇa-sēvita nitya śuddha
nirañjananē
bhūta-nāyaka bhasma-bhūṣita pārvati-priya
paramēśvaranē

O Lord of serpents, Lord Vişhņu worships you, who are the eternally pure Lord of all created beings. O Supreme Lord, adorned by ashes, your consort, Pārvati, loves you dearly.

bhaktara-bandhu kāruṇya-sindhu nandīśvara
narakāntakanē
kaluṣa-bharita kali-dōṣa-sahita iha kāyavidanu
nirmala-goḷisu

You are friend of devotees, an ocean of compassion, Lord of Nandi (the divine bull, Lord Śiva's vehicle), and deliverer of souls destined for hell. Please purify this body, stained by the sins of this dissolute age.

bilva-priyanē bhīma-śaṅkaranē sundarēśa
sarvēśvaranē
rāga-dvēṣa svārtha tumbiha jīvanivana pāvana-
goḷisu

O Bhīmaśankar (a form of Lord Śiva), you are fond of bilva-leaf offerings. You are the Lord of Beauty, nay, the Lord of all. Please deliver me from the likes, dislikes and selfishness, which mar my life.

līlā-jāladi hālāhalava hīrinalida śrī-nīla-kaṇṭhanē
karuṇā-mayanē karpūra-gauranē
karapiḍidennanu kāpāḍu

O Nīlakaṇṭha (blue-throated one), for you, even swallowing poison was divine play. O camphor-hued embodiment of compassion, please save me.

śiva śiva hara hara śaṅkaranē
jaya jaya śaśidhara śubha-karanē

Victory to Lord Śiva, the Destroyer! Victory to the auspicious one, whose locks are adorned with a crescent moon!

nā kaṣṭamlō (Telugu)

rādhē śyām rādhē śyām rādhē śyām rādhē
rādhē śyām rādhē śyām rādhē śyām rādhē
nā kaṣṭamlō tōḍu nīvē
nī nāmamē nāku rakṣa
nī nāmamē nāku dhīram
nī nāmamē nāku balam

When I face hardship, you support me. Your name is my protection. Your name is my courage. Your name is my strength.

ī viśvamlō nālō unnadi nīvē
ī satyam telisēvaraku nīvu nā madilō nilavāli

You are in the universe and in me. Until I realize this supreme Truth, you have to stay in my heart.

nā vijayam lō sukham nīvē
nī nāmamē nāku priyam
nī nāmamē nāku dhanyam
nī nāmamē ānandam

When I succeed, you are my happiness. Your name is my beloved. Your name is my gratitude. Your name is my happiness.

ñān aṙiyāte (Malayalam)

ñān aṙiyāte en antaraṅgē
prēma pravāhamāy amma vannu
ñān aṙiyāte en hṛttaṭatte
uzhutu maṙicciṭunn-ende amma

O Mother! You came to my heart as a river of love, though I knew it not. O Mother! You ploughed well the land of my heart, though I knew it not.

ā mṛdu-sparśattāl niṣkāmamām
sēvanattin vittu pāki ennil
snēhārdra meghaṅgaḷāy ambika
jñānāmṛtam mazhayāy pozhiccu

With your gentle touch, you sowed the seeds of selfless service. O Mother, you became clouds of tender love, and rained down the nectar of immortal knowledge.

haritābha nāmbu poṭicciṭunnu
aham ākum kaḷayum vaḷarnniṭunnu
kaḷakaḷ pizhut-ennil prēma-puṣpam
viṭarān kaniyēṇam amṛtāmbikē

Now my heart is green with foliage, but the weed of my ego still grows. O my Mother, uproot the weeds with your compassion and let the flower of love blossom!

nanmayāṇ-uṇmayām (Malayalam)

nanmayāṇ-uṇmayām lōkamātē
ōmkāra-rūpiṇi nitya-kanyē
śakti-svarūpiṇi śama-dama-dāyini
pāhi mām pāhi mām vēda-mātē

O Mother of this universe! Your true nature is goodness. You are the Omkara, ever pure. You are the embodiment of power, who grants self-restraint. Protect me, O Mother of the Vedas.

viśva-jananiyām vidyā-pradē
kāruṇya-rūpiṇi mukti-pradē
nāda-svarūpiṇi jñāna-pradāyini
pāhi mām pāhi mām dīna-nāthē

You are the giver of knowledge, creatrix of this universe, the form of compassion who grants liberation. Embodiment of sound, you grant knowledge. Please protect me, You who uplift the distressed.

saccit-svarūpiṇi dēvī-mātē
kṣipra-prasādini viṣṇu-māyē
ānanda-rūpiṇi jyōti-svarūpiṇi
pāhi mām pāhi mām varadē mātē

O Divine Mother! You are of the form of Truth and Consciousness. You are easily pleased, and you are the illusory power of Vishnu. You are the form of bliss and effulgence. Please protect me, O Mother, granter of boons!

devi-mātē dīna-nāthē
ambe-mātē lōka-mātē

O Mother, Goddess of the world, you uplift the downtrodden!

nān un ninaiviluṇḍō

nān un ninaiviluṇḍō nandalālā undan
nāvinilen pērumuṇḍō nandalālā
nandalālā yadu nandalālā

O son of Nanda, darling of the Yadu clan, do you ever think of me? Do you ever utter my name?

āṭikkaḷikkayilē nandalālā enne
azhavaittu nī sirippāy nandalālā
pāṭi unai venṭrēn nandalālā undan
pāṭṭinilē enai izhandēn nandalālā – yadu nandalālā
nān un ninaiviluṇḍō nandalālā
nandalālā yadu nandalālā

While playing gleefully, you tease me and laugh heartily. I won you over with my song, and I lost myself in your song. O son of Nanda, darling of the Yadu clan, do you ever think of me?

tēṭi unai piṭikka nandalālā andru
teriyavillai tandiramum nandalālā
tēṭum ulagam unai nandalālā ennai
tēṭivanda deyvamē nī nandalālā – yadu nandalālā
nān un ninaiviluṇḍō nandalālā
nandalālā yadu nandalālā

I know not the secret to find you and catch hold of you, O son of Nanda. The world searches for you, but you have mercifully come in search of me, O Lord. O son of Nanda, darling of the Yadu clan, do you ever think of me?

tattuvaṅgaḷ pēsiṭuvāy nandalālā nānum
tattaḷippēn puriyāmal nandalālā
sattiyattai indruṇarndēn nandalālā anda
tattuvam nī endraṙindēn nandalālā - yadu
nandalālā
nān un ninaiviluṇḍō nandalālā
nandalālā yadu nandalālā

You spoke of the supreme principles and I understood nothing. Today, I understood the Truth that that very absolute principle is you. O son of Nanda, darling of the Yadu clan, do you ever think of me?

nīye niṙainduviṭṭāy nandalālā
endan neñcinilum vākkinilum nandalālā
nandalālā yadu nandalālā
nandalālā yadu nandalālā

O son of Nanda, you alone dwell in my heart; I speak of nothing other but you. O son of Nanda, darling of the Yadu clan!

neñcam negizhndatammā (Tamil)

neñcam negizhndatammā
karuṇai pozhikayile
ennai maṙantēn un
anbu mazhaiyinile

O Mother, when the shower of your compassion filled my heart with joy, I forgot myself in your shower of love.

pātai aṙiyā pētai
vāzha vazhikāṭṭināy
tunbam vanta vēḷai
abhayam tantaruḷpurintāy

You showed the path to this ignorant, lost child. You gave me refuge and protected me when I was afflicted with sorrow.

kāḷī-bhāvam pūṇḍu
kaṇgaḷai niṙaya seytāy
līlaigaḷ pala purintu
en uḷḷam koḷḷai koṇḍāy

My eyes welled up when you manifested Kali bhava. You stole my heart with your many divine plays.

tāyin anbu kāṭṭi
darśana pēru tantāy
piḷḷai yena azhaittu
en uyiril kalantu viṭṭāy

With your motherly love, you blessed me with your vision. You accepted me as your child and became my very life.

nēnēdi nēnēdi (Telugu)

nēnēdi nēnēdi amma, antā nīvaitē amma
dēhamu nīvē amma, jagamu nīvē amma

O Mother, where can I be when you are all-pervading? You are this body and the whole creation.

kannula velugu nīvamma, cevula viniki nīvamma
ūpiri prāṇamu nīvamma, nāluka ruci nīvamma
palukula paluku nīvamma, kaṇṭhapu nādamu nīvamma
vennuku balamu nīvamma, cētula nērppu nīvamma

O Mother, you are the light in my eyes and the hearing in my ears. You are my breath and life energy. You are the taste in my tongue and the words for my speech. You are the sound in my throat, the strength of my backbone, and the skill in my hands.

bhāvana cēsēdi nīvamma, matiki smṛtivi nīvamma
buddhiki sārathi nīvamma, edalō vunnadi nīvamma
manassuku sākṣi nīvamma, nēnanu eruka nīvamma
ahamunu campu ō amma, nīvē migalāli amma

O Mother, you are the source of imagination and memory for my mind. You are the charioteer for my intellect, and you dwell in my heart. You are the witness consciousness and the very awareness of 'I am.' Please kill my ego. May you alone remain within.

bhairavi bhārgavi śaraṇam,
bhārati śārada śaraṇam
śrīlakṣmi kāḷi śaraṇam,
amṛtā śaraṇam śaraṇam

Divine Mother, protect me!

nēnenta śiva śiva (Telugu)

nēnenta śiva śiva nēnenta
nī ananta viśvamulō nēnenta
O Shiva, what am I in your vast universe?
brahmāṇḍamulō sūryuḍenta
sūryamaṇḍalamulō bhūmiyenta
bhūmilō nādēśa menta ūrenta
nā ūrulō nā illenta nēnenta
nēnenta... nēnenta...?

What is the sun compared to the entire Universe? What is the earth compared to the solar system? What is my country and my village compared to earth? What are my house and I when compared to my village?

nī sṛṣṭillō nā āstiyenta
kāluḍi nāṭṭyamlō nā brattukenta
antaṭṭā vunnadi śivuḍē aṇṭṭā
'nēnanu' ahamū vīḍāli anta
nēnenta... nēnenta...?

What is my wealth when compared to your creation? What is my life in the dance of time? Only Shiva is everywhere, leaving the feeling of 'I'!

śiva śiva śiva anāli anta
hara hara hara pāḍāli anta

Let everyone chant 'Shiva Shiva,' let everyone sing 'Hara Hara!'

śambhō śaṅkarā... hara śambhō śaṅkarā

nīla kaṭalinn-agādhata (Malayalam)

nīla kaṭalinn-agādhata pōl en
prēmattin-agādha nīlimayil
ninnuṙi varum virahārdra gānaṅgaḷ
ninn-ōṭakuzhalin gītam-ākkumō
ninn-ōṭakuzhalin gītam-ākkumō

My love for you is deep as the deep blue sea. Will the songs flowing from the pain of separation become a melody in your flute?

niṙa paurṇamiyām enn-uḷḷile niṙayazhakin
anaśvara prēma-pravāha nilāvil
enne maṙannu ñān ninnil uṇarunna
nāḷ ennahō... kaṇṇā

When will the day come that my heart shines with the brilliance of the full moon, and moonlight carries my eternal love for you? O my Lord, when will I forget myself and awaken in oneness with you?

vanamāli muraḷidhāri śrīrādhā hṛdayavihāri
vanamāli muraḷidhāri śrīrādhā hṛdayavihāri

O Krishna! you carry a flute and wear a garland of wild flowers. You reside in the heart of Radha!

kṛṣṇā-priyē ennōti enne nī
ninnōḍu cērttu puṇaravē
enn-ātma nāḷam ninnil layiccu
nin prēma bhāvam ākkaṇē

When will you call out to me, saying, 'O beloved of Krishna,' and hold me close? Let the radiance of my true Self dissolve and merge in your form of love.

nīlamayil pīlikaḷ (Malayalam)

nīlamayil pīlikaḷ cūṭi
nīlakkār mukil-azhak-ēnti
nīrajadaḷa-nētraṅgaḷilāy
nīlāñjanam ezhutiya kaṇṇā
śyāma-sundarā yadukula-bāla mōhanā
dīna-bāndhavā giridhara gōpa-nandanā – hari hari

O Krishna! blue peacock feathers grace your dark hair, and your lotus eyes are dark-rimmed. O dark and beautiful one! O Krishna, young boy of the Yadava clan, you captivate everyone. Friend of the distressed, son of Nandagopa, you lifted the Govardhana mountain.

pārāke panimati pōl nin
pālppuñciri pārttoru bhaktan
pāṭi-pukazhunnu ninnuṭe
pāvanamām mōhanalīla
hē vanacārī hē vanamālī
hē manahārī vandanam

Your devotees see your smile in the silver glow of the moon that illumines the world. They sing praises of your divine sport. You who travel through the forests wearing a garland of wild flowers, you who steal our hearts, we welcome you!

śaraṇāgata-manatāril nin
caraṇāmbujam aniśam teḷiyān
varam ēkuka vāridhi-śayanā
hara-vandita cirasukha-nilayā
hē vanacārī hē vanamālī
hē manahārī vandanam

Bless us that your lotus feet shine forever in the hearts of those who surrender to you! O Lord, you reside in the milky ocean and are adored by Lord Shiva. You are the abode of eternal bliss. You travel through the forests wearing a garland of wild flowers and you steal our hearts. We welcome you!

śyāma-sundarā yadukula-bāla mōhanā
dīna-bāndhavā giridhara gōpa-nandanā – hari hari

O dark and beautiful one! O Krishna, young boy of the Yadava clan, you captivate everyone. O friend of the distressed, son of Nandagopa, you lifted the Govardhana mountain.

ninaittiṭu manamē (Tamil)

ninaittiṭu manamē nittiyamum janmam
nimiḍaṅgaḷ pōle kaṭantu pōkum
dinam tōṙum nī tīṭṭum tiṭṭaṅgaḷ
noṭi pozhutil poṭiyākum maṇalkōṭṭaikaḷ

O mind, understand that this birth will pass in the blink of an eye. In a moment, our daily plans will collapse like sand castles.

munvinaikaḷ manatinai vazhi naṭattave
sēveyum naṭcayalum kavacamākum
vēdaṅkaḷākum guruvākiyam
pinpaṭra ippiṙavi payanpeṭriṭum

Our mind is determined by the results of past karmas. Selfless service and good deeds are our armor. This birth will reach fruition by following the Guru's words, which are essentially the Vedas themselves.

ētoru seyalum gurupūjayāy
ōrō śvāsavum tirumantramāy
erintu maṙayum karppūram pōl
tiruvaṭiyil sēra aruḷīṭammā

Let each action be an offering to the Guru. Let each breath be a mantra. Bless us to reach your holy feet, like camphor that burns for God.

nin nāmam (Malayalam)

nin nāmam ennum japiccu japiccu ñān
ende pērennō maṙannu pōyi
uḷḷil tiḷaṅgiṭum nin rūpa-kāntiyil
en rūpavum cērnn-aliññu pōyi

O Mother! Constantly chanting your name, I have forgotten mine. My form has merged into your resplendent form that shines in my heart.

tulyam-illāttat-ī snēham ammē prēma-
sarvasvamē nammaḷ tammil ennum
anya-cintakk-iṭam tellum illāteyāy
en manam dhanyamāy tīrnniṭaṭṭē

O Mother! Your love is everything to me. Let no thought come between us. Let my mind remain blessed and content.

nirmala-prēmattin ānanda-vīthiyil
raṇdu-pērkk-ill-iṭam ennu kēḷppū
nin manassin kōṇil enneyum cērkkaṇē
onnāyi nammaḷ ā pāta pūkān

I have heard that, on the path of bliss and pure love, there is no room for two to walk together. Please place me in a corner of your heart so that we merge and walk the blissful path as one.

pakalil ñān virahattin-aṅgāra-śayya tan
sahanavum sādhana ākkiṭunnu
rāvil, kināvil nin pādāmbujaṅgaḷil
tala cāyccu, mizhivārtt-uṙaṅgiṭunnu

In my sleeplessness, bearing the intense pain of separation from you becomes my spiritual practice. At night, I rest my head on your lotus feet and cry myself to sleep.

samaya-mēghaṅgaḷ en manujanma-maruvitil
nimiṣaṅgaḷ varṣicc-ozhiññīṭavē
punar darśanattinu vidhi vannu cērumō
ghana-śyāmaḷē dēvi karuṇāmbudē

The clouds of time pour down as wasted seconds in the desert of my life. O Devi, dark and lovely one, ocean of compassion, will I ever see you again?

taḷarum en tanu-mānasaṅgaḷe tazhukiṭān
nī ozhiññ-ārenikk-amṛtāmbikē
tuṭarum ī janmāntaraṅgaḷ tan yātrayil
tuṇa enikk-āru vēṙ-abhayāmbikē

O Mother of immortal bliss! Who but you can caress and bring new life to my tired body and mind? O Mother, you grant fearlessness. Who else will support and guide me in my journey through my future lives?

nin pāda-padmaṅgaḷ (Malayalam)

nin pāda-padmaṅgaḷ tēṭi etti ammē
niravadya prēmattil aṇayuvānāy
paṙayuvān āvātta hṛdayattil nombaram
oru tuḷḷi mizhinīrāy ozhuki ammē
oru tuḷḷi mizhinīrāy ozhuki ammē

O Mother! I have reached your divine lotus feet to merge in the perfection of supreme love. In the flow of my tears, my pain that words could not express reached your feet.

vāri aṇaccu nī endetu mātram enn-
ōtiya madhuramām tēn-mozhikaḷ
tīrātta duḥkhattil amarum en uḷḷattil
nityavum māṫṫoli koṇḍu ammē

O Mother! When I was safe in your embrace, you whispered "You are mine only." Those sweet words of love resonate forever in my aching heart.

aparādham ellām poṙutt-ennil ennum nī
kanivin kaṭākṣam coriyū ammē
prēmāmṛtānanda-lōkattilēkkuḷḷa
nērvazhi kāṭṭiya sadgurō kaitozhām

Forgive my mistakes and shower your grace upon me. O Satguru! I pray to you who have shown me the path to the world of love and joy.

niṙamaṫṫa jīvita-yātrayil (Malayalam)

niṙamaṫṫa jīvita-yātrayil ninnu nī
niṙam ārnna jīvita-ciṙaku tannu
jani-mṛti ākum mahā-nidrayil ninnu
uṇartti nī ende mizhi tuṙannu

In the colorless journey of my life, you gave me resplendent wings of color. You opened my eyes and awakened me from the sleep of life and death.

oru kuññu-pūvilum tēn uṙum vaṇḍilum
tīrattil ala tallum tirayilum kaṭalilum
ammē nin dīptamām mizhi kaṇḍu ñān ende
ātmāvin āzhaṅgaḷil layiccīṭaṇē

O Mother, may I see your radiance in a tiny flower and in a honey-bee. May I see you in a tiny wave, and in the vast ocean. May I dive into the depths of my being.

amṛtābdhiyām ninnil aṇayuvānāy innu
vembunnu jīvande ōrō kaṇaṅgaḷum
amṛtamām nin pāda-padmaṅgaḷil cērnnu
amṛtamāy tīraṇē ende janmam

Every atom of my being yearns to reach you, the ocean of immortality. May I merge in your lotus feet, and attain eternal life.

niṙamayil-pīliyil (Malayalam)

niṙamayil-pīliyil oru śyāma-varṇṇamāy
kuṙunira azhakāy tīrnneṅkil
kaṇṇande kāl-svanam ennum śraviccu ñān
ānanda-pūrṇṇayāy tīrnnēne

If I could become a deep color in the peacock feather adorning Krishna's curly hair, I would be ever blissful, listening to the footsteps of my Lord.

tava tṛppāda-sparśana-mātrayil
pūtt-ulaññā kadambattin caritam
ennōṭ-ōtiya kuḷiriḷam tennal
tazhuki-talōṭi kaṭannu pōyi

The gentle breeze caressed me as she passed, and whispered the story of the kadamba tree that flowered at the touch of your feet.

ī virahattin kanalil eriññu ñān
avaniyil vīṇiṭum munpē en kaṇṇā
varika en cāre nin prēmattin mādhuri
mukarnnu ñānum taḷir-aṇiyaṭṭe

O Krishna! Before I fall to the earth under the scorching heat of my sorrow, come to me. Let me imbibe the sweetness of your love and blossom like the kadamba tree.

nirmala-prēma-svarūpam (Malayalam)

nirmala-prēma-svarūpam ammē
cittattil teḷiyēṇam ninde rūpam

yōgikaḷ tēṭunna ātma-tattvam
ajñānikaḷ kāṇātta nitya-satyam

O Mother, embodiment of pure love, may your form shine in my mind. You are the ultimate principle the yogis seek, the eternal Truth that the ignorant cannot perceive.

aham enna bōdham tyajicciṭumbōḷ
akatāril teḷiyum nin divya-rūpam
mōkṣa-mārgatte labhicciṭāykil
jīvitam arttha-śūnyam allō

When the sense of 'I' disappears, your sacred form shines within. Meaningless is a life that does not come to the path of liberation.

rāga-dvēṣādikaḷ kai-veṭiññāl
bhaktiyāl cittam viśuddham ākum
niścala-cittattil ennum amma
niścayamāyum vasikkum allō

When you relinquish desire and anger, your mind becomes pure through devotion. Mother will always dwell in the still heart.

niśīthiniyuṭe ghōrāndhakārē (Malayalam)

niśīthiniyuṭe ghōrāndhakārē
āzhnnu pōkum jīvane
vāri eṭuttu nī ennammē
kāruṇya-rūpiṇiyām ammē

I was lost and wandering in the dark night of the dense forest. O Mother, embodiment of compassion, you picked me up and embraced me.

māyā-prapañcattin maṙa nīkkukil
atin madhurima nī veḷivākkīṭukil
janma-janmāntara-vāsanakaḷ
uḷkkaṭal enna pōl śāntam ākum

You removed the veil of illusion and revealed the sweetness of the Self. My latent tendencies subsided, and my mind became calm like the depths of the ocean.

manassinde āzhaṅgaḷil uḷḷorā
veṇmuttin prabha ēṙum kānti kāṇke
satyamām ninnil cērnnīṭuvān
vembukayāṇ-ennuḷḷām

I see the radiant beauty of the pearl hidden in my heart, and I long to unite with you, the eternal Truth.

nitya-śuddha-brahmamām (Malayalam)

nitya-śuddha-brahmamām amma
nirmala-prēma-svarūpamāy
makkaḷe nayikkuvānāy
avaniyil avatīrṇṇayāy

To guide Her children, the pure, eternal, absolute Reality has incarnated on earth as the embodiment of pure love.

amṛta-santānaṅgaḷ-āṇ-ennirikkilum
ātma-svarūpikaḷ-ākilum
ajñarāy alayum ī makkaḷe ammē nī
vijñānam aruḷi nayiccīṭaṇē

We are the children of immortality. Even though we are the form of the atman, O Mother, please guide your ignorant children who wander in this land!

ghōramām ī bhava-sāgaram tāṇḍi nin
satyamām dhāmattil ēṙuvān
saccidānandamām ninnil aliññ-ende
janmam saphalamāy tīrnnīṭaṇē

Guide us across the fearsome ocean of samsara to your abode of Truth. Let our lives be fulfilled as we dissolve into your form of Truth, Knowledge and Bliss (satchidananda)!

nitya-śuddha-snēhamē (Malayalam)

nitya-śuddha-snēhamē jagadīśvarī
nin maṭittaṭṭil aṇaññīṭuvān
vembukayāṇ-en hṛdantam ammē
cāratt-aṇayān viḷambam entē

O Goddess of this universe, you are eternal pure love. My heart longs to reach your loving lap. O Mother. Why do you delay in coming to me?

tiru-cintā-malarāl en antaraṅgam
niṙakānti coriyunna malar-vāṭiyāy
madhuvuṇḍu mayaṅgunna madhupan pōl ñān
ānandāmṛtam uṇṇān kāttirippū

The thoughts of my heart have become a beautiful garden of flowers for you. I wait to drink the nectar of your bliss and become like the bee that is full of honey.

sukha-duḥkha-sammiśra bhuvil ammē
ēkāvalambam nin karuṇa mātram
ā prēma-gaṅgayil āṇḍu-muṅgi
ātma-sāphalyam aṭayaṭṭe ñān

This earth is a mix of joy and sorrow. Your compassion is my only refuge. Let me dive into the Ganga of your love, that I may reach the true Self.

nīvu vēṙu (Telugu)

nīvu vēṙu rādha vēṙu
kānē kādulē kṛṣṇā
yugaḷa-manōhara-rūpam atē kadā kṛṣṇā –
atē kadā kṛṣṇā

O Krishna, you are not different from Radha. You are the most beautiful couple!

sṛjana-janani-rūpam nīvē kṛṣṇā
janana-maraṇa-kaṭalī nīvē kṛṣṇā
aṇuvaṇuvu unnadanta nīvē kadā kṛṣṇā
nālōni unikki annadi nīvēlē kṛṣṇā

O Krishna, you are the Mother of creation and the ocean of birth and death. You are present in each and every atom, and you are the existence within me.

sthiramu nīvē calanamū nīvē kṛṣṇā
sāgarappu alavū nīvē kṛṣṇā
terappai āṭe citramu nīvē kadā kṛṣṇā
nā unikkī nā gativī nīvē kṛṣṇā

You are the moving and the non-moving. You are the wave in the ocean and you are the movie playing on the screen. You are my existence and my refuge!

rādhē kṛṣṇā... nā gati nīvē kṛṣṇā...

O Radha Krishna, you are my refuge!

nīyē gati (Malayalam)

nīyē gati nīyē mati
nīyē mozhi ammē nīyē vazhi

You are the goal, the word, and the way. You are the luminous moon.

sundaramām sandhyakaḷil
ambiḷippon rāvukaḷil
andhakāram ārnnor-ende
antaraṅga mandirattil

In lovely evenings, in moonlit nights, darkness fills the temple of my heart.

bandhuramām dīpamāyi
cintakaḷil sāntvanamāy
ennum ennum nī teḷiññu
ende neñcin nōvakannu

When you shone clear as radiant light and gave consolation to my thoughts, the pain in my heart left me.

vāṭiṭumbōḷ pūntaṇalāy
nīṙiṭumbōḷ tūvamṛtāy

viṅgiṭunna mānasattil
vann-aṇayum amma nī

You become gentle shade when I wither and pure ambrosia when I ache. You arrive in my heart when I can no longer bear my sorrow.

amma ninde cētanayil
enneyum aṇaccu nī
annu toṭṭu ñān aṟiññu
ātmānandattin vazhi

O Mother! You held me close and granted me awareness. From that day on, I knew the way to the blissful Self!

nūṟāṟu bhāvanegaḷu (Kannada)

nūṟāṟu bhāvanegaḷu ammā
nūṟāṟu nuḍigaḷu nannamma
hēḷalārade tāḷalārade
sōtihēnammā kṛpe tōru...
kṛpe tōru... daye tōru...

Countless feelings and words rush into my mind that I am unable to express. I cannot bear this anymore. I feel hopeless, O Mother. Please shower your grace and show mercy.

cinteya citayāgidē ī mana
manadāḷada maṟe nīgisu ammā
bhava-sāgarava dāṭisu ammā
kṛpe tōru... daye tōru...
ammā... ammā... ammā... ammā...

Like a funeral pyre, thoughts burn in my mind. O Mother, please remove the coverings of my mind and help me cross the ocean of this life. Shower your grace and show mercy, O Mother.

ninnade āgali nūṙāṙu smaraṇē
ninnade āgali nannella nuḍigaḷu
tumbi tuḷukali prēmabhāvavu
kṛpe tōru... daye tōru...
ammā... ammā... ammā... ammā...

May my thoughts be of you and my every word be yours. Let divine love for you overflow. Kindly shower your grace and show mercy, O Mother!

ō brahmāṇḍ (Hindi)

ō brahmāṇḍ ke bhagavān
kṛpaya mujhe āśīrvād dō

O Lord of the Universe, please shower your blessings upon me.

ō tīnōṅ lōkōṅ ke prabhu
dayālu mujhe ab darśan dō

O Ruler of the three worlds, compassionate one, grant me your darshan.

is sansār mēṅ kyā hai māyā bin
tumhī ēk satya nitya hō

This world is not as it seems. You are the everlasting Truth.

maiṅ tumhāre liyē āsū
bahātā hūṅ tumhē cāhatā hūṅ

I shed tears for you, I yearn for you.

hē viṣṇu maiṅ āpke sāt
ānand sē nṛtya kartā hūṅ

O Vishnu, I long to dance in bliss with you.

ō dharm ke rakṣak tum
sukhadā mujhe ātma-jñān dō

O protector of Dharma, bestower of happiness, grant me knowledge of the Self.

ōm nārāyaṇā hari nārāyaṇā
śrī nārāyaṇā jay nārāyaṇā

I bow down to Lord Narayana.

nārāyaṇā hari nārāyaṇā
nārāyaṇā jay nārāyaṇā

I bow down to Lord Narayana.

ōmkāra-nādam (Malayalam)

ōmkāra-nādam anādiyām nādam
viśvattin-ākeyum ālamba nādam
avasthā-trayattin adhiṣṭhāna-nādam
avasthāntarattin pratīkamām nādam

Omkara, the primordial sound, sustains the universe. Omkara is the foundation for the three states of experience and the symbol of the supreme state.

rūpam ī nādam arūpam ī nādam
nānātva-varṇa prapañcam ī nādam

satyāvabōdha pradāyaka nādam
cit-svarūpattinde samjñayī nādam

This sacred sound is both with form and formless. It is this universe of many colors. This sound grants insight into the Truth. Omkara is the name of absolute consciousness.

ēkam ī nādam anēkam ī nādam
onnāyi mūnnāyi palatāya nādam
sṛṣṭi-sthiti-laya samhāra nādam
sraṣṭāvin jīva-niśvāsam ī nādam

Omkara is one and it is many. It is the One that became the three and the many. This sound is creation, sustenance, and destruction. Omkara is the life breath of the creator.

pulkkoṭit-tumbilum maṇtarikk-uḷḷilum
spandanam ceyyunna nādam
bhūtaṅgaḷ-añcinum saurayūthattinum
ārambham ī nādam ādhāram ī nādam

This sacred sound pulsates in a blade of grass and a grain of sand. Omkara is the origin and substratum of the five elements and of the universe.

ñān pōy maṙaññu 'ñān ār'-ennaṙiyukil
ñān tanne sākalyam ñān āṇ-akhilavum
ñān āṇ-anaśvara-dīptiyum nādavum
ñān tanne sarva-mantrārttha sārāmśavum

When ego disappears and knowledge of the true Self dawns, then I know I am in all and I am everything. I am the eternal flame and the eternal sound. I am the meaning and essence of all sacred mantras.

andhata nīkkunn-anaśvara-dīptiyum
antaraṅgattile ānanda-dhāmavum
ātma-bōdhattinn-akhaṇḍa-prabhāvavum
ōmkāramē... brahma-tatva-pratīkamē

Omkara is the eternal light that destroys blindness. Omkara is the abode of bliss within. It is the indivisible glory of supreme consciousness, the symbol of the Absolute principle!

sāyūjya-mantram sākāra-mantram
sarva-carācara bījam ī mantram
ānanda-mantram anantamām mantram
amma tan ākāra-mantram
jagadamba tan ākāra-mantram
ōmkāra-nādam anādiyām nādam
amma tan ākāra-mantram
jagadamba tan sākāra-mantram

The mantra of oneness with the divine and the mantra with form. It is the source of all things sentient and insentient. It is the mantra of bliss and the mantra of infinity. The sound of Om is beginningless. It is the mantra of the form of the Mother of the universe!

ōmkāra-rūpiṇi (Malayalam)

ōmkāra-rūpiṇi hrīmkāra-rūpiṇi
śakti-svarūpiṇi jagadambikē
akhilāṇḍēśvarī rājarājēśvarī
ānanda-rūpiṇi dēvi-mātē

O Mother of the world, personification of the sacred syllables Om and hrim, embodiment of energy! Goddess of the Universe, supreme empress, embodiment of bliss, Mother Devi!

kāruṇya-mūrti nī kāḷi-mātē dēvi
māmaka cittattil vāṇīṭaṇē
uttamē bhairavi kārttyāyanī śakti
nin pāda-padmam namiccīṭunnēn

Mother Kali, embodiment of compassion, please dwell in my heart. Most supreme one, Mother Bhairavi, Mother Parvati, my salutations at your lotus feet.

rāga-dvēṣādikaḷ nīkki en mānasam
nin prēma-bhaktiyāl śuddham ākkū
āmaya-hāriṇi kaivalya-dāyinī
sāmrājya-śakti nī lōkamātē

Remove all my attachments and aversions, purify my mind and bestow loving devotion to you. Mother of the world, destroyer of impurities, granter of liberation, you are Shakti, the supreme empress!

marttya-rūpam pūṇḍu mānavarkk-āśrayam
ēkunna ninne ñān kumbiṭunnēn
brahma-svarūpiṇi abhaya-pradāyini
amṛtānandamē anugrahikkū

I bow down before you who have taken a human birth to give solace to all of mankind. Absolute Truth, granter of fearlessness, immortal bliss, bestow your blessings!

ōmkārēśvara kailāsēśvara (Sanskrit)

ōmkārēśvara kailāsēśvara bhaktajanapriya
śaṅkarā
advaitapriya saṅgītapriya ḍamarukanāthā
śaṅkarā

Lord of the primordial sound Om, Lord of the mount Kailash, beloved of the devotees, O Shankara! The supreme Truth is dear to you, and so is music, O Shiva, Lord of the damaru drum!

śaraṇam śaraṇam śaṅkarā paripālaya mām
śaṅkarā

O Lord Shiva, Shankara, please grant me refuge and protect me!

trinētradhārī triśūladhārī gangādhārī śankarā
candrakalādhara gaja-carmmāmbara
lōkōddhāraka śaṅkarā

You have three eyes, hold the trident and bear the Ganga, O Lord Shankara! You are adorned with the crescent moon and the elephant skin, O Shankara, uplifter of the world!

tāṇḍava-priya samhāra-priya vairāgya-priya
śaṅkarā
vēdānta-priya vijñāna-priya natajana-pālana
śaṅkarā

The tandava dance, final dissolution and the quality of dispassion are all dear to you, O Shankara! Vedanta and supreme knowledge are dear to you. You protect those who supplicate.

bhakti-pradāyaka jñāna-pradāyaka mukti-
pradāyaka śaṅkarā
śānti-pradāyaka saundarya-dhāma tvamēva
sarvam śaṅkarā

You grant devotion, knowledge and liberation, O Shiva! You bestow peace, and are the abode of beauty. O Lord Shankara, you alone are everything!

oru nimiṣam ōrttu (Malayalam)

oru nimiṣam ōrttu pōyammē – ñān
ninnil uṇarunnat-ennō
uḷppūvin-uḷḷilāy naṙu madhu-kaṇamāy
nī uṇḍenn-ennu ñān aṙiyum

For a moment, I thought, "O Mother, when will I awaken in you?" I know that you are the honey hiding within the flower of my heart.

ā madhu kaṇattin madhura lahariyil
muṅguvān en manam tēṅgiṭunnu
oru nimiṣam ōrttu pōyammē – nin
kṛpa enikkillē ennu

My heart yearns to be inundated with the honey that fills my true Self. For a moment, I thought, "O Mother, am I not worthy of your grace?"

ā pāda padmattil abhiṣēka-madhuvāy
ozhuki paṭaruvān koticcu pōyi
oru nimiṣam ōrttu pōyammē – ñān
ninnil aliyunnat-ennō

I long to flow as the honey that bathes your lotus feet. For a moment, I thought, "O Mother, when will I merge in you?"

oru nōkkil oru vākkil (Malayalam)

oru nōkkil oru vākkil
amṛtam niṙaykkunna ānandamē...
amṛtānandamē...
oru mandahāsattil āyiram veṇṭāram
onniccu minnunnu hṛttaṭattil

O Mother! You are of the form of eternal bliss. Your every word and glance fills us with ambrosial joy. Each smile of yours brightens our hearts like a thousand shining stars.

bhavarōga tāpattāl uzhaṙunna jīvane
māṙōṭu cērkkunna prēma-mūrtē
nērinde pāta aṙiyātta jīvane
nērāya mārgē nayikkunnu nī

You are the embodiment of love who embraces the jiva suffering the unbearable heat of the world. You lead the lost and wandering jiva to the path of Truth.

niṣkāma karmattāl-uḷlam teḷiyumbōḷ
hṛttil teḷiyunna divya-mūrtē
ennum-ennuḷḷil teḷiyēṇam ammē nī
kai piṭicc-enne nayiccīṭēṇē

You are the divinity that shines bright and clear in a heart purified through selfless service. O Mother! please shine forever within my heart. Take my hand and lead me to you.

oru taṭaiyā (Tamil)

oru taṭaiyā iru taṭaiyā orāyiram taṭaiyammā
ulagil unnai vandaṭaiya ēninda nilaiyammā
taṭaiyellām paṭiyākki tandiṭum tāy nīyillaiyō
maṭai tiṙanda kaṇṇīrai māṭruvadun anbillaiyō

Not one, not two, but thousands of obstacles in this world block my way to you. Why? Are you not the Mother who turns obstacles into stepping stones? Is it not your love that transforms a flood of tears into joy?

nī uraitta mozhiyellām nilai uṇarttum poruḷāgum
nī siritta sirippellām nilai uyarttum aruḷāgum
nī vidaitta vidaiyellām endanadu guṇamāgum
nī aṇaitta aṇaippellām enai maṙanda kaṇamāgum

Your words awaken us to our true being. Your laughter blesses us to rise to our true nature. The virtues in me are the seeds you have sown. The moments when I blissfully forget myself are the moments when you embrace me.

nī pāṭiṭum pāṭalellām tittikkum tēnāgum
ninaippirinda en nilaiyum nilattiliṭṭa mīnāgum
nilavulagil nilaitta tuṇai nīyinṭri yārāgum
nīyillā vāzhavenṭrum niccayamāy vīṇāgum

The songs you sing are as sweet as honey. I am like a fish out of water when I am away from you. Other than you, who is my constant support in this world? A life without you is surely in vain.

ōru varam nalkū (Malayalam)

ōru varam nalkū ammē
nin pādam cērān anugrahikkū
māyayāl enne akaṫṫiṭallē
nin kaṭākṣam ēki anugrahikkū
bhavatāriṇī...mūkāmbikē...
dēvī...hṛdayēśvarī...jagadīśvarī... jagadīśvarī...

O Mother, grant me a boon. Bless me that I may be united with your feet. Please don't let maya take me away from you. Bless me with the grace of your glance, O Mother! Mother Mukambika, you take us across the ocean of transmigration. O Devi, Goddess of my heart, Goddess of the world!

nin iccha tanne en iccha ennōtuvān
enn-enikkākum ponnammē
śuddha bhakti nalki anugrahikkū
agati yācikkunnu bhakti-pūrvam
bhavatāriṇī...mūkāmbikē...
dēvī...hṛdayēśvarī...jagadīśvarī... jagadīśvarī...

When will the day come when I can say that your wish is my wish? This child of yours begs for your love. Please bless this child with pure devotion. O Mother, take us across the ocean of transmigration. Mukambika, Devi, Goddess of my heart, Goddess of the world!

nin snēha pāloḷi candrika tuvumbōḷ
en karaḷ ārdramāy tīrnniṭunnu
aṙiyāte nayanaṅgaḷ niṙaññiṭunnu
atu nin kālkkal ñān arccikkunnu
bhavatāriṇī...mūkāmbikē...

dēvī...hṛdayēśvarī...jagadīśvarī... jagadīśvarī...

Your love flows in the form of beautiful moonlight adorning the night. My heart fills with tender affection. My eyes fill with tears that I offer at your holy feet. O Mother, take us across the ocean of transmigration. Mukambika, Devi, Goddess of my heart, Goddess of the world!

avyāja-karuṇā mūrti en amma
vātsalya amṛta varṣiṇi amma
ōṭi vann-ettuk-en ammā
ñaṅgaḷe kākkuken ammā
ammē...dēvī...ādiparāśaktiyē...

My mother of unconditional compassion, you shower affection. O Mother, come running to us. Please take care of us. O Mother, Devi, Supreme Goddess!

ō tāyē mahāmāyē (Kannada)

ō tāyē mahāmāyē paripālisu
karuṇāmayi kāḷi kṛpē tōrisu
anavarata bhajippa ninna makkaḷa
bāḷannu beḷagu hṛdayēśvari

O Mother, divine illusion, take care of us! O Compassionate Kali, shower your grace on us. Goddess of our hearts, illumine the lives of your children who call upon you constantly.

ō tāyē mahāmāyē daye tōrisu paripālisu...

O Mother...divine illusion...be merciful and protect us!

suraṙa bhītiyanu nī nīgide andu
duṣṭaṙakkasara nī damana gaidū
bhava-bandhana-dindemma pārugāṇisū
dōṣa-nāśini durgē harṣa-vardhini

Once, you dispelled the fear of the gods by destroying the wicked demons. Just so, free us from the bondage of worldly existence. Destroyer of all evil, Durga, giver of happiness!

āpattu taruva sampattu ollēvū
daiva-sampatta nīḍi salahū śivē
jyōtiṣām jyōtiyē andhakāra aḷisi
rārāji send endu namma hṛdayadi

We do not want the qualities that bring troubles. Instead, bestow divine qualities and please protect us. O Light of lights, dispell all darkness and shine in our hearts forever and ever!

padamalar-aṭikaḷ (Malayalam)

padamalar-aṭikaḷ tozhunnēn ammē
padatāril abhayam nī ēkīṭaṇē
entināy vannennu ñān maṙannu
puṇyamām ī janmam pāzhākkayō

O Mother! I bow down to your lotus feet! Grant me refuge in them. I have forgotten why I came and I am wasting this gift of a human birth.

nēṭēṇḍat-entenn-aṙiññeṅkilum
nēṭuvān manatāril śuddhiyilla
nin kṛpa uṇḍēlum tan kṛpa illeṅkil
en manam eṅgane śuddham ākum?

I know what I am supposed to gain, but my mind will not stay focused on it. Your grace flows towards me, yet I lack my own grace. How will my mind become pure?

ātma-kṛpaykkāy pariśramam ceyyum ī
ārttanām enne nayikkēṇamē
aparādham akhilavum akaṭṭuk-endammē
aṭimalar akatāril teḷiyēṇamē

O Mother! Won't you guide this helpless one, who is striving to gain the grace of the Self? Free my heart of all faults, and let your lotus feet shine in my heart!

padamalar pārijātam (Malayalam)

padamalar pārijātam
viṭarumō antaraṅgē
viṭarunna nāḷ atināy
tapam irunnīṭām ñān

Will your feet shine in my heart as the parijata flower of heaven? I will perform spiritual austerities and wait for the day when it blossoms within.

uḷḷ-uruki ventu nīṟi
akatār piṭaññorā nāḷ
parāśakti nī kaniññ-en
mānasē padam teḷiññu

Burning grief was scorching my heart. O Primordial Goddess, you felt compassion towards me and your divine feet lit up my heart.

avyāja-karuṇā-mūrttē
tava pada-rēṇuvāyi
ānandattin oru kaṇamāy
ninnil ñān aliññu cērum

O Goddess, who is pure compassion, I will become a speck of dust at your feet. I will become a tiny atom of bliss and merge in you!

pādam nanayāte (Malayalam)

pādam nanayāte sāgaram tāṇḍuvān
kazhivuṫṫōr-uṇḍākilum ennāl
jīvitam ākum arṇṇavam kaṭannīṭān
nayanam nanaykka tanne vēṇam

Some might be capable of crossing the ocean without wetting their feet; but, to cross over the ocean of life, we have to cry.

māmara-kūṭṭaṅgaḷ onnāyi tōnnīṭum
dūrattu ninnu nām kaṇḍīṭumbōḷ
arikattu cellukil aṙiyumāṙ-āyiṭum
akalam uṇḍennuḷḷa satyam

Seen from afar, a cluster of trees seems like one tree; but, when we go near, we can see the gaps between the trees.

uṫṫavar uṭayavar aṭuttu ninnīṭum
akalattu ninnu nām nōkkiṭumbōḷ
cārattu cellukil bōdhyavum āyiṭum
namukku nām enna satyam

From afar, our near and dear ones seem to stand together for us; but, up close, we see the truth that we stand alone. We have only our own Self!

bandhaṅgaḷ duḥkhattin hētu ennākilum
manam alayunnu mōha-bandhaṅgaḷkkāy
en manam ennum bandhurāṅgi ninnil
bandhitam ākuvān kṛpa aruḷū

Attachment is the cause of suffering. Still my deluded mind wanders in search of relationships. O Bandhurangi, bestow your grace that my only bond may be with you alone.

padatārām kalpaka taru (Malayalam)

padatārām kalpaka taruvēkum taṇal ennat-
aṙiyāte maruvunn-ī iruḷ-vazhiyil
padam iṭaṙunn-oru pathikayāyi alaññu
vazhi aṙiyāte ī maru-bhūmiyil

I live here in the darkness of ignorance, not knowing that your lotus feet are the divine tree that grants all wishes. I wander, weak and lost, in this desert, not knowing the way to you.

vazhi-nīḷe kāṇum nāzhika-kallukaḷil
aṙiyāte ēṙe irunnu pōyi
gati entenn-aṙiyāte vazhiyōrakāzhcakaḷil
mati-maṙannirunnu pōy vyartthamāy kālavum

I saw many milestones on the way, and mistook them for the destination. Not knowing my goal, I lost myself in the sights along the path, and time passed.

paritāpam akaṫṫi karatāril ēṫṫi
paricōṭu cāratt-aṇaccu ammā
atirillā kāruṇya-sāgaramē ninnil
aliyuvān ēkaṇē kāruṇya-pīyūṣam

Mother released me from my sorrow and embraced me with love. O Mother, the boundless ocean of mercy, please grant me the ambrosia of your compassion, that I may dissolve in you.

paramārttham entenn-aṙiyāte (Malayalam)

paramārttham entenn-aṙiyāt-alaññu ñān
azhal-ākum āzhiyil tōṇi pōle
sukham ennu ninaccu ñān āññu pulki
vyarthamāy tīrunna bhōga-sukham

Not knowing reality, I wandered like a boat adrift in the ocean of samsara. I hugged the pleasures of the world, and they proved meaningless for me.

ammē nin puñciri-pūnilāvoḷi kaṇḍu
en manam ānanda-sāndramāyi
aṙivinde saurabhyam ennil pakarnn-appōḷ
dhyāna-vilīnayāy dhanyayāy ñān

O Mother! the moonlight of your radiant smile flooded my heart and filled it with joy. When you imparted the fragrance of knowledge to me, I became absorbed in meditation and content with my life.

tanuvalla manamalla matiyalla ñān enna
aṙivine aṙiyānuḷḷ-abhivāñcha nalki nī
aruḷaṇē nin kṛpa enne aṙiyuvān

anubhava-satyamām param-poruḷē

You inspired me to know that I am not the mind, body and intellect. You are the Supreme Self, the Truth we experience in front of our eyes. Please grant me your grace to know my Self!

paramātma-tattva-svarūpiṇi (Malayalam)

paramātma-tattva-svarūpiṇi ammē
paramārttham ennil uṇarttīṭaṇē
hṛdayattil nī sadā maruvunnu eṅkilum
nin māyā-maṙayil ñān uzhalunnat-entahō

O Mother, you are the form of the supreme Truth. Please awaken the knowledge of eternal Truth within me. You ever reside in my heart, so why am I lost in the veils of your illusion?

mujjanma-pāpamō muṫṫum ahantayō
en manam viṅguvān entiha kāraṇam
nin nāma-mādhuryam ennum nukarnn-ende
ajñānam sarvavum nīṅgīṭaṇē

Is it my sins from previous births, or is it my ego, that fills my heart with such sorrow? Let the sweetness of your names destroy my ignorance.

ninn-ahaitukamām kāruṇya-dhārayāl
durguṇam sarvavum sadguṇam ākkaṇē
ennile enne uṇartti en janmavum
nin padē arppitam ākkīṭaṇē

May your unconditional compassion transform all my bad qualities to good. May it awaken the true Self within me, and may I offer my life at your feet.

paramporuḷe (Tamil)

paramporuḷe parāśaktī tāyē... tāyē... tāyē...
paritavikka vaikkāte viraivil varuvāyē
varuvāyē... varuvāyē...
oru varam aruḷvāyē aruḷmazhai pozhivāyē
ammā... anbenum pālūṭṭi vaḷarttāyē

O supreme Goddess, O Mother! We yearn to see you, so, please come quickly. Grant us a boon, and shower your grace upon us. O Mother you nourish us with the milk of your love.

pāl pōl tūya uḷḷam koṇḍa kāḷiyamma
nīlavānam pōl eṅkum paṙantu niṙaintu nilkkum
en amma
endrum aruḷmazhai pozhiyum en amma...
endrum aruḷmazhai pozhiyum en amma
amma... endrum ēn asaiyāmal irukkindrāy

O mother Kali, your heart is as pure as milk. My Mother, you are all-pervading, like the sky. You always shower your grace, O Mother. Why are you unmoved?

tavarizhaitta makkaḷ endru pārāmal
tavarāmal vantu aruḷum, varam aruḷum annaiyē
amma un pirivu tāṅkavillai ammā
amma un pirivu tāṅkavillai ammā
ammā... aṭimalaril aṭaikkalam taruvāyē

O Mother, you continue to bless us, knowing well that we have committed mistakes. I cannot bear this separation, O Mother. Please grant me refuge at your lotus feet!

paribhavam entinu (Malayalam)

paribhavam entinu tōzhī ninde
hṛdayattil illayō kaṇṇan ennum
kaṇṇinum kaṇṇāy-avan vasikkē
entinu maṫṫoru cinta tōzhī

My friend, why do you grieve? Krishna remains forever within your heart. When he resides as the eye of your eye, what need have you for any other thought?

hṛdaya-vṛndāvanam tannilallō
kaṇṇande līlāvilāsam ellām
kaṇṇane mātram ninaccu ninaccu nī
ninne maṙakkukil dhanyayākām

Krishna enacts his divine sports in the Vrindavan of your heart. Remember the Lord and forget yourself. Your love will be fulfilled.

gōvardhanatteyum gōkkaḷeyum
kālimēccīṭunna gōparēyum
kāḷindi tīravum kaṇṇaneyum
kaṇṇaṭacc-uḷḷil nī kaṇḍukoḷka

Close your eyes and see within the Govardhana mountain, the gopas tending the grazing cows, the banks of the Kalindi. See Krishna Himself within your heart.

uḷḷilēkk-ettuka tōzhivēgam
uḷḷil uṇḍā prēma-yamuna ennum
kaṇṇanum rādhayum gōpikaḷum
ottu ninakk-ennum nṛttam āṭām

O friend! Do not tarry. Turn inward. The Yamuna of love is within you. You can dance forevermore with Krishna, Radha and the gopis.

pasi āṙum (Tamil)

pasi āṙum un mukham kaṇḍāl
tiruvaḍi dāham tīrttiḍum tīrttham
aḍittālum aṇaittālum gati nī
nammuḷ pirikka muḍiyāta bandam

The vision of your face appeases our hunger. Your divine feet are holy waters that quench our thirst. Whether you punish or embrace us, you are our sole refuge. Our bond is unbreakable.

kṛpai seyya nī kaḍākṣam seytāl – adai
taḍai seyyum śakti yārkkum illai
karuṇai pravāhamē nī toṭṭāl – oruvan
uyar nilai aḍaivadu uṙudi

If you glance towards a person to bless him, no one has the power to obstruct the flow of your grace. O Devi, torrent of compassion! Your mere touch, is sure to uplift a person.

un peyarum kēṭkādavan avanukkum nīyē gati
un pugazhai pāṭādavan un aruḷai uṇarādadāl
un śakti illai endrāl sarvam iṅgu śavam tānammā
midam miñcum tāyanbu un kūṙa janmam
pōdādammā

You protect all, including those who have never even heard your name. Those who do not praise your greatness have not realized your grace. Without your power, everything is like a lifeless corpse. An entire lifetime is not enough to expound your overflowing motherly affection.

patita-hṛdayatte (Malayalam)

patita-hṛdayatte pāvanam ākkiṭum
parama-pavitrayām kāruṇya-ganga amma
divya-kāruṇya gangayil muṅgum ī
jīvanmār pāpaṅgaḷ pōkkiṭunnu

O Mother, the Ganga of compassion, You purify our fallen hearts and destroy all our negativities when we dive into the waters of your divine compassion.

paṇḍita-pāmara-bhēdamilla
ucca-nīcatvam ētum illa
kāruṇya-tīrttha-pravāhinī nin
kṛpaykk-āruṇḍu atiru kalpikkān

You do not differentiate between the scholar and the ignorant, nor between the high-born and the low-born. No one can limit the boundless flow of your purifying compassion.

maṙakaḷkkum appuṙam maruvunna
nitya-satya-svarūpamē
maṙa nīkkiṭēṇam inn-ende hṛttil nī
janmam nin pādattil cērttiṭaṇē

O embodiment of eternal truth, you transcend the Vedas. Please remove the veil of ignorance from my heart, and unite this life to your feet.

pīlippu (Malayalam)

pīlippu cūṭiya tāmara-kaṇṇane
kāṇuvān entoru bhaṅgi
ārāṇavan sarva-kāraṇan-āṇennat-
aṙiyāte ārānum-uṇḍō

How beautiful to behold is Krishna, wearing the peacock feather on his hair! Who is he? Does anyone not know that he is the origin of all?

kṛṣṇa kṛṣṇā mukundā janārdanā
kṛṣṇa gōvinda nārāyaṇā harē
acyutānanda gōvinda mādhavā
saccidānanda nārāyaṇā harē

O Krishna, cowherd boy, Mukunda, destroyer of enemies! You are the indestructible one, Govinda, Madhava, the form of existence, consciousness, bliss! Narayana, victory to you!

pūvāyapūv-onnum pōrā neṙukayil
cūṭuvān pīlippu vēṇam
cēlottorā mukha kāntikk-itu pōle
cērunna pū vēṙe uṇḍō?
itu pōle cērunna pū vēṙe uṇḍō?
itupōle cērunna pū vēṙe uṇḍō?

All the flowers in this world are not enough to decorate your hair. A peacock feather is needed. Nothing suits the beauty of your radiant face better than a peacock feather!

kāla-varṣam vannu mānam kaṙukkumbōḷ
kēkikaḷ nṛttam āṭumbōḷ
tāne kozhiyunna pīlikaḷ koṇḍoru

pīli-kirīṭam orukkām
kaṇṇanu pīli-kirīṭam orukkām
kaṇṇanu pīli-kirīṭam orukkām

When the sky darkens and the monsoon comes, the peacocks dance and their feathers fall. I shall make a peacock-feather crown for you. O Krishna! I shall make a crown for you from those feathers!

pīr jagī (Hindi)

pīr jagī hai antarman mēṅ
yād mēṅ tērī naināṁ barsēṅ
kōī din nā rāt haiṅ aisē
tērē daras kō jab na tarasēṅ

A pain has risen deep within my mind. My eyes shed tears thinking of you, my Lord! Every single day and night they yearn to behold you!

viraha-vyathā kaisē samajhāūṅ
hṛdaya cīr kiskō dikhalāūṅ
rimjhim kyōṅ barsēṅ yē nisadin
nainan mēṅ chāyā nit sāvan

How can I describe my pain of separation? To whom can I open my heart? Why do my eyes rain tears day and night, like a perennial monsoon?

pīḍā gaharī pyāsā hai man
naināṁ bahatē thamēṅ na aṅsuan
aviral aśru kī dhārā mēṅ
kaisē nihārūṅ tumhēṅ maiṅ bhagavan?

My suffering mind thirsts for you. The flow of tears from my eyes knows no respite. My Lord, how do I behold you through this incessant stream of tears?

karō kṛpā ab mujhē sambhālō
śītalatā kā jal barsā dō
mēghā ban is man par barsō
śōka mōha santāp kō har lō

Shower your grace and embrace me tightly. Please soothe me with your cooling waters. Pour down like rain and rid my mind of its grief, delusion and agony!

ās jagī hai antarman mēṅ
ās jagī hai... ās jagī hai...

Hope has risen in my heart! Hope has risen, hope has risen.

praṇava-śarīrā (Sanskrit)

praṇava-śarīrā prapanna-śaraṇā
pārvati-putrā parātparā
gaṇapati-dēvā gajamukha-ramyā
guruguha-vandyā śivātmajā

O Ganapati, whose body is the syllable Om, who grants refuge, son of Goddess Parvati, most supreme one! Beautiful Lord Ganapati with an elephant face, worshiped by Lord Muruga, son of Lord Shiva!

cāru-śarīrā candana-varṇā
cāmara-karṇā cidātmakā
śōbhana-rūpā śaṅkara-tanayā
siddhida-varadā dayāmayā

gajamukha gajamukha gaṇanāthā
gaurī-nandana gaṇanātha

Your beautiful body is the color of sandalwood, and you have large ears. You are the embodiment of consciousness. Your form is resplendent, O son of Shiva. You are the compassionate bestower of boons. Leader of the ganas, elephant-faced Lord, son of Goddess Parvati!

sādhaka-sukhadā mōhana-caritā
mṛtyuñjaya-suta gaṇēśvarā
vighna-gaṇāntaka viśva-manōhara
vēda-viharaṇa vināyakā
gajamukha gajamukha gaṇanāthā
gaurī-nandana gaṇanātha

You bring joy to ascetics and your story is enchanting. You are the Lord of the ganas, the son of the great Lord Shiva. You destroy obstacles and captivate the world with your beauty. You delight in the Vedas, O Lord Ganapati! Leader of the ganas, elephant-faced Lord, son of Goddess Parvati!

prāṇ māzā (Marathi)

prāṇ māzā... hā... taḷmaḷ lā
prāṇ māzā hā taḷmaḷ lā
darśanās tuzyā
asā hā māzā viṭhal rāyā

O Vithala, my mind longs for the vision of your divine form. Eternal prostrations to your divine form!

parama kṛpāḷā tū guṇ sāgar
kṛpā asē tuzhī sarvāvar
nar janmācē tūc sār
dīnāntsā dayāḷā
asā hā māzā viṭhal rāyā

Most compassionate one, ocean of good qualities, you shower your grace on all, at all times. O essence of human life, you are merciful to the distressed. Eternal prostrations to your divine form!

prāṇ dātā bhaktāntsā tū
ātmā-rāmā māy bāp tū
sarv jagātsā ādhār tū
māzā sāvaḷā
asā hā māzā viṭhal rāyā

O protector of the devotees, the support for the entire world, you are established in the Self. Eternal prostrations to your divine form, O my dark-hued Lord Hari!

duḥkh māzē tulā kaḷāvē
nitya nirantar tulā smarāvē
pāyarīśī tav miḷāvē
rāyā maza visāvā
asā hā māzā viṭhal rāyā

Know my grief, O Lord! May I remember you constantly. Please unite me to your divine feet. Eternal prostrations to your divine form!

viṭhal... viṭhal... viṭhal... viṭhal...

prāṇande prāṇan (Malayalam)

prāṇande prāṇan allāyirunnō... nī en
jīvande jīvan allāyirunnō?
enniṭṭum īvidham enne piriññ-eṅgō
dūra-dūram nī pōyiṭunnu – atō
nin piṭi viṭṭu ñān pōkayāṇō

Are you not my very life breath, are you not the life within me? Then why do you leave me and go far away? Or do I let go of your hand and wander away?

janma-janmaṅgaḷāy ennil svarūpicca
karma-bandhaṅgaḷ tan bāhulyamō
ninnilēkk-ettikkān nī orukkīṭunna
ninnuṭe līlā-vilāsaṅgaḷō...

Is it my many attachments that I have garnered over many lives? Or is it your divine play that brings me to you?

ennirunnālum ī vaikiya vēḷayil
enn-uḷḷilēkk-onn-ettīṭumō
ellā poṙutt-ennu collīṭumō
ellā poṙutt-ennu collīṭumō

Will you come within me, even though time is waning? Will you tell me that you have forgiven everything?

nin puñciri pūm-prakāśattil en mana
paṅkam akannu teḷiññīṭaṇē
prāṇande prāṇanāy tīrnnīṭaṇē kṛṣṇā
jīvande jīvanāy tīrnnīṭaṇē

Let the brightness of your smile purify my mind. Be my life breath, O Krishna, be my very life.

kṛṣṇā kāruṇya-mūrttē
kṛṣṇā kāruṇya-mūrttē
kṛṣṇā kāruṇya-mūrttē

Krishna, O embodiment of compassion!

prārabdha-cumaṭum (Malayalam)

prārabdha-cumaṭum cummi lōbha-kāṫṫil ulaññu
mōha-tērōṭṭum manujā dēhātma-dhī akaṫṫū

O Man! Burdened by your accumulated karma, you sway in the winds of greed and drive your chariot of dreams and desires. Abandon your wrong identification with your body.

haripādē śritanāyi tiru nāmam urukkazhiccu
mālinyam akaṫṫi manasi mallāriyil bhakti tēṭū
vaikuṇṭhanu mukti ēkān vaiṣamyam atētum uṇḍō
vairāgya-jñāna niṙavāl vaikātā padam aṇayū

Surrender to the feet of Lord Hari and chant his sacred names. Purify your mind and seek devotion to Lord Sri Krishna. Vaikuṇṭha's Lord can swiftly grant liberation. Attain his divine feet in the fullness of detachment and knowledge.

sādhu-sēvā paranāyi bhava-bandha
kurukkazhiccu
sāphalyam aṭaññu tapasā maunādiyil niṣṭha nēṭū
kaikoṇḍatu bhakti ēkān kaiṅkaryam atāvatuṇḍō
naivēdyamāka mikavāl caitanyam atāy uṇarū

By serving others, untie the ropes that bind you to this world. Be disciplined in the austerities of meditation and silence. Mere servitude will not grant pure devotion. Offer yourselves to God and awaken to the pure consciousness within.

prēma-pravāhamē (Malayalam)

prēma-pravāhamē jñāna-prakāśamē
kēḷkkunnat-illayō en rōdanam
kāttirunnīṭunna paital āṇ-ī makaḷ
kaṇṇunīr oppīṭān vannīṭaṇē

Mother! you are the river of love and the light of knowledge. Please hear my cries? Your child is waiting for you to wipe away her tears.

antaraṅgattil tuṭikkunnu vēdana
aviṭutte darśana-bhāgyattināy
ī duḥkha-sāgaram nīnti kaṭanniṭān
ammayillāte ivaḷkk-āvatilla

My aching heart yearns for your darshan. Without you, my Mother, I cannot swim across this ocean of sorrow.

tāṅgāy taṇalāy ēzhaye kākkaṇē
kāruṇya-vāridhē kaniyēṇamē
prēma-pravāhattil nīnti tuṭiccu ñān
jñāna-pravāhamāy māṙiṭaṭṭe

O ocean of compassion, be my support and my shade. Protect me! Bathe me in the river of your love and let me merge in the flow of your supreme knowledge.

pūmaṇam cintum (Malayalam)

pūmaṇam cintum ī pūntōppil ēkayāy
kāyāmbu-varṇṇane kāttirikke
vēṇu-gānattināy kātōrttirunna nī
sandhya-tan vērpāṭ-aṙiññillayō?

In this fragrant flower garden, you wait alone for the Lord of the dark blue body. As you listen for the melody of his flute, are you not aware that dusk is leaving?

veṇṇilāvoḷiyilūṭ-oru vēṇu-gānamāy
ninne tiraññavan ettīṭumō?
kaṇṇanāy vēvunna nin manam kāṇāte
kārvarṇṇan eṅgu pōy-ārkk-aṙiyām

Seeing your heart seared in the pain of separation, will He come seeking you as a melody in the moonlight? Who knows where the dark Lord went?

rādha-tan prēma-saugandhika malarinnu
kaṇṇande kazhalil paticcīṭumō?
kōmaḷāṅgī ninde nīṙum manass-atu
kāṇāt-irikkumō gōpa-bālan

Will the delicate saugandhika flower of Radha's love fall at Krishna's feet today? O beautiful one! Will the cowherd boy see the pain in your yearning heart?

rādhaye kāṇuvān kaṇṇan iṅg-ettīṭum
mōhanāṅgī nī maṙaññiṭollē
kaṇṇane kāttirunn-uḷḷam tapikkunna
rādhayāṇ-ennum en kūṭṭukāri!

Do not leave, O lovely one. Krishna will come here to see His Radha. She waits forever, with intense yearning for him, her dear friend!

pūntiṅkaḷāyi (Malayalam)

pūntiṅkaḷāyi prēmam uṇarnnu cidākāśē
pūmukham onnu ñān darśicca mātrayil
puñcirikk-āyiram artthaṅgaḷ uṇḍ-ennu
pūrṇamāy innu nī teḷiccu tannu

Love awoke in my heart, like the full moon. The moment I saw your lovely face, I became absorbed in your smile that contains a thousand meanings.

nērinde vazhiyil nērāyi naṭatti nin
nirmala-prēmatte pulkīṭuvān
ninnilēkk-uḷḷorā nīṇḍa ī yātrayil
nilaykkātta prēmamām ēkāśrayam

You guide me along the straight road to the Truth so that I may embrace pure love. The way to you is long. My only support is your unending love.

kuṫṫam ēṙeyuḷḷa śilpamallō ñānum
kāḷikē līlayil paṅku cērnnu
kālattin-otta kōlaṅgaḷ āṭi ñān
kāruṇyam onnināyi bhikṣa yācikkunnu

Numerous are my faults. Still you have given me a part in your divine play envisioned by time, O Kalika! I beg for the alms of your compassion!

ambā... bhikṣām dēhi
ambā... bhikṣām dēhi

ambā... bhikṣām dēhi

O Mother, I beg alms from you!

pullāṅ-kuzhalinde (Malayalam)

pullāṅ-kuzhalinde māsmara-nādamāy
ennil niṙaññatu nin prēmamō
ā nādam kēḷkke ñān enne maṙann-ennum
ninnil aṇayān piṭaññirunnu

The mesmerizing flute melody filled my heart with love for you. I forgot myself and longed to merge in you.

ā muraḷi etra bhāgyavati annu
tṛkkaram prēmattōṭ-ēṫṫi etra
divya-prēmam ennum nukarum atin puṇya-
lēśattināy ñān tapiccat etra?

O Krishna, how blessed and fortunate is the flute you hold so close in your loving hands! I yearn to share a little of its merit that I may also receive your love.

kṛṣṇa-virahattil tulya-duḥkhitayām
muraḷika ūtaṭṭe rādha alpam
kṛṣṇa-rādhā-muraḷī-bhēdam illahō
kēvala-prēma-saṅgītam mātram!

O Krishna, let Radha play your flute that also aches for your love. Krishna, Radha, and the flute are one. There is only the melody of pure love.

rādhaykku mādhavan (Malayalam)

rādhaykku mādhavan enna pōle
ivaḷkk-āruṇḍu vēṙe śaraṇam ammā
nī ende jīvande śvāsamallē ammē
nī akannāl... maṇṇil ñānum illa

O Mother! Like Madhava for Radha, who else will give me refuge? Mother, you are my life breath. If you leave me, I can no longer remain on this earth.

vazhiyōra kāzhcayil kālam kaṭannu pōyi
āzhiyil sūryanum āṇḍu pōyi
ninnil aṇayātta vēdanayil muṅgi
astamiccīṭumō ī janmam ammē
niṣphalam ākumō ī janmam

Time passed as I stood fascinated by roadside sights. The sun has set in the ocean. Will my life also set like the sun, drowning in the sorrow of not reaching you? O Mother! Will my life be in vain?

indriya-sukham tēṭi alaññoru mānasam
pizhayēṙe ceytupōy māyā-vimōhattāl
ninnil ninnenne akaṫṫallē nī tāyē...
nin mahā-māyayil āzhttiṭollē ammē
nī mātram nī mātram ēkāśrayam

My mind roamed in search of sensory pleasures. Deluded by maya, I have committed many mistakes. O Mother, my only refuge! Do not distance me from you!

lōkam samastavum ninde svantam
amṛtēśvarī... nī mātram ende lōkam...

ninnil aliyān... ammē...
ninnil aliyān alayunnu ñān
nī tanne cērttukoḷk-ende tāyē
nī tanne kāttukoḷk-ende tāyē

O Immortal Goddess, this world is your own, and you are my entire world. I wander in search of you, longing to merge in you. Hold me close and protect me, O my Mother.

śaraṇam śaraṇam śaraṇam ammā
nin maṭiyil tala cāyccu koṇḍu
tīraṭṭe ende ī janmam ammē
śaraṇam śaraṇam śaraṇam...
jagadambikē jagadambikē jagadambikē...

O Mother! I take refuge in you. May my life end with my head resting in your lap. O Mother of this universe, grant me refuge!

rādhē gōvindā kṛṣṇa murārē (Sanskrit)

rādhē gōvindā kṛṣṇa murārē
śyāmā mukundā ghanaśyāma varṇṇā

nanda nandanā jaya gōvindā
nanda nandanā jaya gōvindā
nanda nandanā jaya gōvindā
navanita cōrā gōpālā

śyāmā gōvindā śyāmā gōvindā
śyāmā gōvindā ānanda-candā

ghanaśyāma-varṇā... ghanaśyāma-varṇā
ghanaśyāma-varṇā... ghanaśyāma-varṇā

rādhe rādhē gōvindā rādhē rādhē gōvindā...
rādhē rādhē gōvindā rādhē rādhē gōvindā...

rādhika tan karaḷ (Malayalam)

rādhika tan karaḷ kavarnnu
prēma-rasam nukarnna kaṇṇan
yātra ōti yātrayāyi
tāpam ēki tāpahāri

Krishna stole Radhika's heart and savored the sweetness of Her love. Yet he bid farewell and went away. He who destroys all sorrow gave her sorrow.

akrūran teḷicca tēṛil
kārvarṇṇan pōy maṙaññu
śōkāgniyil āzhnnu rādha
ghōrāgni at-āṙiṭumō

The dark-colored one disappeared in the distance in the chariot driven by Akruran. Radha sank into the burning depths of despair. Will the wild fire raging in her heart ever cool down?

vṛndāvani viṭṭu pōkān
kaṇṇā nī śaktan ākām
enuḷḷam viṭṭu vāzhān
ninnālini sādhyam ennō

O Krishna! You might have the strength to leave Vrindavan, but it is impossible for you to leave my heart and live elsewhere.

uḷḷil nī uḷḷa kālam
koḷḷill-ini uḷḷil onnum
uḷḷāl uḷkkoḷvu ninne
eḷḷil nal eṇṇaye pōl

As long as you stay in my heart, there will be no space for anything else. I have taken you into my heart. You dwell there like oil within the sesame seed.

rāmabhakta hanumān (Tamil)

rāmabhakta hanumān jaya jaya rāmabhakta hanumān
Victory to Hanuman, the devotee of Lord Rama!
añjanamaindā āñjanēyā anbudūtanē anumantā
vānaravīrā vāyukumārā vantōḷ mennaikai vaṭīvazhagā

Hanuman, son of Anjana, you are a messenger of love. You are a strong-faced warrior, the son of wind god. You are charming, with strong shoulders and a beautiful smile.

mōtiram tandu sītaiyin vadanam malarcceydavan nīyallavā
rāmanin śōkam māṭriyadālē sundara-kāṇḍam – unadallavā

You made Sita smile by giving her Lord Rama's ring. Your actions made Lord Rama happy. Hence, you are the hero of the *sundara kandam* of the Ramayana.

rāmanin kadaiyai kēṭpadarkenḍrē varampeṭradālē
- sirañjīvi
rāmanai vaṇangum aṭiyavartamakku kāvalanāga
varuvāy nī

You got the immortal boon to listen to the stories of Sri Rama. You guard those who worship Lord Rama.

jānaki-rāman azhagiya uruvam niṙaintirukkum un
- neñjinilē
añjutal illā āñjanēyan pōlillai bhaktar - bhūmiyilē

The beautiful image of Lord Rama fills your heart. There is no greater devotee on earth than the fearless Hanuman.

rāma rāma jaya rājā rām
rāma rāma jaya sītā rām

Victory to king Rama! Victory to Sita Rama!

rāmacaraṇa sēvakā (Tamil)

rāmacaraṇa sēvakā āñjanēyā
bhakta-bandhu kṛpā-sindhu āñjanēyā
rāma-kārya-sādhakā āñjanēyā
śaraṇam śaraṇam śaraṇam śaraṇam āñjanēyā

O Anjaneya (a name of Hanuman), you serve the feet of Lord Rama, and are the friend of your devotees. O compassionate one, you who accomplished Lord Rama's tasks, I take refuge in you.

yāraiyum vellum balavān nīyē
anpukkum munnē aṭipaṇivāyē
malayinai kaiyyil ēntivantāye
manam taḷarntāl ennai tāṅkiṭuvāye

You have the strength to win over anyone, and you bow down before love. You carried the mountain in your hand. In the same way, carry me when my mind is pulled down by trials and tribulations.

aṙivum paṇivum tantiṭuvāye
anpuṭan ennai nī kāttiṭuvāye
īḍilai rāma bhaktiyil unakku
unpada-bhakti aruḷvāy enakku

Please give me good intellect and humility, and protect me with love. Your devotion to Lord Rama is unsurpassed. Please bless me that I may be devoted to your feet.

rāma rāma rāma rāma rāma rāma rāma
rāma rāma rāma rāma rāma rāma rāma

raṅgā bhajō pāṇḍuraṅgā (Hindi)

raṅgā bhajō pāṇḍuraṅgā bhajō
paṇḍari-raṅgā bhajō purandara-raṅgā bhajō

Sing the names of Lord Vishnu, Panduranga, supreme ruler of the cosmos, presiding deity of Pandharpur!

viṭhalā rakumāyi pāṇḍurangā bhajō
nām tukā jñāna-dēva raṅgā bhajō

Sing the names of Rukmini's Lord, Vitthala. Dwell upon the Lord adored by saints Tukaram and Jnanadev!

rām bhajō raghu-rām bhajō hari
rām bhajō siyā rāma bhajō
antar-vāsi rām avināśi
śaraṇa tihāri rām bhajō

Sing the praises of Rama, of Krishna. Dwell upon the Lord of Sita, sing of SiyaRam. Call upon Lord Ram, indweller of your heart, as your only refuge!

kṛṣṇa bhajō śrī kṛṣṇa bhajō
gōpī-kṛṣṇa rādhā bhajō
sāsōṅ kī mālā mē japakar
prēm aur ānand dil mēṅ bharo

Sing the praises of Krishna. Sing of the Beloved of the gopikas and Lord of Radha. Weave the chant of those holy names into your breath. Fill your heart with love and bliss!

jay giridhārī jay vanamālī
kuñja-vihāri gōvindā
mōr mukuṭ pītāmbara-dhārī
gō hitkārī gōvindā

Victory to the Lord who lifted the mountain. Victory to the One adorned with forest flowers, to the dweller of the forests of Vrndavan. Victory to the enchanting One, adorned with a peacock crown and yellow silk! Sing about Govinda, the Lord who tends and protects cows!

saccidānanda-svarūpamē (Malayalam)

saccidānanda-svarūpamē sadgurō
citprabha tūki en uḷppū viṭarttaṇē
satya-vastu nityam ennil teḷiyuvān
karuṇā-kaṭākṣa-puṣpaṅgaḷ varṣikkaṇē

O Sadguru, embodiment of existence, knowledge and bliss! Let the flower of my heart blossom in your effulgence. Please shower the flowers of your gracious glance that the resplendent Truth may shine within.

kartṛtva-bōdham veṭiññu karmaṅgaḷe
dēha-dharmaṅgaḷāy ñān aṟiññīṭuvān
tṛppāda-sēvaykkāy ammē anugrahicc-
enn-antaraṅgam śuddham ākkīṭaṇē

Let my actions be free of doership, knowing actions are only of the nature of the physical body. O Mother, bless me with a pure heart that I may serve your divine feet.

amma tan prēma-vacassu śravicc-ennil
tattva-bōdhattin prakāśam niṟayaṇē
jñānāgni tannil dahicc-ende karmaṅgaḷ
nin pāda-pūjā-malarukaḷ ākaṇē

O Mother, listening to your words of love, let the light of knowledge shine within. May the fire of knowledge consume all my karma, and may it fall as flowers of worship at your feet.

saccinmayi amba (Sanskrit)

saccinmayi amba sadguru-rūpiṇi
tava kṛpā-varṣam bhavabhaya-bhañjakam
śādhi mām śādhi mām dēvī dayāmayī
pāhi mām pāhi mām lōka-mātē

O Mother, pure consciousness in the form of the Sadguru! Your grace destroys the fear of samsāra. Please instruct me, most compassionate Goddess! Please protect me, O Mother of the world!

bhakti-sandāyini saṅkaṭa-hāriṇi
tava vacanāmṛtam mama mārga-darśakam
maṅgaḷa-dāyini mama mōha-nāśini
pāhi mām pāhi mām lōka-mātē
pāhi mām pāhi mām lōka-mātē

You bestow devotion and destroy our sorrow. Your immortal words light my path. You bring auspiciousness and destroy my delusion. Please protect me, O Mother of the world!

kāruṇya-rūpiṇi kaivalya-dāyini
tava pāda-cintanam jñāna-prakāśakam
tava divya-darśanam mama harṣa-kāraṇam
pāhi mām pāhi mām lōka-mātē
pāhi mām pāhi mām lōka-mātē

You are the embodiment of compassion and the giver of liberation. The very thought of your feet reveals knowledge. The sight of your divine form fills me with joy. Please protect me, O Mother of the world!

sadā hṛday mēṅ (Hindi)

sadā hṛday mēṅ basnēvālī mā tujhē praṇām
tūhī sac hai tū hī prēm aur tū hī dharm kā dhām
tum hī hō sab mēṅ, sab kuch tumhī mēṅ sab haiṅ
tērē nām
lēkin maiṅ yē kaise jānu kaisē karūṅ pēhcān

O Mother, prostrations to you. Ever reside in my heart. You are Truth, love and the abode of dharma. You are in all and all are in you. All names are yours. But how can I know this? How can I recognize this?

bhaktī dē mā prēm dē mā viśvās dē dō mā

Grant me devotion, love and faith, O Mother!

sansār kē is ghōr van mēṅ jab chāyī kālī rāt
hāth thāmkē mayyā mērā tumhī nē diyā sāth
adhyātm kē sundar tāṭ par mujhē bhī diyā sthān
lēkin maiṅ yē kaisē jānu kaisē karūṅ pēhcān

When darkness prevailed in this frightening forest of the world, you held my hand and consoled me, O Mother. On the beautiful shores of spirituality, you made a place for me, but how can I know this? How can I recognize this?

ākhōṅ se māyā timir haṭānē jyōtirmayī padhārō
hṛday mēṅ gnyān kā jōt jalākar satya mujhē
dikhlāvō
divyarūp kā darśan dekar āncal mē sehelāvō
gōd mē tērī mujhē sulākar tujh meṅ līn karādō

Remove the darkness of maya and light the lamp of knowledge in my heart. Please reveal the Truth. Grant me the vision of your divine form and caress me. Let me sleep in your lap and merge in you!

sadguru-rūpiṇi ammē (Malayalam)

sadguru-rūpiṇi ammē
mōkṣa-dāyini ammē
nin jñāna-gaṅgā-pravāhattil ennum
ozhukaṭṭe en janmam dhanyamāy

O Mother, Satguru who grants liberation! May my life flow, forever joyful, in the sacred river of your knowledge!

andhatayil ninnuḷavāya karmattil
en antaraṅgam muzhukīṭavē
śāśvatānandam ninnil āṇennuḷḷa
paramārttham aṙiyāte ñān alaññu

When my mind was intent on actions born of ignorance, I did not know that eternal bliss was in you. I wandered, not knowing my path!

karayallē paitalē janmam vṛthā en
amma tan mozhikaḷ ñān ōrkkavē
viṅgum en hṛttil ā nāda-spandanam
śāśvata-prēmattil enne āzhtti

When I heard Mother say, "Darling child, do not waste your life crying," her words merged with the beat of my sobbing heart and immersed me in eternal love!

sāgarattin agādhatayum (Malayalam)

sāgarattin agādhatayum ākāśattin anantatayum
ammē nin viśvaika-vīkṣaṇavum bhāvana
ceyyuvān āyīṭumō
sāntvanattin tēn-mozhiyum āśvāsattin tṛkkara-
sparśanavum
anirvacanīyamām darśana-bhāgyavum janma-
janmāntara sukṛtam allē

O Mother! Who can ever visualize the depths of the ocean and the expanse of the infinite blue sky? Who can ever imagine your vision of this world as One? Sweet as honey are your words of solace. Your divine touch grants us peace. The bliss of your darshan transcends all worlds. It is the fruit of merits gained from many past lives.

atirukaḷ illāte ozhukunna nin kṛpa
aṙiyāte dina-rātram kozhiññīṭavē
aṙivillāymayāl aparādham anavadhi
arutāte ceytupōy poṙukkukillē

Days and nights pass without knowing your boundless mercy. Won't you forgive my many mistakes committed in my ignorance.?

ahanta tan piṭiyilāy amarum ī paitalinn-
abhayakaram ēki anugrahikkū
aṇayuvān vaikunnuv-enkilum amma nin
akatāril alpam iṭam tarillē

This child is held in the grip of her ego. Bless me to hold your hand and grant me refuge. It may take a long time to reach you, O Mother. Won't you give me a place in your heart?

śambhō śankara sāmba sadāśiva (Sanskrit)

śambhō śankara sāmba sadāśiva
gauri manōhara paramēśa
mṛtyuñjaya hara paśupati-nāthā
candrakalā-dhara bhuvanēśa

O Lord Shiva, Shankara, you are with the divine Mother. Auspicious Shiva, beautiful Lord of Goddess Parvati, supreme Lord! Conquerer of death, Lord of all creatures adorned with crescent moon, ruler of the world!

hara hara ōm namaḥ śivāya bhava hara ōm namaḥ śivāya
hara hara ōm namaḥ śivāya bhava hara ōm namaḥ śivāya

Prostrations to the great Lord Shiva, who rescues us from the ocean of transmigration!

trinētra-dhāri triśūla-dhāri
trilōka pālaka tripurēśā
pārvati nāyaka ganga jaḍhādhara
patitōddhāraka pālaya mām

You have three eyes and hold the trident, protector of the three worlds, Lord of Tripura! You are the Lord of Goddess Parvati and hold the Ganges in your matted locks. Please protect me, O Uplifter of the downtrodden!

śrīkaṇṭhā jaya śitikaṇṭhā jaya
śānta svarūpā śrita-vandyā
mōkṣa-pradāyaka mangaḷa rūpā
cinmaya-rūpā naṭarājā

Victory to Lord Shiva with a blue neck, the peaceful one who is adored by those who take refuge in him! Victory to the auspicious one who grants ultimate liberation, O embodiment of consciousness, cosmic dancer!

samsāra-duḥkha-pūrṇamām (Malayalam)

samsāra-duḥkha-pūrṇamām jīvitam
aviṭuttekk-arppiccu mēvunnu nin makkaḷ
janani tava tiru kṛpāmṛtattināy
anudinam kāttirikkunnu nin makkaḷ

Your children offer you their lives filled with worldly sorrow. O Mother, they wait every day to receive your ambrosial grace.

uḷḷat-uḷḷattil aṙiyān ammē
nin makkaḷkk-ātma-bōdham uṇarttu
ellām orātmāv-ennatu darśikkān
bōdhattāl uḷḷam teḷiccu tarū

O Mother, awaken the knowledge of the Self in your children so that they may know the Truth. Enlighten us so that we become aware that all is the one atman.

māyājālaṅgaḷ kāṇunna kaṇkaḷe
antarātmāvilēkk-ānayāccīṭu
sāndramām saccidānandābdhi pūkuvān

ātma-samarpaṇam ceyyunnu makkaḷ

Guide our eyes, mesmerized by the outer world, to the inner world of the Self. Your children offer themselves to you. Immerse us in the calm ocean of Truth, bliss and consciousness.

sapnē mē dēkhā (Hindi)

sapnē mē dēkhā mā kā svarūp
mā hi sab mē sat hai

In my dream, I saw the form of Mother. She is the Truth within everyone.

ākāś jaisā sarv vyāpi
sab kē man mēṅ mā hai samāyī
antaryāmi hai antaryāmi hai
mā hi sab mēṅ sat hai

All-pervading like the vast sky and within every heart, Mother is the inner witness and the Truth within everyone.

dīpak kē jyōt prakāś jaisē
jīvan kē śvās niśvās mēṅ
antaryāmi hai antaryāmi hai
mā hi sab mēṅ sat hai

Mother is like the light emanating from the flame of a lamp. In every breath, Mother is the inner witness and the Truth within everyone.

līlā karnē mā hai āyī
mā kī māyā ham kaisē jānē
antaryāmi hai antaryāmi hai
mā hi sab mēṅ sat hai

Mother has come to enact her divine play. How can we understand her maya? Mother is the inner witness and the Truth within everyone.

ham sab hai baccē svārth chōḍē
man kō arpit sēvā karē
antaryāmi hai antaryāmi hai
mā hi sab mēṅ sat hai

May we, Her children, give up selfishness. Offering all to Her, may we serve selflessly. Mother is the inner witness and the Truth within everyone.

jay mā jay mā jay jay mā
mā jay mā jay mā

Victory to Mother!

sarva-kāmaṅgaḷum (Malayalam)

sarva-kāmaṅgaḷum astamiccīṭukil
hṛttil orāyiram arkkabimbam pōl
ambika ennum jvalicc-uyarum
jagadambika ennum jvalicc-uyarum

When all our desires end, our Mother will dawn in our hearts with the brilliance of a thousand suns! Our Mother, Goddess of this Universe, will shine within.

ōrō aṇuvilūṭ-ozhukunna nādam
amma tan nāmam enn-aṙivāyiṭum
ā tiru-nāmam kēṭṭu kēṭṭ-en manam
ēkātma-bōdhattil āzhnn-aliyum

I will know that the sound resonating within each atom is the sacred name of our Mother. Hearing Her name everywhere, I will dissolve in the awareness of the one Self.

azhalukaḷkk-ādhāram ahaṃ āṇenn-aṙiyukil
ādhiyat-ellām akale ākum
nin ānandāmṛtābdhiyil muṅgi
ñān onn-ānanda-mattayākum

When we realize that the cause of sorrow is our ego, all our troubles will fall away. Immersed in your ocean of immortal bliss, we will experience unparalleled joy.

sarva-vyāpiyām īśvarī (Malayalam)

sarva-vyāpiyām īśvarī
nī en manassil teḷiyēṇamē
nī en hṛttil viḷaṅgēṇamē

O Goddess, you pervade the entire universe. Please become clear and shine in my heart.

etrayō janmaṅgaḷ ninne tēṭi
alaññu ñān ammē ī marubhūvil
nin kṛpayāl inn-aṇaññu nin savidhē
ninne ñān ī janmam aṙiyumō tāyē
ninne ñān ī janmam aṙiyumō tāyē

I have traversed this wasteland during many previous lives, searching for you in vain. Your compassion has brought me here to live in your divine presence. O Mother! Will I come to know you in this birth of mine?

sarvattilum nī uṇḍenna satyam
enn-ennuḷḷil aṙiyum ñān ammē
oru pulkkoṭiyilum ninne kaṇḍāl
ann-ende janmam saphalamāy-ammē
ann-ende janmam saphalamāy-ammē

When will I know the Truth that you are the substratum of all? When I can see you even in a blade of grass, then my life will indeed be fulfilled!

śāśvata-śānti (Malayalam)

śāśvata-śānti tan siddhauṣadham
guru-smaraṇa at-onnu-mātram
guru-vākyam śraviccittu mānavā nityavum
cintanam ceytu manassil dhariccīṭū

The perfect medicine for eternal peace is the constant remembrance of the Guru. O Man! Listen to the words of the Guru. Contemplate and establish them within your heart!

āsura-bhāvavum garvavum nīkki
smaraṇam ceytīṭu samśuddhar-āyiṭū
karma-yōgattināl pāvanamāy-oru
mānasatāril tattvam viḷaṅgiṭum

Remove your wicked tendencies and ego, contemplate on the Guru's words and become pure-hearted. The essential principle will shine in a heart purified by selfless action.

āśrayicc-ennāl guru kṛpa varṣikkum
ajñānam nīṅgiṭum cittam teḷiññiṭum
sarvavum īśvaramayam enn-aṙiyukil
amṛta-padattil uyarnniṭum niścayam

If we take refuge in her, she will shower her grace upon us and remove our ignorance. Then our mind will become clear. When we experience that all is God, we will surely merge in her divine feet!

śiva hara (Tamil)

śiva hara endrareṇḍu sol irukku – adil
bhavapiṇi tīrkkum marundirukku
śiva śiva śiva śiva - hara hara hara hara
śiva śiva śiva śiva - hara hara hara hara

The names of Siva and Hara contain the medicine to cure the disease of transmigration.

lingamānadāl silaiyalla – cokka
taṅgamānavan kallalla
vīḍu vāsal aṫra yōgi avan...
vīḍu vāsal aṫra yōgi avan – ānāl
vīḍu pēṙu tarum jyōtimayamavan
śiva śiva śiva śiva - hara hara hara hara
śiva śiva śiva śiva - hara hara hara hara

He is not a statue just because his form is the shiva-lingam. He is pure gold, not a mere stone. He is a yogi who has no home of his own. He is effulgent, supreme light that grants deliverance from the cycle of samsara.

jñāna vēṭhkaiyuṭan nāṭi nindrāl – avan
yōga māyai seytu maṙaindiruppān
agniyānavanai oru bhāgam...
agniyānavanai oru bhāgam – sarva
śakti ānavaḷ amaindu taṇittiḍa

śiva śiva śiva śiva - hara hara hara hara
śiva śiva śiva śiva - hara hara hara hara

If anyone approaches him thirsting for spiritual knowledge, he will use yogic powers and hide away. He is the cosmic pillar of fire whose body is shared by his all-powerful consort to mitigate the heat that emerges from him.

śiva-jñāna nīḍi (Kannada)

śiva-jñāna nīḍi ajñāna nīguva
śiva-tattva bōdhini amṛtāmbikē
śaraṇu bandihe ninna caraṇa-kamalake
śaraṇu bandihenamma śaraṇu

I take refuge at the lotus feet of Amma, the eternal Mother who removes ignorance and grants supreme knowledge.

śiva-dhyāna dāyini śakti-svarūpē
bhakti nīḍi naḍesamma bhakta-priyē
dhyāna-rūpa nīnādē divya-yōgini
śaraṇu bandihenamma śaraṇu

O Divine yogini, the form of my meditation, O primordial energy, lead us along the path of devotion. I take refuge in you, O Mother.

niṣkāma sēveya aṙivannu mūḍisi
vairāgya pathadi mūnnaḍesu
jñānadīpa beḷagammā muktidāyini
śaraṇu bandihenamma śaraṇu

O Granter of liberation, you inspire us to do selfless service and keep us steady in the path of dispassion. Please light the lamp of knowledge. I take refuge in you.

śivaśaṅkari śrīśivē śaraṇam śaraṇam
śivajñāna pradāyini śaraṇam śaraṇam
śivātmikē śāmbhavi śaraṇam śaraṇam
śivaśakti aikyarūpē śaraṇam śaraṇam

I take refuge in you, Shiva Shankari, most auspicious one. I take refuge in you, granter of the supreme knowledge. I take refuge in you, Shambhavi, the very essence of divinity. I take refuge in you, who are the union of Shiva and Shakti!

snēhāmṛtam āṇende amma (Malayalam)

snēhāmṛtam āṇ-ende amma
prēma-sāgaram āṇende amma
sāntvana-mizhiyāl enne puṇarnn-amma
karaḷinu kāruṇyam tūkunnu
amma karaḷinu kāruṇyam tūkunnu

My mother is the ocean of immortal, divine love. Her tender eyes embrace and console me. She showers compassion on me.

janmāntaraṅgaḷāy tēṭi alaññ-oru
satyattin sāram endamma
aṙivin uṙavām ātma-svarūpamām
paramātma tattvam āṇ-amma
janma-sāphalya sāyūjyam amma

My mother is the essence of the Truth that I have searched for over many lifetimes. She is the supreme principle, the source of all knowledge, embodiment of the Self. She is the fulfillment and ultimate goal of my life.

laukika-jīvita naśvara-bhāvaṅgaḷ
nirarthakam āṇ-ennu ñān aṙiññu
māyika-bhāvana tan kaṙa puraḷātt-oru
bhāvattin vīkṣaṇam ēkū
ennil prēmattin varṣam coriyū

I understood the transience and futility of material life. May illusion not veil my eyes. Please shower your love on me.

avivēkamāy ceyta karmaṅgaḷ okkeyum
amṛta-svarūpiṇi nī poṙukkū
ajñānam okke kaḷaññ-en hṛdayattil
vijñāna-dīpam teḷikkū – ennil
satyattin mārggam teḷikkū

O embodiment of immortality, please forgive all my unwise actions. Remove the ignorance from my heart and light the lamp of knowledge within. Show me the way to Truth!

śrī kāḷi dēvīm (Sanskrit)

śrī kāḷi dēvīm śirasā namāmi
mātā amṛtēśvarīm hṛdayē smarāmi
tāpasa-mānasa pāvana-kāriṇi
amṛtapurēśvarīm sirasā namāmi

O Goddess Kali, I bow my head before you! In my heart, I meditate upon the form of the Mother of infinite bliss. You purify the minds of ascetics, O Goddess of Amritapuri. I bow down before you!

sarvamaṅgaḷa-svarūpiṇi parāparē
ānanda-dāyini hṛdayē smarāmi

sarvārtti-nāśini sarvārttha-sādhaki
svātma-nivāsini śirasā namāmi

You are the abode of all auspiciousness, the most supreme one. In my heart, I meditate upon the bestower of bliss! I bow down before the destroyer of all sorrow, the granter of all desires, who dwells within!

tuṣṭi-puṣṭi-dāyini bhakti-mukti-dāyini
caṇḍa-muṇḍa-hāriṇi hṛdayē smarāmi
sarva-śatru-nāśini satya-snēha-rūpiṇi
sarva-saukhya-dāyini śirasā namāmi

You grant contentment and nourishment, and you bestow devotion and liberation. In my heart I meditate upon the slayer of the demons, Chanda and Munda! You destroy all enemies, and are the embodiment of true love. I bow before the one who grants all comfort!

ōm kāḷi hṛīm kāḷi ōm kāḷi hrīm kāḷi
ōm kāḷi hṛīm kāḷi ōm kāḷi hrīm kāḷi
kāḷimā... kāḷimā... kāḷimā... kāḷimā...

śrī śaila-vāsinam (Sanskrit)

śrī śaila-vāsinam dēvadēvam bhajē
śrī paramēśvaram dēvam
gaṅgā-dharam śivam candra-cūḍham bhajē
śrī mahādēvam bhajēham

I worship the God of gods, the supreme Lord, who dwells in Sri Shailam. I worship Lord Shiva who wears the Ganga on his head, who is adorned with the crescent moon. I worship the great Lord Shiva!

maṅgaḷa-dāyakam dēvam
sajjana-pūjitam dēvam
pārvati-vallabham pañca-bhūtēśvaram
śrī mahā-dēvam bhajēham
śambhō mahādēva śambhō śambhō mahādēva
śambhō

I worship the Lord who grants auspiciousness, who is worshiped by noble people. I worship the beloved of Goddess Parvati, the Lord of the five elements. I worship the great Lord Shiva! Great lord Shiva!

sarvārtti-hārakam dēvam
śaṅkaram śambhum mahēśam
sadphala-dāyakam sāmba-sadāśivam
śrī mahā-dēvam bhajēham
śambhō mahādēva śambhō śambhō mahādēva
śambhō
gaṅgā-dharā hara gaurī-manōhara

I worship the destroyer of all pain, Lord Shankara, the benevolent one, the great Lord Shiva. I worship the great auspicious Lord, the beautiful Lord of Goddess Parvati, who rewards good deeds. I worship the great Lord Shiva!

sāmba sadāśiva śambhō
Auspicious Lord Shiva!
hara hara hara hara hara hara śaṅkarā
śiva śiva śiva śiva śiva śiva śaṅkarā
hara hara hara śaṅkarā
śiva śiva śiva śaṅkarā

sṛṣṭi-sthiti-laya-kāriṇiyām (Malayalam)

sṛṣṭi-sthiti-laya-kāriṇiyām – amma
sṛṣṭikkum appuṙam mēvunn-avaḷ
mānava-hṛttinnu bōdham uṇarttuvān
sāmōdam āgamicc-amma ī bhuvilāy

O Mother, creator, sustainer and destroyer, you transcend your creation. You came joyfully to this world to awaken us to the pure consciousness in our hearts.

satyam entenn-aṙiññīṭāt-uzhaṙum ī
cittattin-uttama-mārgam teḷiccu nī
māyārṇṇavattinde āzhattil āzhāte
māmaka-jīvitam madhuritam ākki nī

I wandered, ignorant of the Truth, and you showed me the highest path. You filled my life with sweetness and saved me from drowning in the ocean of maya.

bhakti-madhurasam hṛttil niṙacc-ende
marttya-janmattin-orarttham ēkīṭaṇē
ātma-samarpaṇam ākum ā vahniyil
arpicciṭum haviss ākkaṇē enne nī

Fill my heart with sweet devotion, and give meaning to my life. I offer myself into the fire of self-surrender.

śrutiyillāte mīṭṭum (Malayalam)

śrutiyillāte mīṭṭum ī vīṇa pōl ennuṭe
jīvita-nauka takarnn-oru nāḷ
śāśvata-śānti-nikētanam tēṭi
alayavē amma tan savidham aṇaññu

Like a veena playing dissonant notes, the boat of my life was battered as I searched for eternal peace. One day I reached Mother's divine presence.

vīṇa-vādini amma tan sparśattāl
tantrī-layamāy tīrnnor-en jīvita-nauka
saccintayāl śruti mīṭṭiyum
satkarmaṅgaḷāl tāḷavum iṭṭu
amma tan padam aṇaññu

Mother Saraswati touched the veena with her hand, and the boat of my life attained harmony. I reached Mother's sacred feet with the melody of good thoughts and the rhythm of good actions.

sadguru-rūpiṇi jaganmātē
satya-sanātani jagadambē
nityam nin kazhaliṇa pūkān
nitya-nirāmayi kaniyaṇamē

O Mother of the world, Sadguru, ever new, eternal Goddess! O pure one, bless me to remain forever at your feet.

sūryōdayadinda (Kannada)

sūryōdayadinda sūryāstada varege
sūryāstadinda nija sūryōdayada varege

anavarata anusyūta aviratavirali

From sunrise to sunset, and from sunset to the dawning of the true sun, may we ever engage in the following:

nina nāmamantra bhajanē
nina prēmarūpa smaraṇē
nina divyarūpa dhyāna
nina pādapadma namana

May we always sing your holy name and remember your loving form. May we always meditate on your divine form and bow to your sacred feet.

ēkāntadali ō ātmasakhi ninnoḍane
nuḍivenu lalle savinuḍi sihīmātu
bahujanara oḍanāṭṭa bēsarisalāre
avaroḍane nuḍive ninna divyagāthe

O soul mate, when I am alone, I shall converse with you, with sweet endearing words. Since I have no right to turn away people's company, I shall speak to them, and it shall be about your divine life.

bēgadali udayavāgali astamisada sūrya
bēga nīgali samśaya neraḷināṭṭa
onde beḷaku pratiyondarali
endu kāṇva kaṇṇu karuṇisamma

May the never setting sun rise soon. May my doubts leave me soon. O Mother, grant me eyes that see the one light of divine consciousness in all beings.

tālēlō (Tamil)

tālēlō en bāla kaṇṇā tālēlō...
en maṭiyil talaisāyttu ōveṭu kaṇṇā tālēlō
mayilppīli sūḍiya kārkuntalin
menmai ērkka maṭi enna tavam seytatō
ārērō... rārīrō... ārārō...

Sleep my little Krishna. Rest your head on my lap that has been blessed to feel the softness of your head with its beautiful dark hair adorned with a peacock feather.

en kaikaḷil sīrāṭi ōyveṭu kaṇṇā tālēlō
ulagaṅkaḷ ellām paṭaittavaṇe unnai
eṭukka kaikaḷ enna tavam seytatō
ārērō... rārīrō... ārārō...

O Krishna, let me caress you in my arms while you rest. My hands have been blessed to hold you, the creator of all the worlds.

en tālāṭṭu kēṭṭu nī ōveṭu kaṇṇā tālēlō
pullāṅkuzhalin nāthane untan
pukazh pāṭa en kural enna tavam seytatō
ārērō... rārīrō... ārārō...

O Lord, who holds the flute, my voice has been blessed to sing your praises.

tālēlō kaṇṇā en bāla kaṇṇā tālēlō

Sleep O Krishna, sleep my little Krishna.

tan manam tannil (Malayalam)

tan manam tannil iruttām
tānāyi tanne iriykkām
tān ār-enn-ārāññu nōkkil
tannila kaṇḍ-aṅg-iriykkām

Let our mind remain established in our own Self. If we enquire, "Who am I?" we can remain in the knowledge of our true Self.

tānāyi nilkkunna tattvam
anyam allārkkum ennālum
tān tanne dēhamāy-eṇṇum
tan nilakāṇāt-uzhaṙum

The principle of the true Self is natural, yet we identify ourselves with the body and struggle without realizing our own Self.

aṙiyunnat-ellām atanyam
aṙivāṇ-at-ātma-svarūpam
dēha, manō-buddhi onnum
dēhi atall-ennaṙiyū

Whatever we learn is different from us. Knowledge is our true nature. The body, mind and intellect are not the Self!

tān enna dēhōha buddhi
tāne naśikkunnu nityam
tan nijarūpa mām tattvam
kālāti-varttiyām satyam

The ego resulting from identification with the body is destroyed for ever. The principle of our true Self is the Truth that transcends time!

taṇupavanan (Malayalam)

taṇupavanan śruti-mīṭṭum vṛndāvana-kuñjē
rāsalīlā-bhāvam ārnnu rādhikēśvaran

The cool breeze played its melody in the groves of Vrindavan. Radha's Lord decided to dance the rasa leela.

jīvātmā-paramātmā-yōgam allayō! – paran
prakṛtiyōṭu cērnnu sarga-līlayallayō
phulla-bhāvam allayō!

It is the union of the individual self with the supreme Being. It is the divine play of creation. It is the dance of the absolute, primordial nature. It is the blossoming of the Self.

sṛṣṭi-pālan-ātmakanām bhuvana-pālakan
nṛtyavādya-gānaghōṣa-vṛṣṭi ceykayō
svayam hṛṣṭan-ākayō

The Lord of the Universe, the sustainer, the indweller in every being, rains down. Drumbeats accompany a glorious festival of dance and music. He is rejoicing in Himself!

jīvabhāvam ārnna gōpikā-janaṅgaḷe
divya-bhāvam ēki ātma-līnakaḷ ākki
ānanditar ākki

He freed the gopis of Vrindavan from their body-identification and dissolved them into the infinite Self. He granted them divine bliss!

jīvēśvarā murārē... paramēśvarā dayālō

O Lord of my life, destroyer of the demon Mura, O Supreme Lord, most compassionate One!

tava padatārilin (Malayalam)

tava padatāril inn-arppicciṭānāy
padajāla-mālyam nī nalkuk-ammē
paramārttha-satya-pradānam ākunna nin
ānanda-dhāmattil ēṟiṭānāy

O Mother, bestow upon me a garland of words that I may adorn your lotus feet and reach the blissful abode where the ultimate Truth is revealed.

vāg-dēvatē tava maṇi-vīṇa-tannile
gānam āṇinn-ende śvāsa-niśvāsam
attirupāda-kamalābha tannilēkk-
en padamālyavum cērttiṭēṇē

O Goddess Saraswati, the songs from your veena have become my life breath. Please accept the garland of my poetry at your radiant lotus feet.

trailōkya-vanditam ā tiru-pādaṅgaḷ
śritajana-pālakam mōkṣa-mārgam
sindūra-varṇṇābha iyalum ā cēvaṭi
bandhuram ākkaṭṭe en mānasam

The three worlds bow down before your divine feet. They are the path to liberation, and they protect those who take refuge in you. Let my heart be immersed in the crimson beauty of your divine feet.

tavasāra pipāmsu (Sanskrit)

tavasāra pipāmsu madīya cittam
samarppaṇa-bhāvāmbu pānāya
tavāmghri-padma-pāmsu-kāmkṣi
āstikya-buddhi dīyatām
amṛtēśvarī ēkāśrayē śaraṇam tvayī layanam tvayī

My mind yearns to know your true nature. Please grant faith to your child who longs for the dust of your feet, to taste the nectar of surrender. O Immortal goddess, my sole refuge, I seek shelter at your feet, that I may merge in you.

tava śānta sundara-bōdha vīkṣaṇam
vikasati manō-puṣpe nityam
manasi prēma-madhu lava-darśanāt
nitānta kṛpā-varṣaṇam tē
amṛtēśvarī ēkāśrayē śaraṇam tvayī layanam tvayī

The flower of my heart blossoms in the serene beauty of your glance. Just a tiny drop of the nectar of surrender awakens the love in my heart and brings forth a shower of your infinite grace. Immortal goddess, my sole refuge, I seek shelter at your feet that I may merge in you.

tava prēma-citta prasāda kiraṇam
mama duḥkhāraṇya dahanam
durita-nāśita cētōbhuvi
vapatu tava jñāna-bījam
amṛtēśvarī ēkāśrayē śaraṇam tvayī layanam tvayī

When you are pleased, the ray of your grace shines forth and consumes the forest of grief in my mind. Let the land of my mind become devoid of sorrow. Then, sow the seeds of your knowledge. Immortal goddess, my sole refuge, I seek shelter at your feet, that I may merge in you.

tāyum nīyē (Tamil)

tāyum nīyē tantayum nīyē
suṭramum nīyē naṭpum nīyē
kalviyum nīyē selvamum nīyē
entan anaittum nīyē ammā

You are my mother and father. You are the scriptures and you are my friend too. You are knowledge and you are wealth. O Mother, you are my everything!

mātē mātaṅki mahākāḷi śaraṇam
bālē bhavāni parāśakti śaraṇam

O Mother Kali, Matangi (Goddess of speech, music, knowledge and arts), O Bhavani, supreme goddess, I take refuge in you!

tāṅkiyē enayum dharmiṇi nī kāppāy
tavariṇai poruttu dayāpari aruḷvāy
eṅkiṭum enakku enṭrum tuṇai nīyē
ēkkam tanippāy idayam kuḷirvippāy

O Mother, upholder of dharma, please support and protect me. O merciful one, excuse my mistakes and bless me. You are the everlasting support for this yearning child. Rid me of my longing and soothe my aching heart.

ōrōraṭiyilum ōmkārī nīyirukka
ōti nin nāmattai piṟavikkaṭal kaṭappēn
pukaliṭam vērinṭri padamalar sērntēnē
bhayam enbatillai pātayum eḷitē

O Goddess of the sacred syllable 'OM', with you in my every step, I shall cross this ocean of birth and death by chanting your divine name. Having no other refuge, I have reached your lotus feet. This path is simple, so I have no fear.

alaintu tirinta ennai anpāl āṭkoṇḍāy
ānanda vaṭivē nī aruḷāḷ anaittu koṇḍāy
ūzhvinai nīkkiyē tiruvaruḷ purintiṭṭāy
aṭaikkalam nīyē ammā akhilāṇḍēśvariyē

I was wavering and wandering, and you bound me with your love. O blissful one, your grace embraced me. Then you showered your blessings and rid me of my past karmas. You are my sole refuge, O Mother, goddess of the universe!

tazhukunna kāṫṫēṫṫu (Malayalam)

tazhukunna kāṫṫēṫṫu ozhukunna puzhayāyi
tirayunnu ñān ninnil cērunna nāḷ ennu
aliyunnat-ennamme arikilāy ñān ninnil
aṇayuvānāy manam kēzhunnit-amme

Just as the river flows gently with the caressing touch of the breeze, I flow through each day of this life in search of you. When will the day come when I reach you? My mind cries to be with you, O Mother.

akṣiyāl driśyamām viśāla prapañcattil
alasamāy ozhukunna vāhini ñān amme
pala tīram paratumī mātrayil ennumē
paritāpam akaluvān vembum ī hridayaṅgaḷ

I am just like a lazily flowing river in this world. As we flow along each shore, frantically searching for you, our hearts cry to be free from grief.

tirakaḷāy tazhukunna tīraṅgaḷil ennum
viphalamām mōhattāl poḷḷunnu neñcakam
amma tan vātsalyam nukaruvānāyi ñān
kaṇṇima cimmāte kāttirikkunnitā

Each day, as the little waves of this river flow by the river banks, the unfruitful yearning to reach you causes agonizing pain. Yet I eagerly wait to imbibe your sweet motherly love.

ammayām sāgaram darśicca mātrayil
kṣīnam veṭiññu ñān munnoṭṭu ozhukuvān
kūriruḷ mūṭunnu kaṇṇil ennākilum
amma tan prabhayil ñān ozhukunnu pulari pōl

The moment I saw you, O Mother, vast ocean of love, exhaustion left me and I tirelessly continued flowing. Though darkness covers my vision, I flow in the guiding light of your radiance, akin to the first rays of dawn.

tērē prēm sē raṅg (Hindi)

tērē prēm sē raṅg dē mā
jag kā rāg raṅg chuḍā dē...
tērē prēm kī rādhā banākē
śuddha-prēm sē raṅg dē mā

Color my life with your pure love, O Mother. Rid me of the color of the world. Make me the Radha of your love and color me with pure love!

mā... mā... mā... mā...
mā... mā... mā... mā...
na jānu maiṅ is jag kī rīt
na cāhtī jag sē prīt

khōyī rahuṅ bas rādhā kē saṅg
jismē samā hai prēm kā raṅg

I do not know the ways of this world nor do I seek its love. All I want is to be lost with Radha, who is colored in the hue of your love.

mā tū jahāṅ bhī jāyē
banādē mujkō tērā sāyā
nā, na kahnā mērī mā
tērē bin mērā hai hī kaun?

Wherever you go, O Mother, make me your shadow. Do not say, 'No.' Who else do I have but you?

tēṭēṇḍat-onnine (Malayalam)

tēṭēṇḍat-onnine tēṭuvān aṙiyāte
tēṭi taḷarunna manujā
tēṭēṇḍat-uḷḷil āṇennuḷḷat-ōrāte
vāṭi nī vīzhunnu veṙutē

O Man! You do not know how to seek the Truth, yet you wander and become exhausted. Not knowing to seek within yourself, you tire and fall.

nityam allātuḷḷa lōkattil alayāte
satya-svarūpate ōrkkū
nityamāy satyamāy vastu-svarūpamāy
nilpatallō nijasatta

Do not wander in this transient world. Reflect upon the form of Truth, Existence, and pure Consciousness. It is the eternal Truth that pervades all.

karagatamāy-uḷḷor-ātmasukham viṭṭu
nizhal nēṭi alayunna nīyum
tuzha viṭṭu gati viṭṭu tōṇiyil alayunna
pāmaran āṇennat-ōrkkū

You have abandoned the bliss of the Self within and run after shadows. Know that you are adrift in the ocean without an oar or knowledge of the shore.

piṭivāśi nalkumō, dambham niṙañña nin
atibuddhi nalkumō śānti?
vinayavum aparannu hṛdayattil ēkunna
iṭavumē śānti tan mārgam

Will stubbornness, pride and craftiness grant you peace? The way to peace is humility and the space you give to others in your heart.

tozhuda karamum (Tamil)

tozhuda karamum azhuda vizhiyum
ezhudum enadu kathaiyinai
ezhudkōlum muzhudumāga
ezhudiṭāda nilaiyinai
pozhudu alarndu pozhudu vāṭum
pūvaippōlē en manam
pūvaittūvi tozhum enakku
tēnaippōlē unvaram

My tearful eyes and my palms joined in prayer tell my story. Even my pen cannot describe my state. The flower of my mind blooms and wilts like the horizon at dawn and dusk. I worship you with flowers. Your blessings are like nectar.

vāzhumvagaiyai aṙindiṭādu vāzhuminda
siṙumanam
pāzhumkiṇaṙ enṭraṙindum pāyndu senṭru
vizhundiṭum
vīzhum maganai tāṅkivizhinīr tūṭaikka vēṇḍum
unkaram
sūzhumvinaigaḷ tīraśūlam ēndavēṇḍum
nirandaram
ēndavēṇḍum nirandaram

My materialistic mind does not know the right way to live. It knows the external world is a deep well of sorrows, yet still dives in. May your hands hold this falling child and wipe away her tears. With your protective trident, may you always save me from trouble.

azhuvadenṭrāl āṫṫralillā siṙuvarin seyalāgumē
manam tiṙandu unniṭattil azhuvadō tarum āṫṫralē
idayamurugi bhāramiṙaṅki aruḷin pāttiram āgumē
iraṇṭukaṇgaḷ niṙayum kaṇṇīr nanṭrimaṭṭum
kūṙumē
nanṭrimaṭṭum kūṙumē

Only helpless little ones resort to crying, but crying to you with an open heart gives strength. The heart melts and unburdens, becoming fit for your grace. My eyes, filled with tears, express my gratitude.

trailōkya-kāraṇiyāya (Malayalam)

trailōkya-kāraṇiyāya dēvi
mūnnu guṇaṅgaḷkk-atīta nīyē

jāgrat-svapna-suṣupti-trayaṅgaḷkkum
ādhāramāyi viḷaṅgum ammē

O Devi, creator of the three worlds, you are beyond the three gunas. You shine as the support to the three states of waking, dream and deep sleep.

tripuṭi aṭukkātt-orātmasattē
apramēyōjvala tattva-sthitē
nirapēkṣam ākum nija-svarūpē
nirvikārātmikē nityaśuddhē

You are pure existence, transcending the triad (experiencer, experienced, experience). You shine, established in the unknowable Absolute.

nityavum ninne bhajipp-avarkku
nitya-sukhadē sukha-svarūpē
ninne aṙiyān aśaktan ākum
enne aṙivilēkk-ānayikkū

You bestow everlasting happiness on those who constantly worship you. Guide me towards knowledge, I who am unable to know you.

tṛkkaratāril eṭuttu (Malayalam)

tṛkkaratāril eṭuttu vaḷartti nī
lakṣyam entenn-aṙiyāttor-en jīvane
jīvita-vīthiyil ñān taḷarnnīṭavē
tāvaka-snēham āvōḷam pakarnnu nī

O Mother! I did not know the goal of my life. You took me in your divine arms and brought me up. As I walked exhausted on the path of life, you gave me the fullness of your love.

kaṇḍu ñān āmaya-pūrṇam ī lōkam
uḷkkoṇḍū amma tan divya-vacassukaḷ
āśrayamaṫṫ-avarkk-āśvāsam ēkuvān
īśvaran nalki ī dēham enna satyam

I saw the sorrow of this world and understood the meaning of Mother's divine words: 'This life is given by God to serve those who are helpless, who have no refuge.'

sarva-carācara-rūpiyāy mēvunnat-
ammayāṇ-ennuḷḷa satyam aṙiññu ñān
'lōkāḥ samastāḥ sukhinō bhavantu'
ennā mahā-mantram urukkazhikkēṇamē

May I know the Truth that Mother pervades the universe of all things, sentient and insentient. May I chant the great mantra, "May all beings in all the worlds be happy"

tuyilezhuvāy dēvi (Tamil)

tuyilezhuvāy dēvi tuyilezhuvāy
ulakine uṇarttiṭa tuyilezhuvāy

Arise, O Devi, arise and awaken the world!

ādavan veṇmati kaṭaliṇayum
uṇarttiṭavē dēvi ezhuntaruḷvāy
āṇavam kōpatāpam nīkki nal
manadinaiyē dēvi aruḷiṭuvāy

O Devi, arise and awaken the sun, moon and ocean. O Devi, bless me with a pure mind devoid of ego, anger and sorrow.

bhōgattil muzhuki mati mayaṅki

milai maṙakkum ennai uṇarttiṭuvāy
anbenum aṇayā viḷakkiṇayē
oḷittiṭavē dēvi aruḷiṭuvāy

Drowned in materialism, I am deluded and have forgotten my Self. Please awaken me. O Devi, bless me to spread the light of the everlasting lamp of love.

ennuḷḷil uṙayum sattiyattai
uṇarttiṭavē dēvi aruḷiṭuvāy
aruḷpurivāy ennakamakizha
tirupādattil ennai sērttiṭuvāy

O Devi, bless me to awaken to the Truth residing within me. Bestow on me your soothing blessing and unite me with your lotus feet.

udayārdra-kiraṇaṅgaḷ (Malayalam)

udayārdra-kiraṇaṅgaḷ tazhuki talōṭavē
aṙiyāte viṭarunna padma-dalaṅgaḷ pōl
sūrya-kōṭiprabhē nin kṛpā-raśmiyāl
viṭarumō ennuṭe hṛdaya-padmam ammē

Like the lotus that blossoms when caressed by the tender rays of dawn, will the lotus of my heart blossom in the brilliant rays of your grace, O Mother?

mūkam ī vīthiyil iruḷāy niṙayunnu
pāzh-muḷam-taṇḍām ennuṭe nombaram
vātsalya-tēnuṙum puñciri kāṇavē
hṛttil teḷiññ-ēṙe mazhavillukaḷ

The pain of this unworthy bamboo flute fills this dark and silent path. When I see your tender, loving smile, my heart shimmers like a rainbow.

jīvita-pātayil padam onniṭaṙavē
kṣamayāy snēhamāy tāṅgāy vannamma
jīvande uḷppūvil karutt-ēki ennennum
niśśaṅkam gamikkuvān śakti ēkū dēvī

When my steps faltered on the path of life, O Mother, you came as patience, love and support. Grant me inner strength to walk along the path with trust and confidence, O Devi!

ulagin tāyē śaktimayi (Tamil)

ulagin tāyē śaktimayi... un aruḷ irundāl
uḷ oḷi vīsiḍum piṙavi payan peṙum

Primordial energy, Mother of the world, by your grace we can realise the Self. This is the purpose of the human birth.

maṙaiyin poruḷē tatvamayi... nī manam kanindāl
maṙaiyum nīṅgiḍum jñānam veḷippaḍum

O Supreme Principle, the very source of the scriptures! If our hearts melt, by your grace, the veil of ignorance is removed and Self knowledge is revealed.

manadin oḷiyē cinmayi... unai dinam panindāl
malaipōl taḍaikaḷum paṇiyāyi vilagiḍum

O pure Consciousness, you are the light of the mind. When we worship you, mountain-like obstacles vanish like dew drops evaporating in the sun.

guruvin tatvamē amṛtamayi un guṇam aṙindāl
guruvin vākkugaḷ en seyalāgiḍum

Eternal One, you are the Guru principle. When we realize your true nature, our actions will express your words.

satya svarūpiṇi tatvamayi ātma svarūpiṇi cinmayi
sadguru rūpiṇi amṛtamayi satatam pālaya
śaktimayi

Embodiment of Truth, eternal principle, the nature of the Self, pure consciousness! You are the form of the Sadguru. Eternal one, protect me forever, O Shaktimayi!

un seyal enenḍru (Tamil)

un seyal enenḍru purintiṭa iyaḷvatillai
ivai enna viḷayāṭal alakṣiya kaḷiyāṭal
dayai aruḷ tāye tanintaruḷvāyē
viṭutalai tantu kāttaruḷvāyē

I do not understand your actions or your divine plays. Be merciful, be compassionate. Protect me and free me from bondage.

vēda antan tānenḍru bhakta-bālan nānenṭru
yuktanenḍru tyaktanenḍrā āṅkāramatu vēṣamiṭa
'nān' tan talai paṭri munvinai iazhuttiṭavē
vidhi atu ēḷaṇamāy sirunakhai purintatē

You are the learned one who knows the scriptures. I am your devoted child, but ego feigns supremacy. My 'I' is pulled by past karmas, and fate mocks me with a sly smile.

pizhayenten aṙiyātu en manam taḷarntiṭavē
viḷayāṭṭāy naṭampurintu kāṇpittāy entan kurai
maṭitanil iṭam vēṇḍēn atan vilai nān aṙiyēn
aṭitanin iṭam taruvāy saraṇāgati aruḷvāy

When my mind became weak, not knowing my mistake, You playfully danced and pointed out my shortcomings. I don't ask for a place in your heart, as I don't know it's value. Please, grant me refuge at your feet .

un seyal enenṭru purintiṭa iyaḷvatillai
ivai enna viḷayāṭal alakṣiya kaḷiyāṭal
viṭupaṭa aṙiyēn kanintaruḷvāyē
saraṇāgati tantu kāttaruḷvāyē

I am unable to understand your actions or your divine plays. Please have mercy on me. I know not how to free myself.

uṣasin uṇarvē (Malayalam)

uṣasin uṇarvē uṇarvin uṙavē
umayē mūkāmbikayē – en
uṇmayām jīva-poruḷē
uyirē ulakin amṛtē
uṇarū ennil nī

She is Uma, the Goddess Mookambika. She is the freshness of dawn and the source of all wisdom. She is the Truth, the essence of my life. She is life, the nectar of this world. O Uma, awaken within me.

ūnam ezhum ī bhūtalattil
ūrjasvalayāy mēviṭunnu
ūṣara-bhūmi tan jīva-kōṭikaḷil

ūṣmaḷa-lāḷana varṣam ēki

In this world of shortcomings, She reigns with supreme energy and power. In this barren land of millions of lives, She showers the rain of rejuvenating love.

entinu śōkam entinu mōham
enn-uraceytu mugddhar ākki
en jīva-nāthē amṛtānandamē
ennātma-rāgamāy uṇarū nī

She made our lives beautiful, teaching us not to be deluded by sorrow and desire.

O immortal bliss, queen of my life, awaken within me as the melody of my true Self!
uṇarū ennil nī - ammē...
uṇarū ennil nī

O Mother, awaken within me!

uyirin uyirāy avaḷ (Malayalam)

uyirin uyirāy avaḷ
uṭalin uṭamayāy avaḷ
ulakin uṭalāy avaḷ
uṭalāl ulakil udicc-uyarnnu

You are the life of my life and the five elements from which my body is made. You manifest as the universe and have incarnated on this earth.

ulakattin ujjvala-rūpiṇi
ūzhiye uddharikkān uzhaṙi
uṙakkattil uzhalunna uyirine uṇarttān
udayam kāṇikkān umaye kāṇikkān

Your form is resplendent. You travel the world to uplift mankind. You awaken us who are asleep, that we may see the dawn. You grant us the vision of the divine mother.

uṣassil uṇarunna uyirine ennum
upaniṣad uṇmayāl ūṭṭi amma
uṙavine uḷkkaṇṇāl ujjvala-tējassāy
uḷḷattil kaṇḍavar umayāy tīrnnu

Mother feeds the Truth of the Upanishads to her children who have awakened to the dawn. Those who see the brilliant Truth within themselves merge in the divine mother.

vanamāli varum (Malayalam)

vanamāli varum ennu karuti rādhā
vraja-gōpimār ottu kāttirunnu
vana-puṣpamālakaḷ kōrttirunnu
avar vraja-bālane tanne ōrttirunnu

Hoping that her Krishna would come, Radha waited with the Gopis of Vrindavan. They sat making wild-flower garlands, their minds immersed in the boy of Vrindavan.

mathurakku pōkumbōḷ ‘varum’ enn-uraccavan
dinam ēṙeyāyi varāttat-entē?
marataka maṇivarṇṇā maṙannuvō rādhaye
priya-gōpimāreyum muraḷīdharā

When He left for Mathura, He promised to come back. After so many days, why has He not returned? O beautiful Lord, have you forgotten Radha? O flute-bearer, have you forgotten your dear gopis?

hṛdayattil niṙayunnu mṛduhāsa mukhapadmam
muraḷiyil mīṭṭunna surabhila svaragītam
akatāril alatallum avirāmam ōrmakaḷ
aṙiyunnuvō kaṇṇā atulita-guṇadhāmā

Our hearts are filled with your gentle, smiling face, beautiful as a lotus, and the enchanting music flowing from your flute. O Supremely glorious Krishna, do you know that memories of you ceaselessly fill our minds?

vṛndāvanattil patiñña ponpādaṅgaḷ
rāsōtsavattin-advaita nimiṣaṅgaḷ
anupama-sundara… sulabha-saubhāgyam
aviratam aruḷīṭu, azhak-ezhum mukilvarṇā

Your golden feet left their mark in Vrindavan, the moments of non-dual oneness of the rasa dance. O handsome Lord of unparalleled beauty, please grant us the supreme fortune, O dark-colored One.

oru nōkku kāṇuvān oru vākku kēḷkkuvān
oru mātrayeṅkilum kaṇi-kāṇuvān
iruḷ mūṭum hṛdayattil oḷi cintuvatu vare
ima cimmāt-irikkum ī vrajagōpikaḷ

To catch a glimpse of you, to hear a word from you, to have your vision for even a moment at day-break… The gopis of Vrindavan will wait eagerly until you bring light to our hearts filled with darkness.

vānil teḷiyunna (Malayalam)

vānil teḷiyunna mazhavillu pōle
manassil teḷiyunna kārvarṇṇā
manam etra teḷiyēṇam ennil niṙayuvān
kāruṇya-vāridhē colliṭēṇē
kāruṇya-vāridhē colliṭēṇē

O Lord, with the complexion of rain clouds, dawn in my heart like a rainbow emblazoning the sky. O most compassionate one, please tell me how pure my heart must be before you deign to shine within.

māyāte maṙayāte satya-svarūpanāy
ennuḷḷil ennum viḷangiṭuvān
ā divya tējassil ennum layicciṭān
nityam namikkunnu kaiviṭallē

Please dwell in my heart eternally as the indelible and ever-effulgent embodiment of Truth. I offer endless prostrations to you that I may merge once and for all in your divine splendour. Please do not forsake me.

gōvardhanoddhāra gōpāla-bāla
gōpī-lōla gōvinda

O cowherd boy, beloved of the gopis, you lifted Mount Govardhan!

gōkkaḷē mēykkunna gōpāla-kṛṣṇanāy
pullāṅkuzhal ūti nī varēṇam
ā gāna mādhuri ennil niṙayēṇam
en manam ninnil layicciṭēṇam

Please come to me as the cowherd boy who grazed the cows and played the flute. May that divine melody fill my heart and may my mind merge in you.

varttamāna-jīvitam (Malayalam)

varttamāna-jīvitam
suvarddhamānam ākkaṇam
bhaktiyum viraktiyum
vaḷarttiṭunnat-āvaṇam

May our life become meaningful, and may we cultivate devotion and dispassion.

'lakṣya-bōdham ārilum
bhavikkaṇam nirantaram'
amma ēkum ī mozhi
nammaḷil muzhaṅgaṇam

"Everyone should constantly remember the goal." Let these words of Amma resonate within.

śuddhamāya bhaktiye
bhajicciṭām namukk-ini
yuktiyum subuddhiyum
taṭukkukilla mṛtyuve

Hereafter, let us praise pure devotion. Logic and a sharp intellect will not stop death.

āśayatta mānasam
prakāśamānam āyiṭum

īśvarande vāsabhūmi
īhayatta hṛttaṭam

A desire-free mind shines clearly, and God dwells in a desire-free heart.

vēdasāram ākum ā
tyāga-pūrṇa-jīvitam
kāṭṭiṭunnu amma ī
pāriṭattil ākavē

Mother shows the whole world a life of complete sacrifice. That is the very essence of the Vedas.

bhōgavum bhujicciṭām
yōgavum varuttiṭām
ēvam ōrttu pōyiṭunnu
ēṟe mandabuddhikaḷ

Those who imagine they can enjoy sense pleasures and also progress along the spiritual path are fools.

rātriyum veḷiccavum
cērttu koṇḍu pōyiṭān
ārkkum āvatillahō
ōrttu nām gamikkaṇam

Know that no one can bring together darkness and light, and let us move ahead.

kḷēśa-pūrṇam ākum ī
bhōga-lōla-jīvitam
tyāga-pūrṇam ākkiyāl
ārkkum ātma-nirvṛti

This life of pleasure is full of sorrow. Anyone can attain the blissful Self if they make their life a sacrifice.

vāṭikkozhiññiṭum (Malayalam)

vāṭikkozhiññiṭum ende svapnam
nin prēma madhumāri vaiki ennāl
nin mukham kārmukil kāṭṭiṭumbōḷ
vēzhāmbal pōlen manam tuṭikkum

My dream will wither and fall away if the ambrosial rain of your love is delayed any longer. When I see your face in the rain clouds, my heart rejoices like the vezhambal bird waiting for rain!

prāṇēśvarā ninde vēṇu-nādam
kātōrttirikkayāṇ-innu rādha
tōrātta kaṇṇīrumāyi ñān ī
kāḷindi puḷinattilēkayāṇu

O Lord of my life! Radha waits here to hear the melody flowing from your flute. With unending tears, I wait alone by the banks of the Kalindi river.

kāryangaḷ etra uṇḍōtiṭānāy
kaṇṇā nī arikatt-aṇaññiṭumbōḷ
ninnil ninn-akalunna nimiṣam ellām
kaṇṇiril aliyum yugaṅgaḷallō

O Krishna! When you come near, I have so many things to tell you. Every moment away from you is like an eon that melts away in tears.

nī ende arikatt-aṇaññiṭumbōḷ

tiriyātirunnenkil kāla cakram
vyathapūṇḍa manam ende nitya tōzhī
tanuvinum kelppilla kāttirikkān

If only the wheel of time would stop when you come near me! My aching heart is my constant friend, and my body has no strength to wait for you any longer!

vilayēṙum (Malayalam)

vilayēṙum nimiṣaṅgaḷ, kozhiyunnu daḷaṅgaḷāy
aṙiyāte alayunnu, ñān ammē
azhalin vilāpaṅgaḷ, akatāril eppōzhum
ōḷaṅgaḷāy, tira talliṭunnu

The petals of precious moments [of time] are falling away, O Mother! I wander without knowing you, and waves of sorrow surge in my heart.

madhu tēṭi alayunna bhṛṅgaṅgaḷ pōl ende
hṛdayam tirayukayāyirunnu
ennum – ninne tēṭukayāyirunnu

Like bees in search of honey, my heart was always seeking you.

arikilāṇ-arikil āṇ-amma ennā-satyam
uḷḷil, muzhuṅgukayāyirunnu
ñān ninnil aliyukayāyirunnu

Within me resounded the truth, 'Mother is near, nearest to you.' I was dissolving in you.

hṛdaya-śrīkōvilil ennum vasikkunna
snēha-svarūpam āṇende amma
ende – akatāril ennum viḷaṅgiṭēṇē

Mother is the form of eternal love enshrined in my heart. O Mother! Always shine forth in my heart.

vinnapamu vinavā (Telugu)

vinnapamu vinavā ō tallī - cinna
vinnapamu vinavā mā tallī

O Mother! Please listen to my small prayer.

vēdasāramū amṛtasūtramai
nā jīvana yānamuna diksūciyai
akhaṇḍa dīpamai prakāśimpani

You have made the essence of the Vedas into aphorisms. Please let them be a beacon of light guiding me on my journey of life.

oke dāramunaku memu pūsalaṇṭivi
sandrānna vēru dīvulu kādaṇṭivi
nīṭilōna vennalāga telamaṇṭivi
antarārtham edo telupavammā
vivēka pradāyini amma

You said we are like beads on the same string, and not isolated islands in the ocean. But you also teach us to float in the ocean of samsara like butter! O Mother, bestower of discernment, please explain the inner meaning.

dhavaḷakānti pala raṅgulaina tīruna
udbhavince nā nuṇḍi nāma rūpa jagamu
sūryuḍu tējamu vēru kādaṇṭivi
paramārtham edo telupavammā
svayam prakāśi amma

Just like white light becomes all colors, this world of names and forms arises in me. You said the sun and its light are not different. O Mother, self-effulgent one, please explain the true, deep, meaning.

ammā nī kāryāniki karaṇam nēnavvanī
viśvamunu nī svarūpamai cūḍani
nā cinna yatnamu nī pādārpitam avvanī
svārtha maraka lēni prārthana nādavvanī
vinnapamu vinavā – nā vinnapamu vinavā

Mother, please make me an instrument in your work, and let me serve this universe as your form. Let my every little effort be an offering at your feet. Let my prayers be untainted by selfishness. O Mother, please hear my prayer.

You and Me, Amma (English)

You and me Amma, you and me,
all just you and me.
Clouds and the sky, waves and the sea,
all just you and me.

My soul dances to the symphony.
I revel in the sweetness of your love.
Fragrance of flowers, song of the birds,
silences of the night.

Remembering you with a surge of love,
I merge and melt into existence.
Losing you is losing me,
core of love is eternity.

www.ingramcontent.com/pod-product-compliance
Lightning Source LLC
Chambersburg PA
CBHW071207090426
42736CB00014B/2738
* 9 7 8 1 6 8 0 3 7 8 6 3 4 *